About the Author

Pierre Berton, well-known and well-loved Canadian author, journalist, and media personality, hailed from Whitehorse, Yukon. During his career, he wrote fifty books for adults and twenty-two for children, popularizing Canadian history and culture and reflecting on his life and times. With more than thirty literary awards and a dozen honorary degrees to his credit, Berton was also a Companion of the Order of Canada.

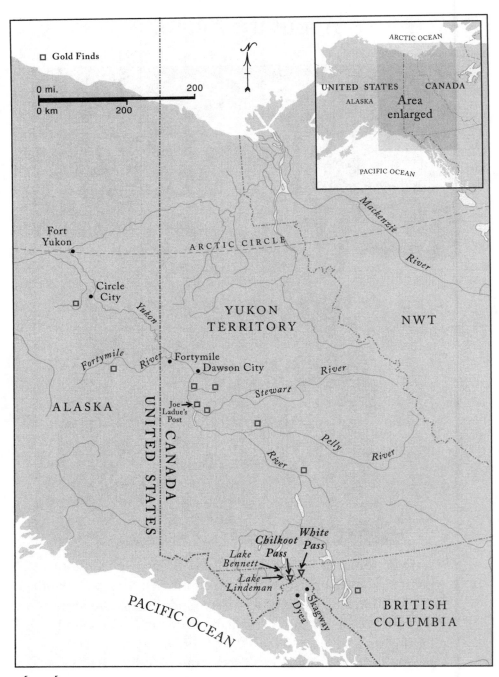

The Yukon

The Great Klondike Gold Rush
An Omnibus

Pierre Berton

FIFTH
HOUSE

Cover and interior design by John Luckhurst
Cover image courtesy Library and Archives Canada, PA126210
Edited by Dallas Harrison
Proofread by Kirsten Craven
Scans by ABL Imaging
Maps by Brian Smith / Articulate Eye

The type in this book is set in Minion.

The publisher gratefully acknowledges the support of The Canada Council for the Arts and the Department of Canadian Heritage.

THE CANADA COUNCIL | LE CONSEIL DES ARTS
FOR THE ARTS | DU CANADA
SINCE 1957 | DEPUIS 1957

We acknowledge the financial support of the Government of Canada through the Book Publishing Industry Development Program (BPIDP) for our publishing activities.

Printed in Canada

2007 / 1

First published in the United States in 2007 by
Fitzhenry & Whiteside
311 Washington Street
Brighton, Massachusetts, 02135

Library and Archives Canada Cataloguing in Publication

Berton, Pierre, 1920-2004
The great Klondike gold rush / Pierre Berton.

(Pierre Berton's history for young Canadians)
Includes index.
Collection of 6 previously published works: Bonanza gold, The Klondike stampede, Trails of 98, City of gold, Kings of the Klondike and Before the goldrush.
ISBN 978-1-897252-05-5

1. Klondike River Valley (Yukon)—Gold discoveries— Juvenile literature. I. Title. II. Series.

FC4022.3.B465 2007   j971.9'102   C2006-906387-7

Fifth House Ltd.
A Fitzhenry & Whiteside Company
1511, 1800-4 St. SW
Calgary, Alberta T2S 2S5

1-800-387-9776
www.fitzhenry.ca

CONTENTS

Foreword *by Ken McGoogan*

On the last day of August 1896, a twenty-nine-year-old man named Antone Stander strode down hill along a rough forest path in the Yukon. He was following Bonanza Creek, a tributary of the Klondike River, and he was feeling anxious and excited at the same time. Nine years before, Stander had sailed from Austria to New York City. He had arrived almost penniless and speaking hardly any English.

Stander had learned the language while working as a cowboy, a sheep herder, a coal miner, and lately as a prospector—but he had remained dirt poor. He had travelled across North America to this far northwest corner of the continent in hopes of getting rich. Recently, he had heard that some other gold seekers had staked claims to sections of land along Bonanza Creek. They had pounded wooden stakes into the ground and then registered their claim with a local official.

With four friends, Stander had decided to check out the area. Reaching a spot where a small stream trickled into the creek, he stopped to look more closely. He walked a few yards up the stream, dipped his pan into the flowing water, and scooped up pebbles and sand. He sifted out the lighter materials by carefully shaking the pan, and suddenly his eyes went wide. He was staring down at a scattering of gold nuggets.

Years later, Antone Stander would recall this moment as the most important turning point of his life. And no wonder. He and his friends had discovered the richest creek in the world—a rivulet that would soon be known as Eldorado Creek. Each of the claims they staked that afternoon would produce more than one million dollars worth of gold. Antone Stander was rich—rich beyond his wildest dreams.

This is just one of many stories that the legendary Pierre Berton brings to life in *The Great Klondike Gold Rush*. Berton was a larger-than-life figure—a giant who came roaring out of the North to dominate the Canadian landscape while writing fifty books, among them *The Last Spike, The Invasion of Canada*, and *The Arctic Grail*. Because he grew up in Dawson City, Yukon, in the afterglow of the greatest gold rush this continent has ever known, no story was closer to his heart than the one he tells in this volume.

The saga begins in ancient history, with geological forces depositing a winding streak of gold in the mountains along the west coast of North America. But the human adventure that Berton found fascinating did not start until July 1896, when prospectors like Antone Stander discovered that gold streak near the Klondike River in the Yukon. Because communications were so slow—no radio, no telephone, no television, and certainly no Internet—the news did not reach the outside world until the following summer. But when, in July 1897, two ships carrying miners with suitcases full of gold sailed into San Francisco, North America went crazy.

During the next few months, more than one hundred thousand people would set out to reach Dawson City, a town that sprang up overnight near where the Klondike River flows into the Yukon River. Fewer than forty thousand would reach their destination. The rest would either turn back or die along the trail. Still, for one year, starting in the summer of 1897, Dawson City became the largest Canadian city west of Winnipeg. With eighteen thousand people in town and another five thousand in the surrounding forest, the gold-rush centre made Vancouver and Victoria look small.

Berton tells horrific tales of the hardships involved in reaching that isolated settlement, which he describes as located "a thousand miles from nowhere." Almost none of the gold seekers were prepared for rough-country travel. But at one point, when the winter ice melted, more than seven thousand boats set out to voyage eight hundred kilometres down the Yukon River and found themselves bashing through canyons and white-water rapids.

People who travelled overland faced even worse conditions. They had to carry food and equipment across the coastal mountains through one of two passes. In the famous Chilkoot Pass, two disasters occurred. First, part of a glacier came crashing down onto the trail and killed three climbers. Then, a blizzard caused an avalanche that buried hundreds of people and killed more than sixty. Still, the gold seekers kept coming, bent on getting rich overnight.

One reason Pierre Berton was such a successful writer was that he could spot an intriguing detail or a compelling anecdote where others would see a speck of dust in the distance. In Dawson City, he tells us, doing laundry became so expensive that men would wear a shirt until they couldn't stand the smell, then they would throw it away and buy another. When one woman, Mrs. Berry, needed pocket money, she would walk out to the dump where her husband washed himself. She would poke around with a sharp stick, break apart a few clods of earth and collect nuggets of gold.

Berton describes how the mayor of Seattle quit his job to seek gold in the Klondike. He sailed north in a steamer that got frozen into the winter ice 1,287 kilometres from Dawson City, and spent the next nine months trapped in the wilderness with dozens of other unhappy dreamers. The gold rush cast a spell on the entire continent. From New York City, five hundred widows set sail in a ship, hoping to find rich husbands in the gold fields. They sailed around the bottom of South America, but got no farther north than Seattle.

But the worst nightmare voyage, according to Berton, was that of an ancient steamship called the *Eliza Anderson*. The oldest side-wheeler on the west coast, she had served for years as a floating gambling hall. But the owners fitted her out and sent her out of Seattle to sail 4,800 kilometres along the coast. Before long, most of the passengers were begging the captain to turn back. But he proved to be a roaring madman bent on reaching his destination "come hell or high water." When the vessel ran out of fuel, the captain ordered the furniture burned and kept sailing. After ten months of desperate hardship, some of the passengers reached Dawson City. They felt so disillusioned that they turned around and went straight home.

Those who survived that experience were lucky compared with the trekkers who set out to reach the Klondike by walking across the Malaspina Glacier, the largest sheet of ice on the continent. Starting in the spring of 1898, about one hundred men tried to cross. They took various routes, and forty-one of them died in the attempt.

One group of nineteen New Yorkers spent three months crossing the glacier. When they reached the mountains, heavy snows forced them to make a rough camp. During the cold, dark, winter months, men died of fever and scurvy and got buried in avalanches. In the spring, seven of them, half-crazy, reached the Pacific Ocean. Four men lived long enough to be rescued by a passing ship, and two of those had been blinded by the glare of the ice.

Pierre Berton makes these true stories live again partly because of his skill as a writer and partly because he grew up in Dawson City a couple of decades after the gold rush. He actually met some of the old-timers who had come north during the stampede. Only a few men struck it rich in the Klondike Gold Rush. But nobody who survived the adventure ever forgot it. The same can be said of this book. If you read it, you will never forget it.

Ken McGoogan
Author of *Lady Franklin's Revenge* and
winner of the 2006 Pierre Berton Award

George Carmack never took himself seriously
as a prospector. But he and his friends Charley and
Jim discovered the rich gold claim that began
the great Klondike Gold Rush.

BONANZA GOLD

CONTENTS

The Golden Highway

A LINE OF GOLD STRETCHES NORTH ALONG THE CONTINENTAL SPINE FROM THE LAND OF THE INCAS IN PERU TO THE CHILL SANDS OF NORTON SOUND ON THE BERING SEA, OPPOSITE SIBERIA.

People have searched for gold ever since the fabled days of El Dorado, the legendary treasure city of South America. There was gold there in the mountains—the Incas made jewellery from it that can be seen to this day— and there was gold farther north in Mexico, the land of the Aztecs.

Gold in the Sierras produced the great California stampede in 1849. Gold strikes in Arizona and Colorado helped make the American West wild. There was gold in the Fraser River of British Columbia and gold in the fabled Cariboo, gold at Lake Atlin on the Yukon border, gold in the sandbars of the Yukon River, gold along the watershed of the Klondike and the Fortymile, gold in Alaska at Fairbanks, on the Tanana, at Circle City, and at Nome near the mouth of the Yukon.

The gold had bubbled up, hot and molten within the backbone of the continent. Over the eons, as the mountains were ground down by wind, water, and ice, the gold was ground down too and washed down the mountainsides in ancient streams. The coarse gold, being heaviest, was caught in the crevices of the bedrock. The finer gold was pushed farther down the slopes, while the finest gold—fine as sifted flour—ended in the sandbars at the mouths of creeks and rivers. There it stayed as the streams changed course, while the vegetation turned to soil and covered the old creek beds in a mantle of clay. To find it, men had to burrow deep into the bowels of the earth, building shafts to bedrock and then scraping out tunnels or "drifts" to find the old channels where the "pay streak" glittered.

Men still stampede for gold today whenever a new find is announced, but it isn't the same. In the nineteenth century, before the airplane and the helicopter, every gold strike was remote. But none was quite so remote as the Klondike, on a river that wasn't even named on the maps.

There are several reasons why the Klondike Gold Rush appeals to us as romantic. First, it contained the richest ground in history. Second, it was far enough away to be glamorous yet still within the reach of those men and women determined enough to get there by foot and homemade boat.

Finally, it was a "poor man's" stampede. One or two men could actually sink a shaft in the frozen ground, find the pay streak at bedrock, and haul up the gold by themselves. The only capital they needed was money for food and enough left over to build a cabin and a sluice box. Thus paupers became millionaires, almost overnight—and that was the appeal of the gold find on the Klondike in 1896.

CHAPTER ONE

A Fateful Meeting

THIS IS A STORY OF A MAN WHO SPENT ALL HIS LIFE SEARCHING FOR GOLD, ONLY TO LET A FORTUNE SLIP THROUGH HIS FINGERS BECAUSE HE MADE A RACIST REMARK ABOUT INDIANS. ROBERT HENDERSON DIDN'T LIKE INDIANS. THAT COST HIM DEARLY. IF HE HADN'T OPENED HIS MOUTH, HE WOULD HAVE BECOME A MILLIONAIRE.

He hailed from Big Island off the coast of Nova Scotia. A lighthouse-keeper's son, he could scarcely remember the time when he hadn't thought of gold. As a child, he'd read Alaskan histories and wandered about Nova Scotia searching for gold, finding nothing. As a boy of fourteen, he decided to spend all his life seeking gold.

He thought that the southern hemisphere held out the best hope and so signed aboard a sailing ship to search the seven seas. He panned and picked in New Zealand and Australia and other corners of the globe and found nothing. After five years, he tried the northern hemisphere, working his way up through the Rocky Mountain states to the mines of Colorado. Then, after fourteen years of fruitless search, he was carried north with a human tide flowing toward Alaska. He searched for gold on the Pelly River, a great tributary of the mighty Yukon, but found no gold in the Pelly. And still he kept looking.

He was tall and lean, with a gaunt, hawk's face, fierce brows, and piercing eyes. His full moustache, drooping slightly at the edges, gave him a stern look that revealed his Scottish ancestry. He wore his broad-brimmed miner's hat proudly, as if it were a kind of badge. All his life he wore it, on city streets and wilderness pathways. It proclaimed to the world that Robbie Henderson was a prospector.

In 1894 he reached the trading post of Joseph Ladue on the upper Yukon

River. Ladue was at the mouth of the Sixtymile River sixty miles (100 km) upstream from Fort Reliance, and Henderson persuaded Ladue to back him in his search. Ladue had spent twelve years on the river. He too had been obsessed with the idea of gold. He was a stocky man of French (not Quebec) ancestry, and gold had a very real meaning for him. Without it he could not marry his sweetheart, Anna Mason, whose wealthy parents continued to think of him as a penniless drifter. She was faithfully waiting for him, three thousand miles (4,800 km) away, while he sought his fortune in a plain log cabin on the banks of the Yukon.

That post lay about a hundred miles (160 km) from the border between Yukon and Alaska. Between that point and the border, two other rivers flowed into the Yukon—the Indian River about thirty miles (50 km) downstream, and the Thron-diuck River, another thirty miles farther down. Ladue had explored the Thron-diuck in the old days and had sworn that there was gold in its streams. Now, however, he believed that the neighbouring Indian River was ankle-deep in nuggets. He told every prospector who stopped at his post, including Henderson, that it was rich with gold.

"Let me prospect for you," Henderson told Jack Ladue. "If it's good for me, it's good for you. I'm a determined man, I won't starve."

And so, for the next two years, Robert Henderson stubbornly combed the Indian River and its tributaries looking for gold. He searched with that same restlessness that had governed his life, shifting from creekbed to creekbed but never settling for long at any given spot.

He found gold, but he never found enough to satisfy him. On the sandbars of the main river, he found gold as delicate as lace. He dragged his sled up Quartz Creek, and there he found gold as coarse as sand. It still was not what he was seeking. Possibly, even if he had found a cache of twenty-dollar gold pieces or a mountain of solid gold, he would have felt vaguely disappointed, because with Henderson it was the search itself that counted.

Bad luck dogged him, but he didn't give up. He suffered the agonies of leg cramps from wading in the chilling streams and snow blindness from the glare on the white slopes. On Australia Creek, he had the terrifying experience of falling across a broken branch, being impaled through the calf, and hanging over the rushing torrent like a slab of beef on a butcher's hook. For fourteen days, he lay crippled in his bivouac. Then he was away again, living off the land, eating caribou or ptarmigan, limping through the forests, or travelling the shallow streams in a crude boat made from the skins of animals.

Occasionally, he would raise his eyes northward to examine a curious round mountain—known as a "dome"—whose summit rose above the other hills. The creeks of Indian River flowed down the flanks of this dome, and Henderson guessed that on the other side more nameless creeks flowed into another river—probably the Thron-diuck, or "Klondike," as the miners mispronounced it. At last his prospector's curiosity got the better of him. He climbed the dome to see what was on the other side.

When he reached the summit, a sight of breathtaking majesty met his gaze. To the north, a long line of glistening, snow-capped peaks marched off like soldiers to vanish beyond the lip of the horizon. In every other direction, the violet hills rolled on as far as the eye could see, hill upon hill, valley upon valley, gulch upon gulch—and each hill about the same height as its neighbour. The whole effect, seen through half-closed eyes, was of a great plateau creased and gouged and furrowed by centuries of running water.

From the summit on which Henderson was standing that spring of 1895, the creeks radiated out like the spokes of a wheel, with himself at the hub, three falling off toward the Indian River and three more, on the far side, running to some unknown stream. He could not know it, but these were six of the richest gold-bearing creeks in the world. They wound through beds of black muck and thick moss, bordered by rank grasses from which the occasional moose lifted its dripping snout. They twisted across flat valley floors whose sides, notched by steep gulches, rose in steps marking the pathways of once mighty tributaries.

Almost at Henderson's feet a deep cleft dropped off from the dome. Henderson walked down a little way and dipped his pan into a small creek. When the gravel and sand washed away, there was about eight cents' worth of gold left behind. Henderson weighed it out with the pair of scales that every prospector carried. *Eight cents to the pan!* In those days, that was a good prospect; he felt that he had at last found what he was looking for.

Back he went over the mountain to the Indian River, where about twenty men, lured by Ladue's tales, were toiling away on the sandbars. He persuaded three to return with him to the creek, which he named "Gold

Bottom" because, as he said wistfully, "I had a daydream that when I got my shaft down to bedrock it might be like the streets of New Jerusalem."

By midsummer of 1896, the four men had taken out $750, and it was time for Henderson to head back to Ladue's post for more supplies. To each man he met, he told the story of a V-shaped valley back in the hills. This free exchange of information was part of the prospector's code, in which Henderson fiercely believed. He not only told strangers of the gold, but he also urged them to turn back in their tracks and stake claims by hammering in peeled-log posts at the four corners of their five-hundred-foot (150 m) find. In this way, he emptied the settlement at the mouth of the Sixtymile. Every man except Ladue headed downstream.

His order filled, Henderson drifted back the way he had come in his skin boat. It was late summer, and the water was low. The Indian River was so shallow that Henderson, fearing he might tear his craft to shreds trying to navigate it, determined to continue on down the Yukon toward the Thron-diuck, guessing correctly that Gold Bottom Creek must flow into it. Thus, on a fateful summer's day, he approached his meeting with George Washington Carmack. The bitter memory of that moment was to haunt Henderson all the days of his life.

As he brought his boat around a broad curve in the river and past a rocky bluff, he could hear on his right the roar of the Thron-diuck, or Klondike, as it poured out from between the flat-topped hills to join the Yukon. Directly before him now, just beyond the Klondike's mouth, rose a tapering mountain, its pointed peak naked of timber. Slashed across its flank was an immense and evil scar in the shape of a stretched moose hide, the product of slow erosion by underground springs. At its base, a wedge of flat swampland covered with scrub timber bordered the riverbank for a mile and a half (2.4 km)—ugly, foul, and mosquito-infested. It seemed an almost impossible place for settlement, yet this was to be the site of the gaudiest city in the North.

The Thron-diuck was known as the finest salmon stream in the Yukon—hence its name: an Indian word meaning "Hammer-Water," which, pronounced in the Native fashion, sounded like a man in the throes of strangulation. It was so called because the Indians had hammered stakes across the shallow mouth in order to spread their nets. Henderson could smell the stench of the fish drying in the sun, and on the bank just below the river's mouth he could see a white man moving about.

The idea of anyone fishing for a living when there was gold to be had appalled him. He later recalled his first thought: "There's a poor devil who hasn't struck it."

As was his habit, he decided to share his good fortune with the fisherman, and a moment later he was up on the bank talking to George Washington Carmack, or "McCormick," as he was often called.

The two men, who would later be called "co-discoverers of the Klondike" and around whom so much controversy was to swirl, were opposites in almost every way. Henderson, with his chiselled features, serious and intense, bore little resemblance to the easygoing, ever-optimistic salmon fisherman with his heavy jowls, his sleepy eyes, and his rather plump features. But they had one quality in common: an incurable restlessness controlled their lives.

Carmack was the child of an earlier gold rush. His father had crossed the western plains in a covered wagon in '49, heading for California, and Carmack had been born at Port Costa, across the bay from San Francisco. He had gone to work at sixteen years of age aboard the ferryboats, shipped to Alaska as a dishwasher on a man-of-war, jumped ship at Juneau, and pushed steadily north. In 1887 William Ogilvie, the Canadian surveyor, encountered him at Dyea. By that time, Carmack could speak both the Chilkoot and the Tagish dialects and had considerable influence over the Han or "Stick" Indians from the interior or the "Stick" country.

At a time and place when every man was a prospector, Carmack appeared to be a misfit. He alone of all men did not want gold. Instead he wanted to be an Indian in a land where the Natives were generally scorned by the white man and the white word *Siwash* was racist. His wife, Kate, a member of the Tagish tribe, was the daughter of a chief, and it was Carmack's ambition to be chief himself. (Among the Tagishes, descent is through the chief's sister.)

He worked with the other Indians as a packer on the Chilkoot Pass, and by the time he moved into the interior with his wife and her two brothers he had three or four children of mixed blood. He had grown an Indian-type moustache that drooped over his lips Oriental style, and when anybody said to him, "George, you're getting more like an Indian every day," he took it as a compliment. He did not in the least mind his nicknames, "Stick George" and "Siwash George," for he considered himself a true Indian, and he was proud of it.

While other men scrabbled and mucked in the smoky shafts of Alaskan mining camps, Siwash George was slipping up and down the river with Indian comrades. His easygoing mood matched that of the Natives, who were a different breed from the fiercely competitive and ambitious Tlingit tribes of the coast.

When it suited Carmack, he bragged of gold discoveries he had made. It was certainly true that he had discovered a seam of coal on the Yukon River, but nobody took him seriously as a prospector, including Carmack himself. In the words of a Mounted Police sergeant at Fortymile, the nearest mining camp to the Alaska-Yukon border, he was a man "who would never allow himself to be beaten and always tried to present his fortunes in the best possible light." The men at Fortymile summed him up more tersely with a new nickname. They called him "Lying George."

When it suited Carmack, he bragged of gold discoveries he had made. It was certainly true that he had discovered a seam of coal on the Yukon River, but nobody took him seriously as a prospector, including Carmack himself.

Yet he was no dummy. He had an organ, of all things, in his cabin near Five Finger Rapids on the Yukon and a library that included such journals as *Scientific American* and *Review of Reviews*. He liked to converse on scientific topics, and occasionally, as on Christmas Eve in 1888, he wrote sad, sentimental poetry. ("A whisper comes from the tall old spruce, And my soul from pain is free: For I know when they kneel together to-night, They'll all be praying for me.")

He was also something of a mystic. In May of 1896, he was sitting on the bank of the Yukon near the ruins of old Fort Selkirk at the mouth of the Pelly, and there, if one believes his later recollections, he had strange feelings. He stared into the blazing sunset and came to the conclusion that something unusual was about to take place in his life. On a whim, he took his only coin, a silver dollar, from his pocket and threw it in the air. If it came down heads, he told himself, he would go back up the river, but if it showed tails he would go downstream to test whatever fate had in store for him. Tails it was, and Carmack loaded his boat and started to drift the two-hundred-odd miles (320 km) to Fortymile.

That night he had a vivid dream in which he saw himself seated on the banks of a stream watching grayling shoot the rapids. Suddenly, the fish scattered in fright, and two enormous king salmon shot upstream and came to a dead stop in front of him. In place of scales they were armoured in gold nuggets, and their eyes were twenty-dollar gold pieces. It reveals a great deal about Carmack that he took this as a sign that he go fishing; prospecting never entered his head. He determined to catch salmon on the Thron-diuck and sell it for dog-feed. So there he was, with his catch hanging to dry under a small birch lean-to, when Robert Henderson encountered him.

His Indian friends had joined him at the Klondike's mouth: Skookum Jim, a giant of a man, supremely handsome with his high cheekbones, his eagle's nose, and his fiery black eyes—straight as a gun barrel, powerfully built, and known as the best hunter and trapper on the river; Tagish Charley, lean and lithe as a panther and, in Carmack's phrase, "alert as a weasel"; the silent, plump Kate with her straight black hair; and Carmack's daughter, known as Graphie Gracey because no white man could pronounce her real name. It was this group that Henderson approached with news of the strike at Gold Bottom. Carmack later set down his version of the conversation, which does not differ substantially from Henderson's briefer account:

"Hello, Bob! Where in the world did you drop from, and where do you think you're going?"

"Just came down from Ogilvie; I'm going up the Klondike."

"What's the idea, Bob?"

"There's been a prospect found in a small creek that heads up against the Dome. I think it empties into the Klondike about fifteen miles up, and I'm looking for a better way to get there than going over the mountains from the Indian River."

"Got any kind of a prospect?"

"We don't know yet. We can get a prospect on the surface. When I left, the boys were running up an open cut to get to bedrock."

"What are the chances to locate up there? Everything staked?"

Henderson glanced over at the two Indians who were standing nearby. Then he uttered the phrase that probably cost him a fortune. "There's a chance for you, George, but I don't want any damn Siwashes staking on that creek."

He pushed his boat into the water and headed up the Klondike. But his final remark rankled.

"What's matter dat white man?" Skookum Jim asked, speaking in Chinook, the pidgin tongue of the traders that prevailed on the river. "Him killet Inchen moose, Inchen caribou, ketchet gold Inchen country, no liket Inchen staket claim, wha for, no good."

"Never mind, Jim," said Carmack lightly. "This is a big country. We'll go and find a creek of our own."

And, as it turned out, it was to be as simple as that.

CHAPTER TWO

Striking It Rich

CARMACK DID NOT IMMEDIATELY FOLLOW HENDERSON'S SUGGESTION TO GO UPRIVER AND STAKE AT GOLD BOTTOM. HE WAS LESS INTERESTED IN GOLD THAN HE WAS IN LOGS, WHICH HE HOPED TO CHOP ON RABBIT CREEK, A TRIBUTARY OF THE KLONDIKE, AND FLOAT DOWN TO THE MILL AT FORTYMILE NEAR THE BORDER FOR TWENTY-FIVE DOLLARS PER THOUSAND FEET (305 M).

Skookum Jim had already explored the creek and in passing had panned out some colours, for, just as Carmack wished to be an Indian, Jim longed to be a white man—in other words, a prospector. He differed from the others in his tribe in that he displayed the white man's kind of ambition. He had, in fact, earned his nickname of Skookum (meaning "husky") by his feat of packing the record load of 156 pounds (71 kg) of bacon across the steep Chilkoot Pass that led across the mountains into the heart of the Canadian Yukon. In vain he tried to interest Carmack in the prospects along Rabbit Creek; Carmack was not intrigued.

It was as much Carmack's restless nature as his desire for fortune that took him and the Indians to the site of Henderson's strike some days after the meeting at the Klondike's mouth. They did not follow the river but decided to strike up the valley of Rabbit Creek, which led to the high ridge separating the Klondike and the Indian watersheds. The ridge led to the head of Gold Bottom.

They poled up the Klondike for two miles (3 km), left their boat, shouldered their packs, and began to trudge through the wet mosses and black muck and the great clumps of grass that marked the mouth of the Rabbit. As they went, they prospected, dipping their pans into the clear water that rippled in the sunlight over sands white with quartz. As Carmack sat on his haunches, twirling the gold-pan, he began to recite Hamlet's soliloquy, "To be or not to be," for he felt that all prospecting was a gamble.

"Wa for you talket dat cultus wa wa?" Tagish Charley asked him. "I no see um gold."

"That's all right, Charley," Carmack told him. "I makum Boston man's medicine."

He raised the pan with its residue of black sand.

"Spit in it, boys, for good luck."

They spat, and then Carmack panned out the sand and raised the pan to show a tiny stream of colour.

On they trudged, stopping occasionally to pan again, finding minute pieces of gold, wondering whether or not to stake. They came to a fork in the frothing creek where another branch bubbled in from the south, and there they paused momentarily. They did not know it, but at that instant they were standing on the richest ground in the world. There was gold all about them, not only beneath their feet but also in the hills and benches that rose on every side. In the space of a few hundred feet, there was hidden gold worth several millions of dollars. The south fork of the creek was as yet unnamed, but there could be only one name for it: Eldorado.

But they did not linger there. Instead they hiked on up the narrowing valley, flushing a brown bear from the blueberry bushes, stumbling upon Joe Ladue's eleven-year-old campfires, panning periodically and finding a few colours in every pan, until they reached the dome that looked down over the land of the Klondike. Like Henderson, they were struck by the splendour of the scene that lay spread out before them like a Persian carpet: the little streams tumbling down the flanks of the great mountain, the hills crimson, purple, and emerald green in the warm August sunlight (for already the early frosts were tinting trees and shrubs), the cranberry and salmonberry bushes forming a foreground fringe to the natural tapestry.

Below, in the narrow gorge of Gold Bottom Creek, a pale pillar of smoke marked Henderson's camp.

"Well, boys," said Carmack, "we've got this far, let's go down and see what they've got."

Skookum Jim hesitated; Henderson's remarks about Siwashes still bothered him. But in the end, the trio clambered down the gorge to the camp where Henderson and his three companions were washing out gold from an open cut.

Exactly what happened between Carmack and Henderson has long been in dispute. Carmack later insisted that he urged Henderson to come over to Rabbit Creek and stake a claim. Henderson always swore that it was he who urged Carmack to prospect Rabbit—and if he found anything to let Henderson know.

Two facts are fairly clear. First, Carmack did promise Henderson that if he found anything worthwhile on Rabbit he would send word back; Henderson offered to pay him for his trouble if the occasion arose. Second, the Indians tried to purchase some tobacco from Henderson, and Henderson refused, possibly because he was short of supplies, but more likely because of his attitude toward Indians, since it was against his code to refuse a fellow prospector anything. This action was to cost him dearly.

Carmack tried the prospects at Gold Bottom, but did not stake, and the trio headed back over the mountain. The way was hard. They struggled over fallen trees and devil's clubs, a peculiarly offensive thorn, and they forced their way through tangled underbrush, brier roses, and raspberry bushes. On the far side of the mountain, they floundered into a swamp that marked the headwaters of Rabbit Creek, and there they had to hop from clump to clump on their slippery moccasins or sink to their thighs in the glacial ooze. Hordes of gnats and mosquitoes rose about them as they stumbled on, unable to swat the insects for fear of losing their balance.

Thus they came wearily to the fork of Rabbit Creek once more and pressed on for about half a mile (0.8 km) before making camp for the night. It was August 16, the eve of a memorable day that is still celebrated as a festive holiday in the Yukon Territory.

Who found the nugget that started it all? Again, the record is blurred. Years afterward, Carmack insisted it was he who happened upon the protruding rim of bedrock from which he pulled a thumb-sized chunk of gold. But Skookum Jim and Tagish Charley always claimed that Carmack was stretched out asleep under a birch tree when Jim, having shot a moose, was cleaning a dishpan in the creek and made the find.

At any rate, the gold was there, lying thickly between the flaky slabs of rock like cheese in a sandwich. A single panful yielded a quarter of an ounce (12.5 g) or about four dollars' worth. In a country where a ten-cent pan had always meant good prospects, this was an incredible find. Carmack flung down the pan and let out a war-whoop, and the three men began to perform a wild dance around it—a sort of combination Scottish hornpipe, Indian foxtrot, Irish jig, and Siwash hula, as Carmack later described it. They collapsed, panting, smoked a cigarette apiece, and panned out some more gravel until Carmack had gathered enough coarse gold to fill an empty Winchester shotgun shell. Then they settled down for the night, the Indians chanting a song of praise into the embers of the fire while Carmack, staring at the dying flames, conjured up visions of wealth—of a trip around the world, of a suburban mansion rimmed with flower borders, of a suitcase full of gilt-edged stock certificates. In that instant of discovery, something fundamental had happened to Siwash George: suddenly, he had ceased to be an Indian. And he never thought of himself as an Indian again.

The following morning the trio staked claims on Rabbit Creek, which would soon be renamed Bonanza. Under Canadian mining law, no more than one claim may be staked in any mining district by anyone except the discoverer, who is allowed a double claim. Carmack blazed a small spruce tree with his hand-axe and on the upstream side wrote with a pencil:

TO WHOM IT MAY CONCERN
I do, this day, locate and claim, by right of discovery,
five hundred feet, running up stream from this notice.
Located this 17th day of August, 1896.
G. W. Carmack

The claim, also by law, straddled the creek and ran for five hundred feet (150 m). Carmack then measured off three more claims—one additional for himself, by right of discovery; *One Above* discovery for Jim; and another below for Charley, which, under the claim-numbering system, became *Two Below*. Jim's story, later, was that Carmack took the additional claim for himself, having persuaded Jim that, although he had made the discovery, as an Indian he would not be recognized as discoverer.

That done, and with no further thought of Robert Henderson, waiting for news on the far side of the hills, the three set off through the swamps to emerge five hours later on the Klondike again, their bodies prickling with thorns.

They had moved only a short distance downriver when they came upon four beaten and discouraged men wading knee-deep in the mud along the shoreline and towing a loaded boat behind them. These were Nova Scotians who had come to the Yukon valley by way of California and had since tramped all over the territory without success. They were starving when they reached the Klondike looking for salmon, but there they had heard of Henderson's strike. Now, in the intense August heat, their hunger forgotten, they were dragging their supplies (or their "outfit," as it was known) upstream, searching once again for gold.

The leader, Dave McKay, asked Carmack if he had heard of Henderson's strike.

"I left there three days ago," Carmack said, holding his boat steady with a pike pole.

"What do you think of it?"

Carmack gave a slow, sly grin. "I don't like to be a knocker, but I don't think much of it."

The faces of the four men fell: all were now at the end of their tethers.

"You wouldn't advise us to go up there?" Dan McGillivery, one of the partners, asked.

"No," said Carmack, still grinning, "because I've got something better for you." With that, he pulled out his nugget-filled cartridge case, like a magician plucking a rabbit from a hat.

As the Nova Scotians' eyes goggled, Carmack gave them directions to his claim. Without further ado, the four men scrambled upriver, the tow line on their boat as taut as a violin string. This chance meeting with Carmack made fortunes for all of them.

"I felt as if I had just dealt myself a royal flush in the game of life, and the whole world was a jackpot," Carmack later remarked, when recalling the incident.

He reached the salmon camp at the Klondike's mouth, and there he hailed two more discouraged men—Alphonse Lapierre of Quebec and his partner, another French Canadian. These two had been eleven years in the north, and now, en route downriver to Fortymile, almost starving, out of flour and bacon, their faces blistering in the sun, they had reached the low point of their careers.

"If I were you boys, I wouldn't go any farther," Carmack told them as they beached their boat. "Haven't you heard of the new strike?"

"Oh, yes, we know all about heem. I tink hee's wan beeg bluff."

"How's this for bluff?" Carmack shouted, producing the gold. Again the effect was electric. The two men unloaded their boat, filled their packs, and fairly ran across the flat, waving their hands and chattering in a mixture of French and English. The abandoned boat would have floated off with the current if Carmack had not secured it.

As Carmack made preparations to set out for Fortymile to record his claim, he continued to tell anyone he encountered about the gold on Rabbit Creek. He made a special trip across the river to tell an old friend, then sent Jim back to guard the claims and drifted off with Tagish Charley down the Yukon, still spreading the news. He told everybody, including a man who, on hearing the tale, called him the biggest liar this side of hell.

One man Carmack did not tell. He sent not a whisper back to Robert Henderson.

CHAPTER THREE

The Triumph of Lying George

LATE IN THE AFTERNOON CARMACK LANDED AT THE MINING CAMP OF FORTYMILE, NEAR THE ALASKA BORDER, AND WENT STRAIGHT TO BILL MCPHEE'S SALOON. FORTYMILE WAS A WEIRD AND LONELY VILLAGE NAMED FOR THE RIVER THAT FLOWED INTO THE YUKON AT THAT POINT, FORTY MILES (64 KM) NORTH OF FORT RELIANCE. IT WAS TOTALLY REMOTE FROM THE WORLD, EXISTING FOR EIGHT MONTHS OUT OF TWELVE AS IF IN A VACUUM, ITS RESIDENTS SEALED OFF FROM THE REST OF CIVILIZATION.

The nearest outfitting port was San Francisco, almost five thousand water miles (8,000 km) distant, and the only links with the sea were two cockleshell sternwheelers, the *New Racket*, and the Alaska Commercial Company's *Arctic*, built in 1889. These boats seldom had time to make more than one summer trip upstream from the old Russian seaport of St. Michael, near the river's mouth on the Bering Sea.

The little steamboats were the town's only lifeline. If one sank, the miners starved. On her maiden voyage in 1889, the *Arctic* was damaged and unable to bring supplies to Fortymile. The AC Company sent Indian runners sixteen hundred miles (2,500 km) from the Bering Sea to the settlement to warn the miners that no supplies would be arriving and that they must escape from the Yukon valley or starve. As the October snows drifted down from the dark skies, the Fortymilers jammed aboard the *New Racket*, and the little vessel made a brave attempt to reach St. Michael at the Yukon's mouth before the river froze. She was caught in the ice floes 190 miles (305 km) short of her goal, and the hungry passengers had to continue the journey on foot. Those who remained at the community of Fortymile spent a hungry winter: indeed, one man lived for nine months on a steady diet of flapjacks.

There was one alternative route to the outside world once winter set in. That was the gruelling trek upstream from Fortymile to the Chilkoot, more than six hundred miles (1,000 km) distant. It was seldom attempted. Four men who tried it in 1893 were forced to abandon fifteen thousand dollars in gold dust on the mountain slopes and were so badly ravaged by the elements that one died and another was crippled for life.

Who were these men who had chosen to wall themselves off from the world in a village of logs deep in the sub-Arctic wilderness? On the face of it, they were men chasing the will-o'-the-wisp of fortune—chasing it with an intensity and a determination that had brought them to the ends of the Earth. But the evidence suggests the opposite. They seemed more like men pursued than men pursuing, and if they sought anything it was the right to be left alone.

Bill McPhee's saloon was crowded with such men when Carmack arrived. Autumn was approaching, and many had come in from their claims to acquire their winter outfits before snowfall. Behind the bar was Clarence Berry, a one-time fruit farmer from Fresno, California. He didn't know it, but Carmack's arrival and discovery would make him a wealthy man for the rest of his life.

Berry had gone north in 1894 as a last resort—a victim of the depression of the 1890s. He borrowed money at a high rate of interest to buy his outfit and passage. A giant of a man with the biceps of a blacksmith and the shoulders of a wrestler, his magnificent strength had sustained him when his fellows faltered. Out of a party of forty that had crossed the passes into the Yukon that year, only Berry and two others reached Fortymile. The rest had turned back discouraged after a storm destroyed their outfits.

But Berry wouldn't give up. He pushed ahead with little more than the clothes on his back. A year later he trekked back to California, married his childhood sweetheart, a sturdy waitress from Selma named Ethel Bush, and again headed for Alaska. He strapped his bride to a sleigh, which he dragged over the mountains and down the river. He found no gold, so he went to work tending bar for Bill McPhee, and it was here that he encountered Carmack.

Carmack was no drinking man, but on this occasion he felt the need for two whiskies. It was not until he swallowed these that he was ready to break the news. After more than a decade, his moment had come, and he savoured it. He turned his back to the bar and raised his hand.

"Boys, I've got some good news to tell you. There's a big strike up the river."

"Strike, hell!" somebody shouted. "That ain't no news. That's just a scheme of Ladue and Harper to start a stampede up the river."

"That's where you're off, you big rabbit-eating malamute!" Carmack cried. "Ladue knows nothing about this." He pulled out his cartridge full of gold and poured it onto the "blower," upon which gold was weighed. "How does that look to you, eh?"

"Is that some Miller Creek gold that Ladue gave you?" someone asked sardonically.

A wave of suspicion swept the room. Nobody believed that Lying George had made a strike. Nevertheless, they crowded to the bar and examined the gold curiously. A seasoned prospector could tell from which creek a given amount of gold came simply by looking at it, and this gold was certainly strange. It did not come from Miller Creek, nor from Davis, nor from Glacier; it did not come from the bars of the Stewart or the Indian. In texture, shape, and colour, it was different from any gold that had been seen before in the Yukon valley.

The men in Bill McPhee's saloon looked uneasily about them. All of them had been on stampedes before, and almost all of those stampedes had led them up false trails. And yet …

One by one they started to slip away. Bewildered, some went to see William Ogilvie, the Canadian government surveyor, to ask his opinion, and Ogilvie pointed out that Carmack must have found the gold *some-where*. That was enough.

Silently, in the twilight hours of the August night, one after another, the boats slid off. By morning, Fortymile was a dead mining camp, empty of boats and empty of men. Even the drunks had been dragged from the saloons by their friends and tied down, protesting, in the boats that were heading for the Klondike.

Meanwhile, Carmack and Charley crossed the mouth of the Fortymile and went into the police post to record their claims. The recorder took one look at Lying George and laughed at him. Once again Carmack produced his shell full of gold dust. The recorder stopped laughing. From that moment on, few men laughed or called him Lying George again.

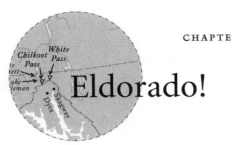

CHAPTER FOUR

Eldorado!

UP AND DOWN THE YUKON VALLEY, THE NEWS SPREAD LIKE A GREAT STAGE WHISPER. IT MOVED AS SWIFTLY AS THE BREEZE IN THE BIRCHES AND MORE MYSTERIOUSLY. MEN SQUATTING BY NAMELESS CREEKS HEARD THE TALE, DROPPED THEIR PANS, AND HEADED FOR THE KLONDIKE. MEN SEATED BY DYING CAMPFIRES HEARD IT AND STARTED UP IN THE NIGHT, SHRUGGING OFF SLEEP TO MAKE TRACKS FOR THE NEW STRIKE. MEN POLING UP THE YUKON TOWARD THE MOUNTAINS OR DRIFTING DOWN THE YUKON TOWARD THE WILDERNESS HEARD IT AND DID AN ABRUPT ABOUT-FACE IN THE DIRECTION OF THE SALMON STREAM WHOSE NAME NO ONE COULD PRONOUNCE PROPERLY.

Some did not hear the news at all but, drifting past the Klondike's mouth, saw the boats and tents and the excited figures, felt the hair rise on their necks, and then, still unbelieving, joined the clamouring throng pushing up through the weeds and muck of Rabbit Creek.

Joe Ladue already was on the scene. His quick merchant's mind had swiftly grasped the situation. Others were scrambling to stake claims, but Ladue was more interested in staking out a townsite on the swamp below the scarred mountain at the Klondike's mouth. That was the start of Dawson City. It was worth all the gold of Bonanza. Within two years, lots sold for as much as five thousand dollars a front foot on the main street.

Ladue headed for Fortymile to register his site, but on the way he met a man who wanted timber to build a house. Ladue's lively imagination saw a thousand houses rising on the swampland. Back in his tracks he turned, sending his application down to the police by runner. At his trading post at Sixtymile, he loaded his raft with all the available dressed lumber, then floated his sawmill to the new townsite. Soon he had a rough warehouse built, and a little cabin for himself, which did duty as a saloon. It was the first building in the new mining camp, which Ladue had already named after George M. Dawson, a government geologist.

It was the old-timers who were skeptical of Bonanza. The valley was too wide, they said, and the willows did not lean the proper way, and the water did not taste right. It was too far upriver. It was on the wrong side of the Yukon. It was moose pasture. Only newcomers, known as *cheechakos*, were too green to realize that it could not contain gold. That made some of them rich.

The men who first staked the Klondike were men who saw it as a last chance—men in poor luck, sick and discouraged, with nothing better to do than follow the siren call of a new stampede. Many of these sold their claims in the first week, believing them worthless. Many more tried vainly to sell, so that in that first winter two-thirds of the richest properties in the Klondike could have been bought for a song. Most men were too poor to work their claims; they went back to Dawson or Fortymile to try to get jobs to raise funds. Others, infected by the excitement of the moment, simply wandered back and forth aimlessly up and down the valley.

Carmack himself could not start work at once. He was forced to cut logs for Ladue's mill to earn enough to feed himself. Even then he was so short of funds he could build only three lengths of sluice box. As he had no wheelbarrow, he carried the gravel in a box on his back for one hundred feet (30 m) to the stream to wash out the gold. In spite of this awkward arrangement, he cleaned up fourteen hundred dollars from surface prospects in less than a month. It would be worth thirty times as much today. But even in the face of this evidence there were only a few men who believed that there actually was gold in the valleys of the Klondike.

By the end of August, all of Bonanza Creek had been staked, and new prospectors, arriving daily, were fanning out across the Klondike watershed looking for more ground. None realized it, but the richest treasure of all still lay undiscovered.

Down Bonanza, in search of new ground, trudged a young Austrian immigrant named Antone Stander. For nine years, ever since he had landed in New York City, Stander had been seeking his fortune in the remote corners of the continent, working as a cowboy, as a sheep herder, as a farmer, as a coal miner, and now as a prospector. When he arrived in the

New World, unable to speak a word of English, he had just $1.75 to his name. After mastering the language and walking over most of North America, he was no richer. All his funds had been spent on the trip north in the spring of 1896. Now, on this last day of August, he was embarking on a final gamble.

He was a handsome man, just twenty-nine years old, with dark, curly hair and sensitive, romantic-looking features. As he reached the south fork of Bonanza Creek, a few hundred feet above Carmack's claim, he stopped to examine it curiously. Later Stander would look back upon this as the most important moment of his life, for after this day nothing was ever again the same for him. The narrow wooded ravine, with a trickle of water snaking along its bottom, still had no name. The prospectors referred to it in Yukon parlance as "Bonanza's pup." It would soon be known as Eldorado.

After mastering the language and walking over most of North America, he was no richer. All his funds had been spent on the trip north in the spring of 1896. Now, on this last day of August, he was embarking on a final gamble.

Stander arrived at the fork with four companions, all of whom had already staked on Bonanza. They had little faith in their property, but on an impulse they walked up the pup in a group and sank their pans into the sand. Like Stander, each had reached the end of the line financially. Now they stared into the first pan and, to their astonishment, saw that there was more than six dollars' worth of gold in the bottom. They had no way of knowing it, but this was the richest creek in the world. Each of the claims staked that day eventually produced one million dollars or more.

As Stander and his companions drove in their stakes, others up and down Bonanza began to sense by some curious kind of telepathy that something tantalizing was in the wind. Louis Emkins, a lean-faced and rangy prospector from Illinois, was struggling up Bonanza when he saw the campfires flickering among the bushes of the unexplored creek. It was enough to send the blood pulsing through his veins. He and his three companions quickened their pace and burst upon Stander and the others, who tried to discourage them, claiming that the prospects were small and only on the surface.

Two of the men turned back at once, a fortune slipping from their grasp, but Emkins and his partner George Demars stayed on. *Seven* had already been staked illegally for a friend in Fortymile, but Emkins, a determined figure with a forbidding black moustache, would have none of it. He tore up the stakes and substituted his own and by that single action made himself wealthy. Within a year, he was able to sell out for more than $100,000.

William Johns, a black-bearded and raw-boned ex-newspaper reporter from Chicago, was at the mouth of the Eldorado when Emkins's two discouraged comrades emerged, talking disconsolately of "skim diggings" on a moose flat. Some sixth sense told Johns to prospect the pup anyway. He had a strange feeling that something important was afoot. This sensation increased when he met Emkins and Demars, who were suspiciously casual about their prospects, and then Frank Keller, Stander's companion, who was curiously evasive about what he had found.

When Johns and his three Norwegian companions headed up the new creek the following day, one of them pointed to the water:

"Someone's working; the water's muddy!"

The four men crept upstream, alert and silent—"like hunters who have scented game," as Johns put it. Suddenly, they surprised Stander crouching over a panful of gold with three of his companions crowding about him. They looked "like a cat caught in a cream pitcher," and Johns and his friends needed no further encouragement to stake. One of the Norwegians who had read a great deal named the new creek Eldorado, more or less as a joke. But, as it turned out, the title fitted.

To the newcomers, however, this narrow cleft in the wooded hills was just another valley with good surface prospects. These really meant very little, for gold lying in the gravel on the creek's edge did not necessarily mean that the valley was rich. Before that could be determined, someone would have to go through the hard labour of building fires to burn one or more shafts down through the permafrost for at least fifteen feet (4.5 m) to bedrock, searching for the "pay streak" (which might not exist). Then the muck must be hauled up by windlass to the surface and washed down a sluice box to find out how much gold there really was.

The sluice boxes were long, three-sided wooden troughs with crossbars, known as "riffles," and cocoa matting on the floor. By damming the creek and building up a head of water, the prospector could wash the paydirt down the incline of the sluice box, shovelling it in from the "dump" that had been hoisted by buckets from the bottom of the shaft. The coarse gold was caught in the riffles, for it was nineteen times as heavy as the rushing water; the fine gold sank into the mesh of the cocoa matting. Every three days, the miners turned off the water from the dam and removed the gold and black sand from the riffles and matting.

The final "cleanup," as it was called, was done by panning the sand—an exhausting task that involved squatting on the ground and rotating the pan with a movement of the shoulders until the water had washed away the lighter sand, leaving the specks of glistening gold behind.

This back-breaking toil could easily occupy two months. Until the muck was washed down the sluice box, it was pure guesswork to estimate a claim's true worth. Until the spring thaw came and the rushing creek provided enough head of water to wash the gravels drawn up the shaft that winter, no one could really say exactly how rich Eldorado was—if, indeed, it was rich at all.

CHAPTER FIVE

Robert Henderson's Bad Luck

MOST OF THE MEN WHO STAKED CLAIMS ON THE NEW CREEK IN THAT FIRST WEEK HAD ALREADY DONE THEIR SHARE OF PROSPECTING. THEY HAD SUNK SHAFTS AND SHOVELLED GRAVEL ON CREEK AFTER CREEK IN THE YUKON WATERSHED WITHOUT SUCCESS. TO THEM, THIS LITTLE PUP LOOKED EXACTLY LIKE ANY OTHER IN THE TERRITORY. IF ANYTHING, IT LOOKED SCRAWNIER AND LESS ATTRACTIVE.

To most men, then, Eldorado was as much of a gamble as the Irish sweepstakes. Some, such as Stander, determined to take the gamble and hold their ground and work it to see whether it really did contain gold. Others decided to sell out at once for what they could get. Still others bravely set out to take the risk and then got cold feet and sold before the prize was theirs.

Nobody then knew, of course, that this was the richest placer creek in the world, that almost every claim from *One* to *Forty* was worth at least half a million, that some were worth three times that amount, and that half a century later dredges would still be taking gold from the worked-over gravels.

But in that first winter, paper fortunes changed hands as easily as packages of cigarettes, and poor men became rich and then poor again without realizing it. Jay Whipple, for instance, sold claim *One* almost immediately, for a trifle. The purchaser, a lumberman from Eureka, California, named Skiff Mitchell, lived for half a century on the proceeds.

So the wheel of fortune spun around on Eldorado. Al Thayer and Winfield Oler had staked out *Twenty-Nine* and, believing it worthless, returned to Fortymile, looking for a sucker on whom to unload it. They found one in Jimmy Kerry's saloon in the person of Charley Anderson, a thirty-seven-year-old Swede with a pinched face, who had been mining for several years out of Fortymile. Anderson was so doubtful of the Klondike that he had delayed his trip to the new field until all the ground was gone. Now he was drinking heavily, and Oler, a small and slender man from Baltimore, saw his chance. Anderson woke up the next morning to find he had bought an untried claim for eight hundred dollars.

Anderson went to the Mounted Police post to ask Inspector Charles Constantine to retrieve his money for him, but the policeman pointed out that his signature was on the title. Anderson glumly headed for Eldorado. He had no way of knowing yet that a million dollars' worth of gold lay in the bedrock under his claim and that for the rest of his life he would bear the tag of "the Lucky Swede." As for Oler, he became the butt of so many jokes that he fled the country in disgust.

And yet who is to say which were the lucky ones in the Eldorado lottery? Many who sold out and left the country ended their lives in relative comfort. Many who stayed behind to dig out fortunes lost all in the end. William Sloan, a Nanaimo dry goods merchant, sold his interest in *Fifteen* for fifty thousand dollars and turned his back on the Klondike forever. He invested his money wisely and rose to become a cabinet minister in British Columbia's provincial government. His son became chief justice of that province. But the Lucky Swede died penniless and alone.

All this while, on the other side of the Bonanza watershed, Robert Henderson continued to toil at his open cut on the creek he had wistfully named Gold Bottom. Boats were arriving daily at Dawson; shacks were being clapped together helter-skelter on valley and mud flat; Bonanza was staked for fourteen miles (22.5 km) and Eldorado for three (5 km); and men were spreading across the whole of the Klondike country searching for new discoveries.

Henderson knew nothing of this; he had seen no one but his partners since that August day when Carmack had gone off, promising to send word back if he found anything on the other side of the blue hills.

Then one day—some three weeks after the strike—Henderson looked up and saw a group of men coming down from the divide. He asked them where they had come from, and they replied: "Bonanza Creek."

The name puzzled Henderson, who prided himself on a knowledge of the country. He did not like to show his ignorance, but finally curiosity overcame pride. Where was Bonanza Creek?

The newcomers pointed back over the hill.

"Rabbit Creek! What have you got there?" Henderson asked, with a sinking feeling.

"We have the biggest thing in the world."

"Who found it?"

"McCormick."

Henderson flung down his shovel, then walked slowly over to the bank of the creek and sat down. It was some time before he could speak. McCormick! *Carmack!* For the rest of his life, the sound of that name would be like a cold knife in his heart. Why, the man was not even a prospector!

When he gathered his wits about him, Henderson realized that he must record a claim at once before the human overflow from Bonanza arrived at his creek. He had explored a large fork of Gold Bottom and discovered much better ground yielding thirty-five cents to the pan. Here he had staked a discovery claim, and it was this that he intended to record at Fortymile. He divided up his small gleanings of gold with his partners and set off at once.

But fate had not yet finished with Robert Henderson. He had moved only a short way down the creek before he encountered two long-time prospectors. He knew them both. One was Charles Johnson, tall, bearded, and tough, a farmer and logger from Ohio; the other was Andrew Hunker, better known as "Old Man Hunker," a native of Wittenberg, Germany, a man with sharp features and a dogged face who made a practice of reading Gibbon's *Decline and Fall of the Roman Empire* nightly. (Indeed, he carried six volumes about with him.) Both men were veteran prospectors of the Yukon valley.

Hunker now revealed to Henderson that he, too, had staked a discovery claim on the other fork of Gold Bottom Creek. The partners had got as much as $2.50 a pan from a reef of high bedrock, and they were carrying twenty-five dollars' worth of coarse gold with them, all of it panned out in a few minutes. Obviously, the Hunker claims were far richer than the ones Henderson had staked.

What was Henderson to do? A discovery claim was twice the size of an ordinary claim. He could insist on his own earlier discovery and take a thousand feet (305 m) of relatively poor ground. But the richer ground was obviously in the area of Hunker's find. The only answer was to allow Hunker the discovery claim and for Henderson to stake an ordinary claim of five hundred feet next to it. Thus the entire watershed became known as Hunker Creek, and only the fork that Henderson originally located was called Gold Bottom.

Henderson, having swallowed this second bitter pill, pushed on down the Klondike valley. Soon a new prize was dangled before him. He ran into a Finn named Solomon Marpak who had just made a discovery on another tributary of the Klondike called Bear Creek. Henderson staked next to Marpak, his spirits rising; Bear Creek looked rich.

> *"I only want my just dues and nothing more, but those discoveries rightly belong to me, and I will contest them as a Canadian as long as I live," he said with force and bitterness. And so began the long controversy over which man was the rightful discoverer of the Klondike.*

He now believed he had three claims to record—on Gold Bottom, on Hunker, and on Bear—but when he reached Fortymile, fate dealt him a third blow. He was told that the law had been changed. No man was allowed more than one claim in the Klondike mining district, and that claim must be recorded within sixty days of staking. In vain Henderson protested that when he had staked his ground the law had allowed a claim on each creek, with no deadline for recording. The mining recorder did not know him. Henderson swallowed hard and recorded only the Hunker Creek claim.

"I only want my just dues and nothing more, but those discoveries rightly belong to me, and I will contest them as a Canadian as long as I live," he said with force and bitterness. And so began the long controversy over which man was the rightful discoverer of the Klondike. It rages still and almost always along national lines: the English and Canadians say that Henderson should have the credit; the Americans stand by Carmack.

CHAPTER SIX

The News No One Would Believe

CLARENCE BERRY QUIT HIS JOB AS BARTENDER IN FORTYMILE AND WAS ONE OF
THOSE WHO LEFT TOWN IMMEDIATELY ON HEARING CARMACK'S NEWS. HE WAS
HELPED BY HIS OLD BOSS, BILL MCPHEE, THE OWNER OF THE SALOON, WHO
LENT HIM ENOUGH MONEY TO BUY FOOD TO KEEP HIM GOING. WHEN BERRY
REACHED BONANZA CREEK, HE WAS ABLE TO STAKE CLAIM NUMBER *FORTY
ABOVE* DISCOVERY. IT WASN'T A TERRIBLY RICH CLAIM, BUT IT WASN'T A POOR
ONE EITHER. BERRY'S REAL FORTUNE LAY AHEAD, HOWEVER. HE OWED IT TO
ANTONE STANDER, THE AUSTRIAN WHO HAD STAKED ON ELDORADO.

The handsome Stander was back in Fortymile, without funds, without
food, and, to his pain and bewilderment, without credit at the Alaska
Commercial Company's store, which wouldn't advance him any provisions
until he got somebody to back him. Stander was desperately seeking a friend
when Berry volunteered to help. In gratitude Stander gave him half of
his Eldorado property in exchange for half of the claim that Berry had
staked on Bonanza. With that simple gesture, Clarence Berry laid the
foundation for one of the largest personal fortunes to come out of the
Klondike.

That fall, while Ladue's sawmill was turning out rough lumber for the
first of Dawson's buildings, while Carmack was treating his friends to drinks
in the tent saloons at fifty dollars a round, while old-timers continued to
jeer and newcomers scouted the valleys for new ground, the industrious
Berry and one or two others set about the slow work of burning shafts to
bedrock to find out just how much gold there was in the Klondike valley.

On *Twenty-One Above* Bonanza, Louis Rhodes was also reluctantly
grubbing his way down through the frozen muck. He felt a bit of a fool,
for his neighbours were laughing at him, but when he tried to sell out for

$250 there were no takers, and so he kept working. On October 3, at a depth of fifteen feet (4.6 m), he reached bedrock.

The results were electrifying. In the soft rock, he could spy, by guttering candlelight, broad seams of clay and gravel streaked with gold. This was the "pay streak." He had hit the old creek channel squarely on his first try. It was so rich that he was able to hire workmen on the spot and to pay them nightly by scooping up a few panfuls of dirt from the bottom of the shaft.

Heartened by this news, Berry kept working until, early in November, he too reached bedrock. From a single pan of paydirt, he weighed out fifty-seven dollars in gold and knew at once that his days of poverty were over. (Gold in those days was worth sixteen dollars an ounce. Today the price is close to four hundred dollars.) He and Stander began to hire men to help them haul the dirt up by windlass and pile it on the great "dump" that, when the spring thaw came, would be shovelled into sluice boxes so that the gold could be washed free of the clay and gravel.

Berry and Stander were also able to pay their workmen with gold dug out on the spot. They bought the two adjoining claims, *Four* and *Five*, from the original stakers of Eldorado and eventually split this block of claims in half, Stander taking the lower half and Berry the upper. Berry alone took $140,000 from his winter dump the following spring.

Now the Klondike was a frenzy of excitement as every claim owner began to burrow into the frozen earth. Glowing in the long nights with a hundred miners' fires, the valleys looked like the inferno itself. Those who had scoffed at Rhodes and Berry could now peer down their shafts and literally see the nuggets glittering in the candle's ray.

Meanwhile, a tent town was forming along the margin of the Yukon near the mouth of the Klondike River. By January there were only four houses in Dawson besides Ladue's, but the tents, like dirty white sails, were scattered in ragged order between the trees on the frozen swampland. It was not an ideal townsite, but it was close to the source of gold.

No one in the outside world yet knew of the existence of the new camp or of the gold that nourished it. In Fortymile, William Ogilvie, the Canadian government surveyor, was searching about for some means to inform his government of the situation.

Scarcely anyone would attempt the dangerous journey up the river to the Chilkoot Pass, but Captain William Moore, a remarkably tough seventy-three-year-old, offered to take a short message. Moore was a steamboat man who had been in almost every gold rush from Peru to the Cassiars and who now made his home on Skagway Bay, at the foot of the Coast Mountains. At an age when most men were over the hill of life, the white-bearded old pioneer was still going strong. He had a contract to bring the Canadian mail across the mountains and into the interior of the Yukon, and when his U.S. counterpart failed to deliver Moore took on his job too.

That fall of 1896 Moore had already been down the river to Circle City (in Alaska) and was now heading back again like a man on a Sunday jaunt when he picked up Ogilvie's message. Moore put all other mushers to shame; three young men, strong and vigorous, had all started from Fortymile the previous week in an attempt to make a record trip to the coastal Panhandle. When the aged mail carrier overtook the trio, they were exhausted and starving. Moore popped them onto his dogsled and whisked them out to Juneau without further mishap. As far as Ogilvie was concerned, the trip, though memorable, was a waste of time. His report went on to Ottawa, where nobody paid any attention to it.

At an age when most men were over the hill of life, the white-bearded old pioneer was still going strong. He had a contract to bring the Canadian mail across the mountains and into the interior of the Yukon.

As the town of Dawson slowly took shape around Ladue's sawmill and saloon, a subtle change began to work among those prospectors who for years had had nothing to call their own. Accepted standards of wealth vanished. There was a desperate shortage of almost everything that a man needed. But there was no shortage of gold. Those who had struck it rich could claw the legal tender from the dumps with their bare hands; thus, to many, gold became the cheapest commodity in the world.

No other community on Earth had a greater percentage of would-be millionaires. Yet all its citizens were living under worse conditions than any sharecropper. Food became so scarce that all but the most expensive dogs had to be killed because the owners did not have enough to feed them. Only the fortunate arrival of a raftload of beef cattle saved the camp from starvation. Willis Thorpe, a Juneau butcher, sold the meat for sixteen thousand dollars; within a year, he was worth $200,000.

There was no writing paper in Dawson and nothing to read. The only eggs came from two hens owned by a policeman's wife, and these cost a dollar apiece. Laundry was so expensive that most men wore their shirts until they couldn't stand them any longer and then threw them away. One French Canadian turned a net profit by retrieving these garments, laundering them, and reselling them, often enough to the former owners. The camp's single bathhouse consisted of a small tent with a stove and an upended log as a stool; for five minutes in a wooden laundry tub, the unclean paid a dollar and a half.

Some men could no longer eat or sleep at the thought of mining so much gold. One, who had washed out thirty thousand dollars, became so obsessed by the fear of being robbed that he suffered a mental collapse and shot himself.

The ante at stud poker was one dollar, but it might easily cost five hundred to see the third card. A night on the town—which meant a night in Joe Ladue's bare-boarded saloon, drinking watered whisky—could cost at least fifty dollars. Few minded the expense; it was so easy to pan out a few shovelfuls of dirt from the dump to pay for the fun.

One man went to work in the morning and came to town at night with fourteen hundred dollars in gold. In Ladue's he ordered two whiskies, toasting his former self in the one and making believe his former self was drinking the other, then stuck two cigars in his mouth and smoked them together.

This behaviour was less peculiar than it seemed. Every man's life had been changed by the strike. On the day he reached the pay streak and realized that he was rich, he became a different person. Some men could no longer eat or sleep at the thought of mining so much gold. One, who had washed out thirty thousand dollars, became so obsessed by the fear of being robbed that he suffered a mental collapse and shot himself.

By midwinter the frenzied staking on the creeks had brought about a state of complete confusion. The original staking of Bonanza had been so unorganized that both the ownership and the size of many claims were in dispute. Work stopped; men argued and fought; by January, when William Ogilvie arrived to survey the Ladue township, the miners begged him to re-survey Bonanza and Eldorado. Ogilvie agreed on the condition that his decisions should be accepted as final.

Few men were better fitted for the task of unsnarling the Klondike tangle, where the shifting of stakes by a few feet might mean the loss or gain of thousands of dollars. No one would dare to bribe Ogilvie. He firmly believed that no government servant should enrich himself because of his job. Alone among hundreds, he stubbornly refused to stake an inch of ground or to turn a single cent of profit from the Klondike strike. The sense of what was right had become an act of faith with Ogilvie, and he insisted that his son, Morley, who was with him, keep the same standard. Only one other man in the Yukon felt the same way, and that was Charles Constantine, the North-West Mounted Police superintendent, who also left the country poor but respected, though some of his constables staked out fortunes.

With his round, solemn face and his dark beard, Ogilvie had the features that were later to be associated with reigning British monarchs, but this

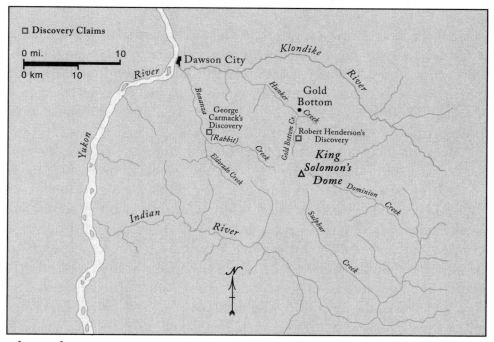

The Creeks, 1896

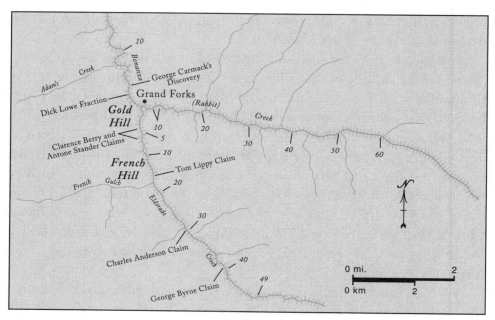

The Rich Ground, 1896–97

solemn appearance masked a puckish sense of humour. His whole character, indeed, was an unlikely mixture. The face that he presented to the public was that of the dedicated government official, conscientious and sedate. But in private he was a clever mimic, a punster, a practical joker, and a good storyteller known also for his ability to play anything on the piano, especially Scottish reels.

He went about his tasks on Bonanza and Eldorado with professional seriousness, for his tidy civil servant's mind was shocked by the raggedness of the original staking. At the same time, he carefully filed away in the neat pigeonholes of his memory a small collection of anecdotes that served him as after-dinner stories in the years that followed. He was both dismayed and amused, for instance, to discover the way in which one prospector—a Mounted Policeman at that—had located a claim in the twisting section of Lower Bonanza. Instead of measuring off five hundred feet in a straight line, he followed the creek, which doubled back on itself in such a way that, when Ogilvie surveyed it, he discovered that the unfortunate policeman had got eight feet (2.4 m) *less* than a claim.

CHAPTER SEVEN

A Friend in Need

OGILVIE HAD MANY STORIES TO TELL ABOUT THAT FIRST WILD YEAR. AS THE MAXIMUM LEGAL STAKE WAS FIVE HUNDRED FEET (152 M), MANY OVERSIZE CLAIMS WERE CHOPPED DOWN BY HIS SURVEY, LEAVING THIN WEDGES OF LAND SANDWICHED IN BETWEEN THE NEW BOUNDARIES. THESE FRACTIONAL CLAIMS COULD BE VERY VALUABLE: ONE ON ELDORADO, FOR INSTANCE, JUST TEN FEET (3 M) WIDE, WAS THOUGHT TO BE WORTH BETWEEN TEN AND TWENTY THOUSAND DOLLARS.

And another, a mere five inches (12.7 cm) wide, was sold to the owner of the adjacent claim for five hundred dollars. Jim White, an Irishman from Circle City, Alaska, was convinced there was a fraction between *Thirty-Six* and *Thirty-Seven* Eldorado. He staked it and used the ground in an effort to bully the owners on either side to come to terms with him. He waited on tenterhooks for Ogilvie's survey to set the proper dimensions. In order to madden White, whom he considered a scoundrel and a blackmailer, Ogilvie deliberately delayed the work. When the ground was finally surveyed, the fraction turned out to be just three inches (7.6 cm) wide. For the rest of his days, its owner smarted under the nickname of "Three-Inch White."

It was a bitterly cold spring day, about ten below zero (-23° C), and a biting wind was whistling up the trough of Eldorado when Ogilvie reached the upper limit of Clarence Berry's *Five*. Dusk was falling, and, as his assistants gathered up his instruments, the surveyor stood working out the figures in his notebook to see how long the claim really was. Around was gathered the usual group of miners, all guessing at the claim's size; for months they had been searching and measuring on their own, hoping without success to discover a fraction on Eldorado.

Now Ogilvie whistled in surprise when he discovered that *Five* was forty-one feet, six inches (12.6 m) too long. It was on this section of his claim and this section only—one of the richest locations in the history of placer mining—that Berry had done his winter's work. Hundred-dollar pans were the rule there; five-hundred-dollar pans were not unusual. Now it turned out that Berry didn't own this rich sliver of land. And he could not stake it because he had used up his staking rights. His entire dump of pay-dirt stood on the fraction; it could not be washed out until spring. Meanwhile, anyone could stake it.

Ogilvie realized at once that, if he announced the fraction, Berry would lose everything he had worked for that winter and also that a riot would probably follow as dozens fought to stake ground known to be worth hundreds of thousands. And now in that conscientious mind, so used to the rule book, a struggle ensued; should he cling to procedure and take the consequences, or should he depart from the rigid path he had set himself? His solemn, bearded face did not change expression as, turning to Berry, who was standing nearby, he said: "Let's go to supper. I'm cold enough and hungry enough to eat nuggets."

A ripple of suspicion ran through the throng, and Berry sensed it as Ogilvie hurried toward the cabin.

"Is there anything wrong, Mr. Ogilvie?"

"Come out of hearing," the surveyor whispered. He had made his decision.

"What's wrong?" cried Berry, in an agony of impatience. "My God, what's wrong?"

Ogilvie maintained his cracking pace. "There's a fraction of forty-one feet, six inches on claim number five, and nearly all your winter's work is on it." "My God!" Berry almost shouted. "What will I do?" Ogilvie's civil servant mask returned. "It is not my place to advise you," he said. And then—another rent in the rule book—"Haven't you a friend you can trust?"

"Trust—how?"

"Why, to stake that fraction tonight and transfer it to yourself and partner."

Berry thought at once of George Byrne, who was at work on a claim five miles (8 km) up Eldorado. He rushed to the cabin, told his wife to get supper for Ogilvie, then dashed up the creek.

He returned with Byrne about half past nine, and, in the presence of a baffled Mrs. Berry, a strange little act took place. The two men carefully questioned Ogilvie about the proper method of legally staking a fraction, and Ogilvie replied politely. There was no suggestion that this was anything but an academic discussion, but the surveyor took the trouble to draw a detailed plan of the method of staking on a sheet of wrapping paper, which he handed to Byrne.

In the small hours of the morning, Byrne staked the fraction, which in that single season produced for Berry $140,000; in return Byrne got an equal length off the lower unworked end of the property so that Berry's block of land would remain unbroken. As Ogilvie wrote, "A friend like that, in such a need, is a friend indeed."

Ogilvie himself later that spring washed out a pan of dirt taken at random from Berry's shaft. On it was $119 worth of gold or, as he remarked, "about half a year's salary for many a good clerk."

And yet Berry and his wife lived under the most primitive of conditions in a twelve-by-sixteen-foot (3.7 m by 4.9 m) hovel without floor or windows, whose only furniture was two homemade chairs and two rickety bedsteads built of unplaned lumber and curtained with calico. By the door stood a sheet-iron stove that the Berrys had packed in over the trail. Beside it was the panning tank of dirty water in which one of Berry's twenty-five workmen periodically tested the paydirt. A small glass kerosene lamp and a pair of copper gold scales supplied the only other ornament.

When Mrs. Berry needed pocket money, she merely walked to the dump and, with a sharp stick, smashed apart the frozen clods and pulled out the nuggets.

The gold was everywhere. The wages Berry paid totalled $150 a day, which he washed out himself each evening. When Mrs. Berry needed pocket money, she merely walked to the dump and, with a sharp stick, smashed apart the frozen clods and pulled out the nuggets. One day she went to call her husband for supper and, while she was waiting for him to come up the shaft, picked up fifty dollars' worth of coarse gold.

Ethel Berry's only female neighbour was Tom Lippy's wife, Salome, a sinewy little woman from Kinsman, Ohio, who lived with her husband in another tiny mud-roofed cabin, about a mile (1.6 km) up the valley. Lippy, like Berry, was industrious, sober, level-headed—and lucky. A sudden and inspired hunch had brought him to the Yukon.

He had started life as an iron moulder in Pennsylvania, but his almost fanatical belief in physical culture had led him into the YMCA and then west to Seattle as a physical-training instructor. As a volunteer fireman, he had once held the title of world's champion hose coupler. Like everybody else who came in over the trail, he was tough: solidly built, dark, good-looking, and clean-shaven. An injury to his knee had forced his retirement from the YMCA, and a strange intuition had sent him north in 1896 on borrowed money. Now he had one of the richest claims in the Klondike. Although this was the most memorable winter of Thomas Lippy's life, it certainly was not the happiest, for the Klondike, which gave him his fortune, took the life of his adopted son, who was drowned in the Yukon River. Not all the gold in Eldorado could have saved him.

CHAPTER EIGHT

The End of the Line

THE WINTER PASSED SLOWLY, DREAM-LIKE FOR MANY. IT WAS HARD SOMETIMES TO SEPARATE REALITY FROM FANTASY. IN THEIR DARK HOVELS, THE MINERS WATCHED IN FASCINATION AND DISBELIEF AS THE SMALL HEAPS OF GOLD PILED UP IN JARS AND BOTTLES ON THE WINDOWSILLS. IT SUPPLIED THE ONLY ORNAMENT ON THE NAKED WALLS, GLITTERING IN THE FLAT LIGHT OF THE SUNLESS NOONS OR IN THE FLICKERING OF HOARDED CANDLES.

But with the coming of the summer of 1897, Dawson was to become front-page news, its isolation from the world at an end. The camp waited impatiently for the arrival of the first steamboat in June. The Klondike's newly rich were ready to return to a civilization that some had rejected ten years before. There were more than eighty, each owning a fortune that ran from twenty-five thousand to half a million dollars.

Some were determined to leave the North forever and had already sold the claims, content to live modestly but securely for the rest of their lives. Others were looking for a brief celebration in the big cities of the Pacific coast before returning to the Klondike for more treasure. All felt the desperate need to escape from the dark confines of their cabins and tents and from the smoky depths of their mine shafts, just as they had once felt a similar need to escape the smoky, populous cities.

Then, early in June, a shrill whistle was heard out in the river, and the Alaska Commercial Company's tiny sternwheeler *Alice* rounded the Moosehide Bluff and puffed into shore. The entire town poured down to greet her. She was loaded with equal quantities of liquor and food, and the whole community went on a spree, as every saloon served free drinks across the counter. A couple of days later a second steamboat, *Portus B. Weare*, arrived, and the performance was repeated. When the two boats left for the trip downstream, they carried with them the men who would bring the first news of the great strike out to the unsuspecting world. When the Klondikers finally reached Seattle and San Francisco, they were mobbed by would-be gold seekers.

One prospector, J. C. Miller of Los Angeles, was reduced to a state of nervous prostration by the swarms of gold-crazy men who visited him. Another, William Hewitt, who came out with a five-gallon (22 l) can filled with dust and nuggets, received more than a hundred callers a day for weeks and letters from every state in the union.

But Ladue had perhaps the most frantic time of all, for the papers quickly dubbed him mayor of Dawson City, and he was pursued by such a throng of reporters, well-wishers, fortune hunters, and cranks that he fled to the East. He stepped off the train in Chicago into the arms of another waiting mob, and even when he reached his farm at Plattsburg in the Adirondacks of New York State there was no relief. A bushel basket full of mail awaited him. The people crowded into the parlour and began to finger the nuggets that he poured onto a table. Ladue left them to it and went off into a barn to hide. There he was cornered by Lincoln Steffens, the most persistent reporter of his day. "He was the weariest looking man I ever saw," Steffens wrote in *McClure's*.

It was a prophetic remark, for Ladue's days were numbered. His life reached its climax in a Cinderella ending, made to order for the press. At long last he married Anna Mason, his lifelong sweetheart, whose parents were now more than happy to welcome the most renowned figure in America into the family.

Ladue's name by this time was a household word. He was worth, on paper, five million dollars. His picture appeared in advertisements endorsing Dr. Green's Nervura blood and nerve remedy. The financial pages were soon reporting that he had been named president and managing director of the Joseph Ladue Gold Mining and Development Company, whose directors included some of the biggest names in New York finance.

Alas, for Ladue, the thirteen winters spent along the Yukon had taken their toll. A few months after he came out of the North, his aging partner, Arthur Harper, who had followed him down the coast in the next boat, died of tuberculosis. The following year Ladue also succumbed to the disease, at the height of the great stampede he helped bring about.

And what of Robert Henderson, the man whose tip to Carmack had started it all? Tragically, his troubles never ended. The old injury to his leg prevented him from doing any work on his claim on Hunker Creek. All through the fall and winter he lay ill from that injury. And then he was off again, searching for gold. A less restless man might have gone to work on the Hunker claim, which was obviously a good one, but it was typical of Henderson that he ignored it in order to search for new goldfields.

He trudged the length of Too Much Gold Creek, which contained no gold at all, and then, still supremely optimistic, headed for the Stewart River country. There, too, he searched in vain, though he left his name behind on one of the Stewart's smaller tributaries.

Ladue's name by this time was a household word. He was worth, on paper, five million dollars. His picture appeared in advertisements endorsing Dr. Green's Nervura blood and nerve remedy.

At last he decided to return to his wife and children in Colorado, whom he had not seen for four years. He boarded a steamboat for St. Michael, anxious to be away, and there, for the fifth time, bad luck descended upon him. The steamer was frozen in at Circle City, and Henderson, trapped in the country that had brought him nothing but misfortune, fell sick again. In order to pay his medical bills, he was forced to sell his claim on Hunker Creek. He received three thousand dollars for it; that represented the total amount that he took from the Klondike district. Yet each of the claims that he had staked and tried to record was worth a great deal. The Hunker claim eventually paid a royalty of $450,000, after which it was sold for another $200,000. For decades it continued to be a valuable property, but Henderson got none of it.

He reached St. Michael ultimately, the following spring, and boarded a steamer for Seattle. He had eleven hundred dollars left in Klondike gold, but his troubles were still not over. The years spent in the country of the open cabin door had not equipped him for civilization's wiles. Before he reached Seattle, all his gold had been stolen. Disgusted, he tore an emblem from his lapel and handed it to Tappan Adney, the correspondent for *Harper's Illustrated Weekly*.

"Here, you keep this," he cried. "I will lose it, too. I am not fit to live among civilized men."

Adney examined the little badge curiously. It was the familiar insignia of an exclusive lodge, the Yukon Order of Pioneers, with its golden rule and its motto: "Do unto others as you would be done by."

The statistics regarding the Klondike stampede are diminishing ones. One hundred thousand persons, it is estimated, actually set out on the trail; some thirty or forty thousand reached Dawson. Only about one half of this number bothered to look for gold, and of these only four thousand found any. Of the four thousand, a few hundred found gold in quantities large enough to call themselves rich. And out of these fortunate men, only the merest handful managed to keep their wealth.

The kings of Eldorado toppled from their thrones one by one. Antone Stander drank part of his fortune away; his wife—a one-time dance-hall girl—deserted him and took the rest, including the Stander Hotel, which he had built in Seattle with profits from his claim. One cannot entirely blame her, for when Stander was drinking he was subject to crazy fits of jealousy; on one occasion, he tried to cut her to pieces with a knife. Stander headed north again, seeking another Klondike, working his passage aboard ship by peeling potatoes in the galley, but he got no farther than the Alaska Panhandle. He died in the Pioneers' Home at Sitka. His wife, who lived until 1944, left an estate worth fifty thousand dollars.

Win Oler died in the Pioneers' Home too, plagued to the last by the knowledge that he had sold a million-dollar claim to the Lucky Swede for eight hundred dollars. But Charley Anderson, the Lucky Swede, fared no better. His dance-hall-girl wife divorced him; the 1906 San Francisco earthquake shattered his fortune, since he had invested heavily in real estate.

He remained, in spite of these setbacks, an incurable optimist, so convinced he would strike it rich again that he vowed never to shave off his little pointed beard until he became wealthy again. He was still wearing it in 1939 when he died, pushing a wheelbarrow in a sawmill near Sapperton, British Columbia, for $3.25 a day. It had always annoyed him when people referred to him as a millionaire. "I never had a million dollars," the

Lucky Swede used to say. "The most I ever had was nine hundred thousand."

It is pleasant, in the light of all this, to report that the two most industrious men on Bonanza and Eldorado enjoyed continued success and fortune for the rest of their lives. Louis Rhodes and Clarence Berry, who sank the first two shafts to bedrock in the Klondike while their fellows twiddled their thumbs, did not squander their riches but, on the contrary, added to them.

Berry took $1,500,000 from his claims on Eldorado. Then he and his brothers moved on to Fairbanks, where they struck it rich a second time on Esther Creek. They returned to California, purchased oil property near Bakersfield, and made another enormous fortune. At various times, they owned both the Los Angeles and the San Francisco baseball clubs.

Berry never forgot his original benefactor, Bill McPhee, the saloon keeper. In 1906 McPhee's saloon at Fairbanks was destroyed by fire, and the aging barkeeper lost everything but the clothes he wore. Berry wired him from San Francisco to draw on him for all the money necessary to get back into business again. In his declining years, McPhee lived on a pension from Berry, who died of appendicitis in San Francisco in 1930, worth several millions.

> *Louis Rhodes and Clarence Berry, who sank the first two shafts to bedrock in the Klondike while their fellows twiddled their thumbs, did not squander their riches but, on the contrary, added to them.*

Louis Rhodes invested his Klondike fortune in mining property in Mexico and lost everything. Without a moment's hesitation, he turned prospector again and headed for Alaska. With all the industry that he had shown in the early Bonanza days, he began to explore the newly staked country near Fairbanks. He found gold-bearing quartz on a tiny outcropping of unstaked land and parlayed it into a mine that yielded him a profit of $300,000. He retired to California's Valley of the Moon and lived out the rest of his days in comfort.

And what of the original discoverers of the Klondike? Carmack abandoned his Indian wife, Kate, in 1900. She had not been able to cope with civilization and returned to her home at Caribou Crossing on Lake Tagish, where she lived on a government pension, still wearing her cheap cotton clothing but always with a necklace of nuggets taken from the famous claim on Bonanza. She died about 1917.

Carmack was married again to a pretty, dark woman named Marguerite Laimee, who had been on the fringe of three gold rushes—in South Africa, Australia, and the Klondike. She and Carmack lived happily until his death in Vancouver in 1922. He died wealthy and respected, and his wife inherited his money.

Tagish Charley sold his mining properties in 1901 and spent the rest of his years at Carcross on the Yukon-BC border, where he operated a hotel, entertained lavishly, and bought diamond earrings for his daughter. He was treated as a white man and allowed to drink heavily. As a result, one day when he was on a drunken spree, he fell off a bridge and was drowned.

Skookum Jim was treated as a white man too—but that was not enough for him. He wanted to *be* a white man. And so, although his mining property was paying him royalties of ninety thousand dollars a year, he continued to live the hard life of the prospector, travelling ceaselessly across the North vainly seeking a quartz load, often going for days without food, so fierce was his quest. In the end, his magnificent physique was weakened. He died, worn out, in 1916.

Robert Henderson outlived them all. The Canadian government at last recognized him as a co-discoverer of the Klondike. It awarded him a pension of two hundred dollars a month. But for the rest of his life, he continued to look for gold. He sought it on Vancouver Island, in northern British Columbia, and on the Pelly River. In 1932 he joined two mining promoters in a gold discovery on the Upper Pelly. A party was organized to fly into the area on a prospecting trip. When the time came, he was not with them. He died of cancer in January of 1933, still talking of the big strike he hoped to make.

INDEX

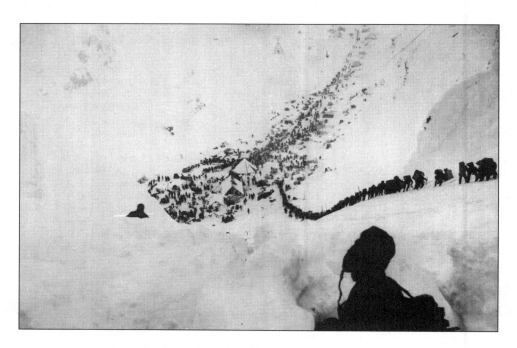

The mode of travel on the Chilkoot Pass at the height of the Klondike Gold Rush. Losing your place in line might mean waiting for days to rejoin the masses making the trek upward.

(P124-42, ALASKA STATE LIBRARY, ERIC A. HEGG PHOTOGRAPH COLLECTION)

THE KLONDIKE STAMPEDE

CONTENTS

CHAPTER ONE

"Show Us the Gold!"

SOMETHING WAS IN THE WIND THAT JULY MORNING IN 1897; THE LOUNGERS WAITING ON THE SAN FRANCISCO WHARF FELT IT. BUT WHAT WAS IT? WAS THERE ANY TRUTH TO THESE STRANGE WHISPERS DRIFTING OUT OF THE NORTH? WAS THERE TREASURE ABOARD THE STUBBY LITTLE STEAMER, STAINED AND RUSTY, PUFFING SLOWLY TOWARD THE DOCKSIDE? THE *EXCELSIOR* WAS NINE DAYS OUT OF A DISTANT PORT ON THE BERING SEA CALLED ST. MICHAEL, NEAR THE MOUTH OF A RIVER KNOWN AS THE YUKON. SOMEWHERE ALONG THAT WATER-WAY, SO THE RUMOURS HINTED, SOMETHING ELECTRIFYING HAD HAPPENED.

As the ship drew closer, a murmur rose from the crowd. A long line of men in miners' hats was clustered at the deck railing. Now, as their features began to emerge from the blur, you could see that these were men aged beyond their years, gaunt and unshaven, their faces leathered by the sun but with eyes that glittered feverishly—picture-book prospectors, in fact. The buzz increased as it was noticed that their tattered clothing was still stained with the mud and clay of some far-off northern valley.

An outlandish scene followed. Down the gangplank they staggered, wrestling with luggage that seemed too heavy—old leather grips bursting at the hinges, packing cases about to break apart, bulging valises, blanket rolls barely secured by straps and so heavy that each one required two men to hoist it to the dock.

It dawned on the onlookers that this was not common baggage: these suitcases, canvas sacks, old cartons, and boxes were stuffed not with socks and shirts but with gold. And these men, who had been paupers a few months before—some driven nearly to suicide by despair—were now rich beyond their wildest fantasies.

In that moment, the Klondike stampede began, not quietly or gradually, but instantly and with explosive force. Before the *Excelsior* could turn north again, her agents were forced to refuse tickets to ten times her passenger list. For *gold* was a magic word in that dark and dreadful decade that history has mistakenly called the Gay Nineties. In those drab years, when depression destroyed hope and men and women literally died in the gutters of starvation, gold was the rarest of prizes, hoarded in socks and sugar bowls by those who had lost faith in paper money.

Now, it appeared, there was a magic land far to the north where the treasure lay thickly on the ground waiting to be shovelled into club bags. And anybody could dig it out—a one-time YMCA worker, an ex-laundryman, a former muralist! For such were among the fortunate ones traipsing off to Selby's Smelting Works with their golden burden, a chattering mob at their heels.

By the time a second treasure ship docked at Seattle, two days later, a kind of mass lunacy had seized the continent. Five thousand people jammed Schwabacher's Dock to greet the *Portland* at 6 AM, July 19. By 9:30, every road leading to the wharfside was crammed with men and animals, carts and drays. It was as if everyone had been waiting for an excuse to break free. Somewhere just beyond the horizon—few knew exactly where—lay wealth, adventure, and, perhaps more important, release from the dreariness of the decade.

"Show us the gold!" cried the watchers on the wharf, and the miners on board obligingly hoisted their sacks. One man had $100,000 in dust and nuggets tied up in a blanket and had to hire two others to help him drag it away.

"We've got millions," Frank Phiscator, one of the kings of Eldorado (the richest creek in the Klondike), shouted to the crowd. William Stanley, an aging bookkeeper whose wife had been living on wild blueberries, was now so wealthy that she could immediately call in a dressmaker to design a new set of clothes. As one newspaper put it, "Seattle has gone stark, staring mad on gold."

The key phrase was coined by a Seattle newspaper reporter who figured that there was at least a ton of gold aboard the *Portland*. That phrase, "a ton of gold," electrified the nation. In fact it turned out that the reporter had been too cautious: when the results were added up, there were at least two tons of gold on the *Portland*. Within a week, tens of thousands of people were scrambling to reach the Klondike—even though they didn't know where the Klondike was.

In the first twenty-four hours, two thousand New Yorkers tried to buy tickets to the Yukon. In the first week, hundreds quit their jobs; within a month, thousands more followed suit. Streetcar operators deserted their trams, policemen their beats, clergymen their congregations. Clerks walked out of offices, salesmen jumped counters, reporters quit their desks. The mayor of Seattle, attending a convention in San Francisco, did not bother to return home but wired in his resignation and joined the herd.

The world caught the disease. Maoris, Kanakas from Hawaii, Scots, and Serbs were infected. People wore buttons proudly proclaiming, "Yes, I'm going this spring"; it was the thing to do. Men in Klondike outfits were treated free in the saloons. Any druggist's clerk, brought up on dime novels, could walk into a photographer's studio, put on a set of furs or mackinaw and high boots, and feel that he too was a seasoned prospector heading for high adventure in a far-off land.

The world caught the disease. Maoris, Kanakas from Hawaii, Scots, and Serbs were infected. People wore buttons proudly proclaiming, "Yes, I'm going this spring"; it was the thing to do.

One million people, it is said, laid plans to go to the Klondike. One hundred thousand actually set off. And so the Klondike saga is a chronicle of humanity in the mass—of thousands squeezed onto wharfs, jamming street corners, choking roadways; of men, women, horses, and dogs crushed together below decks on overloaded steamers; of beaches crowded with prospectors and pack animals; of dense lines of gold seekers struggling up mountain slopes; of rivers and lakes alive with water craft; of gutted valleys buzzing like hives and ramshackle villages bursting into cities. For the next eighteen months, the Yukon interior plateau became a human anthill.

San Francisco, Seattle, Portland, and Victoria teemed with men, every hotel filled to suffocation, the restaurants overcrowded, the lodging houses roaring. Near the dock areas, a river of humanity moved sluggishly between ten-foot (3 m) stacks of supplies. Hundreds clogged the roadways dressed in the approved garb (garish mackinaws, wide-brimmed hats, iron-cleated top-boots), buying beasts of burden: dogs, goats, sheep, oxen, burros, mules, ponies, even reindeer and elk—anything on four legs—at outrageous prices.

As they waited for the ships to take them north, as the salesmen from the outfitting houses moved among them, and as the smooth-talking gamblers took their savings, they babbled about gold, caressing the word as if the metal were an end in itself and not a means to a better life. The press caught the feeling and reproduced it with such phrases as "rich, yellow gold," "hard, solid gold," "shining gold." It was up there, somewhere, glittering among the mosses.

Blinded by the prospect of gold, the tenderfeet had only the vaguest idea of what lay ahead. Yet almost everyone who fought for passage on the leaky boats bound for Skagway and Dyea was convinced that he would return with a fortune. Some even took gunny sacks to hold the nuggets they expected to scoop from the gravels of Bonanza and Eldorado Creeks.

In the Yukon, autumn was already in the air, the birches on the hillsides yellowing, the buckbrush on the treeless peaks turning purple, the shallow ponds bearing a thin skin of morning ice. The stampeders had themselves photographed proudly swathed in furs and so must have had some inkling of the conditions facing them: of the numbing cold on the beaches, the winds howling through the passes, the ghostly fog of the northern winter. But fantasy possessed them: it was as if the gold by its very nature—by its glitter, by its shine—could warm them. Experienced voices sounding notes of caution were drowned out by the thunder of the stampede.

The nineties was the decade of the swindler and the confidence man, and it might be said that every white- and blue-collar worker who joined in the scramble that winter was conning himself. He *had* to believe he would find what he was seeking, otherwise he could not go—could not desert his job, his family, his home.

But *not* to go was unthinkable. So, in that era of insecurity, when mortgages were foreclosed on a whim, when robber barons prospered and most others grew more wretched, when the workhouse, the sweatshop, and the pauper's grave were realities and not figures of speech, each man who set off on the golden trail was forced to believe not only in the future but also in himself.

Thus, in an odd way, the Klondike quest gave the continent a new optimism. "Hurrah for the Klondike!" the crowds on the dock shouted, as each overladen ship limped out of harbour. It was a kind of war cry, a mass call of hope that somehow, in some magical way, things were going to be better.

It was an era, not unlike our own, when success was worshipped almost as a religion and when the accumulation of riches was the evidence of that success. And so no scheme was too harebrained, no project too lunatic, to shatter the confidence of the true believers. A diver who announced that he would trudge beneath the foaming waters picking up nuggets was taken seriously. So was a man who proposed to suck gold from the creeks using compressed air, and another who claimed to have trained gophers to dig for treasure, and a group of clairvoyants who planned to find the elusive pay streak by gazing into crystal balls.

Scores set off for the promised land on bicycles or on ingenious adaptations of them—on "ice bicycles" or "bicycle skates." Others planned to soar across the mountains by balloon or chug up the icy passes on motor sledges or snow trains with gigantic sprocket wheels. No device was too bizarre to attract the gullible.

The idea of gold begot gold. Once it had been so scarce that a gold dollar was worth twice as much as a paper dollar. Now the coins came out from beneath the floor boards as the gold seekers spent their hoards on anything bearing the magical name "Klondike"—there were Klondike glasses, Klondike medicine chests, even Klondike soup. The word was used on anything designed to lighten the burden on the long trail north—on coffee lozenges, evaporated eggs, dried onions, beef blocks, peanut meal, saccharine and pemmican—and on less practical devices: mechanical gold pans, nugget-in-the-slot machines, patented gold rockers, collapsible beds, knock-down boats, portable cabins, scurvy cures, even X-ray machines designed to detect the presence of golden treasure.

Like those thrill seekers who gaped at stage magicians, the stampeders were caught up in the fantasy. Some set off for the mystic land of gold as cheerfully as they might depart for London, Paris, or Bombay. They took caged canaries, parrots, upright pianos, portable bowling alleys, lawn tennis sets, magic lanterns. The marvel is that some of this bric-à-brac actually reached the city of gold. Some of it is there to this day.

Their optimism seems strange, because this was not an optimistic age. But it was an age of yearning, and the Klondike had become more than a goldfield, more than a piece of geography: it was Happyland, Paradise, the Promised Land—a cure for all the fears and torments of the era, an answer for the lonely, an inspiration to the God-fearing, a defence against the weaknesses of the flesh. For if the creekbeds were said to be paved with gold, were not also the streets of heaven itself?

Thus no one was much surprised when the Beecher Memorial Church of Brooklyn announced that it would build a second Brooklyn in the clear air of the Yukon, free of drinkers, gamblers, and non-Christians, at the foot of "a mountain which is said to be the fountainhead of the gold-field"; or when a leading female professor developed a plan to transport four thousand single women from the sweatshops of New England to the free and open spaces of the Klondike; or when a Pittsburgh promoter launched a matrimonial agency to secure jobs in Dawson City for groups of one hundred "poor but respectable women"; or when the Bowery Mission of New York sent an expedition north headed by a reformed gambler, whose job was to convert his fellow stampeders while digging for gold.

So strong was their faith in the magic of the Klondike that five hundred widows seeking rich husbands chartered a steamer and set off from New York around Cape Horn for the goldfields. In spite of shipwreck and Patagonian cannibals, the vessel managed to limp into Seattle before its passengers' funds were gone and their dreams shattered.

Few knew exactly where the Klondike was, and, perhaps because they feared the truth, a surprising number didn't bother to find out. A man who planned a regular balloon route to the Klondike—the round trip, he said, would take only two weeks—was besieged with offers from hundreds who had obviously never consulted a map. And there were other schemes, equally nutty: a reindeer service modelled on the pony express; a bicycle path to the goldfields to service a chain of trading posts; even a postal system using carrier pigeons.

This blindness to geography was a symptom of the fever that gripped the continent. One Canadian company actually received a government charter to build a railway across seven hundred miles (1,100 km) of unmapped tundra from Hudson Bay to Great Slave Lake and on to Dawson.

That journey, an enthusiastic Toronto newspaper reported, would take a mere seven days.

There was something about the Klondike disease that caused normally sensible businessmen to indulge in pipe dreams. But then these fantasies were supported by those who saw profit in madness and gold in gold fever: outfitters, eager to turn a dollar; Chamber of Commerce boosters, booming their communities; promoters organizing syndicates in exchange for cash on the barrelhead. For every man in the crowd scrambling northward seeking a gold mine, there was at least one con man on the lookout for a sucker.

As the winter progressed, a grotesque flotilla of oddly assorted craft, many of them little more than floating coffins, shuttled up and down the Pacific coast crammed with stampeders. By February there were forty-one regular ships operating out of San Francisco harbour alone—enough to carry up to six million pounds (2,700 tonnes) of freight to Alaska. A few vessels attempted the all-water route—the "rich man's route" to the gold-fields—booking passage for a three-thousand-mile (4,800-km) ocean journey around the Aleutian Islands to the mouth of the Yukon on the Bering Sea and then transferring to a riverboat for the 1,700-mile (2,700 km) trip upstream to Dawson City. But only a few could afford the fare. Most chose the shorter, cheaper passage.

Ships that had long been condemned were resurrected from boneyards, hastily patched up, and put into use. Yachts, sloops, barques, scows, barges, ancient steamboats, and sailing schooners—anything that could float was pressed into service. This included a San Pedro ferryboat, a private yacht of an Indian rajah, and a creaky Chinese freighter, *The Ning Chow*, brought across the Pacific for the coastal trade and fitted out with rough lumber bunks, four tiers high.

By September, twenty-eight steamers had left for Alaska, and new ones were being chartered daily. Space was short, and comfort meant little. Horses were wedged side by side so tightly they couldn't lie down.

A passenger aboard the Canadian steamer *Amur* described it as "a floating bedlam, pandemonium let loose, the black hole of Calcutta in an Arctic setting." The vessel was supposed to hold a hundred people. It managed to cram five hundred aboard together with almost as many dogs—every kind of dog: Great Danes, mastiffs, collies, Saint Bernards, Newfoundlands, and wolfhounds, all yapping, howling, and struggling. None of them, as it turned out, was of the slightest use under northern conditions. Because the ship's dining room could hold only twenty-six people comfortably, every meal took seven hours to serve. The famished passengers fell into the habit of lying in wait for the stewards as they passed by and hungrily snatched morsels of food from the trays.

There were many accidents, some ludicrous, some tragic. The *Nancy G*, billed as "a fine schooner in tow of a powerful ocean tug," started off twenty days behind schedule and sank on her return voyage. Another ship, the *Clara Nevada*, ignoring the laws against booking passengers when the cargo contained dynamite, blew sky-high between Skagway and Juneau with a loss of all sixty-five souls—a dog survived. The *Blakely*, a square-rigged brigantine, condemned two years before, survived a storm so fierce that one seaman was flung overboard by the wind, and one passenger died of starvation because he was too seasick to eat. Conditions were so bad that many of the dogs on board died in their crates.

And yet, so eager were the gold seekers to reach the foot of the two passes that led to the interior of the Yukon, they were prepared to pay any amount and suffer any discomfort in order to reach the beaches at the head of the inland passage that leads up the coast of British Columbia and Alaska. And there, at the foot of the Coastal Mountains, two strange little boom towns were quickly taking shape. Skagway lay at the foot of the White Pass. A twin community only a few miles away, Dyea, lay at the foot of the Chilkoot Pass. When the gold seekers clambered out of the ships and waded or were ferried ashore, they may have thought their ordeal was over. In fact it had just begun.

CHAPTER TWO

The Dead Horse Trail

AS THE WINTER WINDS BEGAN TO HOWL DOWN THE WHITE PASS AND ACROSS THE SHINING TIDAL FLATS OF SKAGWAY, SHIP AFTER SHIP POURED IN UNTIL THE LONG BAY WAS SPECKLED WITH HUNDREDS OF CRAFT. THESE RANGED FROM GREAT, GRIMY FREIGHTERS TO SLIM PETERBOROUGH CANOES. SNUB-NOSED OVERLOADED SCOWS, CREAKING WITH THE STRAIN, SHUTTLED FROM BEACH TO BEACH AND BACK AGAIN, OR LEFT FOR DYEA THREE MILES (5 KM) AWAY, PICKING THEIR WAY BETWEEN THE THRASHING FORMS OF GOATS, DOGS, MULES, AND OXEN LEFT TO FEND FOR THEMSELVES IN THE COLD WATERS.

Each incoming ship was forced to anchor a mile (1.6 km) off shore and then dump men, outfits, and animals into the shallow sea. Horses were swung from the decks in special boxes whose bottoms opened up, plunging the terrified creatures into the water. Trunks and packing cases were dropped into the waiting scows, where they were often smashed to kindling, and then cast helter-skelter onto the gravel beach, where they were often lost or stolen. There was nobody to help. Every working stevedore had deserted for the goldfields.

The beach was a human anthill, a confused mixture of swearing men and neighing horses, of rasping saws and sputtering campfires, of creaking wagons and yelping dogs—a jungle of tents and sheet-iron stoves and upturned boats scattered between the piles of goods and hay.

On top of these heaps, knee-deep in flour sacks and frying pans, perspiring men bawled out the names on every outfit and tossed them down to the waiting owners. The most far-sighted of the stampeders organized themselves into committees to rope off areas and to stand guard over their stacks of provisions at gunpoint. But none was able to cope with the problems posed by international geography.

Those outfits that had been bought in Canada couldn't be opened in Skagway, because it was an American town. They had to be escorted across the White Pass in bond. The escorts had to be fed and paid ten dollars a day by the owners. On the other hand, those who had bought their outfits in the United States were charged duty by the Canadian customs officer on the border.

Night and day the beach was never still, for rubber-booted men in constantly shifting streams were forever dragging their outfits across the tidal ooze in an effort to get above the high-water line. The extreme rise and fall showed a difference of thirty feet (9 m), and the onrushing tidal waters advanced at such a speed that many returned to their sacks of goods only to find they had been covered in saltwater.

Above the beach, the town of Skagway was being hacked out of the forest. The main street was nothing more than a single rut of black mud, down which a river of men and animals flowed ceaselessly. Through a mish-mash of hovels and tree stumps moved all sorts of strange contraptions.

Two men pushed a pedal-less bicycle on which frames had been mounted suitable for carrying two hundred pounds (90 kg) of goods. A group of stampeders laboured up toward the pass carrying little carts mounted on buggy wheels. Another sloshed through the mud striving to maintain the balance of an enormous single wheel, around which a platform had been built.

And threaded in between these grotesque devices were three thousand pack horses, loaded to the breaking point. Panic was already mirrored in their eyes, but their agony had only begun.

Of all the routes to the Klondike, the Skagway Trail across the White Pass more than any other brought out the worst in men. None who survived it ever forgot it, and most who remembered it did so with a sense of shame and remorse. It looked so easy: a walk through the rolling hills on horseback, not much more. Yet the men who travelled it were seized by a kind of madness that drove them to the pit of brutality. Like drug addicts, they understood their craziness but could not control it.

Unlike the Dyea Trail that led directly to the base of the Chilkoot and then crossed the mountain barrier in a single leap, the Skagway Trail straddled a series of obstacles. Its beginnings were deceptive—an attractive wagon road that led for several miles over flat timber and swampland. Then began a series of steep hills, each one separated by the marshy riverbed, which had to be zigzagged by the narrow pathway.

Five thousand men and women attempted to cross the White Pass in the fall of '97. Only the tiniest handful reached their goal in time to travel the Yukon River before it froze. One who succeeded compared the slow movement with that of an army in retreat—those in the forefront struggling against hopeless odds, followed by a line of stragglers moving forward like a beaten mob.

On the coastal side of the divide a cold drizzle shut out all sunlight, producing streams of gumbo mud. The trail wasn't wide enough to allow two animals to pass, and so, time and again, all movement ground to a stop. Fires sputtered and smouldered in the misty half light, while shivering men hovered over them, waiting for the human chain to resume its slow movement across the dark hills.

During these tedious delays, the horses for miles back had to stand, often for four hours, with crushing loads pressing down on their backs. No one would unload them because they were afraid the movement might suddenly start again. An animal could remain loaded for twenty-four hours, and that was why scarcely one survived out of the three thousand horses that were used to cross the pass in the fall of '97.

This was the shame of the Skagway Trail. Many of these doomed horses were ready for the glue factory anyway. They had been purchased for outlandish prices. Some had never been broken or felt the weight of a pack. Few of their owners had ever handled animals before. It was not unusual for two partners to spend an entire day just trying to load a single horse.

By the time they got to the summit of the mountains—the border between Alaska and Canada—horses that had cost two hundred dollars in Skagway weren't worth twenty cents. The Klondikers wanted to get across the mountains at any cost—and that cost always included an animal's life. A quarter of a mile (400 m) before the border was reached, each owner performed a grisly act. He carefully unloaded his pack animal, then smoothed a blanket over its back to hide the sores the horse had suffered. For the Mounted Police would shoot a sore, injured horse on sight if it was brought across the line.

No one who travelled the Dead Horse Trail could ever forget those scenes. One veteran horseman, Major J. M. Walsh, one of the most famous officers of the original North-West Mounted Police, climbed the trail that fall with a government party and was horrified at what he saw.

He wrote that "such a scene of havoc and destruction ... can scarcely be imagined. Thousands of pack horses lie dead along the way, sometimes in bunches under the cliffs, with pack-saddles and packs where they had fallen from the rocks above, sometimes in tangled masses filling the mud holes and furnishing the only footing for our poor pack animals in the march ... The eyeless sockets of the pack animals everywhere account for the myriad of ravens along the road. The inhumanity which this trail has been witness to, the heartbreak and suffering which so many have undergone, cannot be imagined. They certainly cannot be described."

One man, Dufferin Pattullo, a future premier of British Columbia, reported that the tortured animals were actually trying to commit suicide rather than travel farther. To his dying day, Pattullo insisted he saw an ox trying to fling itself over a cliff. Others reported similar incidents.

Within a month, the trail became impassable. By September all movement had ceased. It was obvious to all that no one else was going to reach the Klondike until spring. Thousands were already in retreat and vainly trying to sell their outfits, which were strewn along the right of way for more than forty miles (65 km).

The tidal flats of Skagway were still black with a thousand horses. "For Sale" signs hung over their backs, and blood streamed down their torn thighs. Everywhere a pall of gloom hung over the multitude. One reporter came upon a huge, strapping gold seeker in a red shirt seated on a rock. He was a picture of despair. He couldn't get his goods across the first ridge in the pass. His money was gone, his adventure was at an end, and he was sobbing his heart out.

Men had been willing to pay any sum to reach the lakes beyond the mountains. Scores had given fifty cents apiece just to use a log that one enterprising stampeder had flung over a stream. One packer who landed in Skagway without a dollar made $300,000 in transport fees before he blew out his brains. As the gold seekers were to learn over and over again, money alone was not enough to take them to the Klondike.

When the mud froze as hard as granite and the rivers turned to ice, and the snow swept down from the mountains so thickly that a man could scarcely see his neighbour, the Dead Horse Trail reopened. Thousands again took up the struggle to cross the White Pass.

By this time, the Mounted Police at the border were enforcing a new regulation. Nobody could enter the Yukon territory of Canada without a year's supply of food—about 1,150 pounds (520 kg). Together with tents, cooking utensils, and tools, this made a ton (900 kg) of goods. Think of what was needed: lime juice and lard, black tea and chocolate, salt, candles, rubber boots and mincemeat, dried potatoes and sauerkraut, string beans and cornmeal, cakes of toilet soap and baking powder, coal oil and lamp chimneys, ropes, saws, files, mukluks, overshoes. There were no stores in the Yukon, so the gold seekers had to bring in everything.

All these goods had to be carried on the backs of animals or men or dragged on sleds and parcelled up into loads of about sixty-five pounds (30 kg)—the most the average man could carry. He would move it five miles (8 km), hide it, and return for another load. He continued that process until his entire ton of supplies was shuttled across the pass.

Thus a man who depended on his own back for transportation might have to make up to thirty round trips to move his outfit. His total mileage before he reached the lakes would exceed 2,500 miles (4,000 km). Many contrived to pull sleds with larger loads. But even these found they were covering more than one thousand miles (1,600 km). That explains why even a hard-working man took at least ninety days to move through the White Pass.

All along the trail, often buried in twelve or more feet (4 m) of snow, lay the packs and equipment of those who were backtracking in this way. After days and days of slow forward movement, men were ready to fling themselves down by the side of the trail and sob their hearts out in frustration.

Others got so mad they attacked their animals. One beat his dogs so badly they couldn't go farther. Then he pushed them one by one into a water hole and drowned them. Another was frustrated because his oxen became exhausted and couldn't continue. He built a fire under them, then began to poke at them with burning brands, but they still couldn't move and so were slowly roasted before his eyes. Nobody paid any attention.

Everybody was too occupied with his own misfortunes to mind anybody else's business on the Dead Horse Trail. A dead man sat beside the right of way for hours with a hole in his back staring glassily out at the passersby who trudged on with scarcely a second glance.

As the winter wore on and the snow continued to fall, the trail changed its shape and rose above the surrounding countryside. What happened was this: the soft snow on either side was blown off down the valley by the screaming gusts; the trail itself was kept packed so hard by the boots of thousands that no wind could budge it. When more snow fell, it too was packed down hard as cement, until in certain places the pathway was ten feet (3 m) high.

Bert Parker, a teenaged boy from Ontario, crossed the pass that winter. He likened the trail to a huge pipeline, six to eight feet (2 to 2.5 m) in diameter. The men moving along it looked to him like a chain gang. The wind-blown snow on either side was so loose that if a man toppled off the trail he had trouble climbing back up again.

Young Parker noted that, "if a man forgets for a moment what he is doing, his sled is liable to get off the trail and upset in the snow. The minute this happens the man behind him steps up and takes his place and he stays there till the whole cavalcade passes by. Sometimes you would think that a man had gone crazy and that his sled had upset off the trail. They would throw their caps in the snow, shake their fists, throw their heads back and ask Jesus Christ to come down there on the trail so they could tell Him what they thought of Him for playing a trick like that on them."

The solid line was so closely packed with men that it could take four or five hours to pass a given point without a gap appearing—and there was no level place to sit down. Here each man became a robot—part of the human serpent that wound slowly through the mountains. On it moved with its thousand identical vertebrae, each figure bent forward in its jack-knife attitude of strain, each face purple with the stress of hauling a heavy sled, a rope over every shoulder, a pole for steering purposes gripped in the right hand.

The summit, when they reached it, turned out to be a symphony of white. Here the sun glittered on the dazzling peaks. The flanks of the mountains, blue-white in the shadows, merged with a white fog that rose from the seacoast. In the intense cold, men walked in a cloud of vapour made up of the lazy white steam that rose from the campfires and the white jets that burst from the snouts of the animals and the nostrils of the struggling climbers.

Through this eerie world moved the shadowy, frost-covered forms of the stampeders. Here were people of every kind, made brothers and sisters for this brief moment. A man with a string of reindeer pulling a sled, for instance, a group of Scots in furs and tam-o'-shanters led by a bagpiper, a woman with bread dough strapped to her back so it rose with the heat of her body. Every kind of human animal struggled forward with a single purpose.

A. J. Goddard, a steamboat man, and his wife moved two entire stern-wheel vessels in bits and pieces across the mountains that winter. A photographer, E. A. Hegg, arrived with a darkroom fastened to a sled drawn by a herd of long-haired goats.

There was a boxing champion among the climbers too. His name was Jim Carroll, but he wasn't tough enough for the journey. He dropped exhausted on the trail and called to his young wife that he was turning back. She turned on him.

"All right, Jim, we'll split the outfit right here on the trail. I'm going on to Dawson."

That spurred him forward. The following summer he gave boxing lessons in Dawson, and she opened a roadhouse that earned three hundred dollars a day.

But for every person who found the strength to press on, there was at least one who turned back. And so the leaderless mob swarmed forward—leaderless except for the small band of North-West Mounted Police who officially took possession of the summit in February 1898, on orders from the Canadian government.

Until that time, nobody had paid much attention to the boundary. Now it was in dispute. But the Mounties took possession simply by building a customs house on the razor's edge of the divide. To get there, firewood and cabin logs had to be hauled uphill for twelve miles (19 km). There the wind howled ceaselessly, and the snow fell day and night. And there twenty policemen endured conditions so terrible that no stampeder lingered longer than necessary.

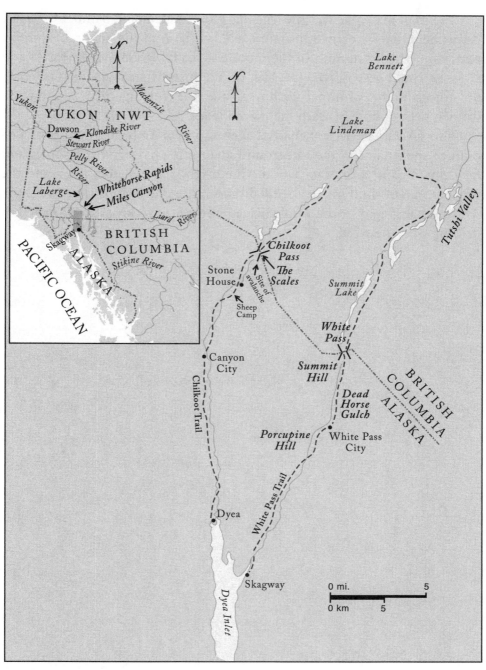

Gateway to the Klondike

The man in charge was the legendary superintendent, Samuel B. Steele. It was here that he earned his name as "The Lion of the Yukon." From his perch on the very summit of the mountain wall, high above the forest and river, he could gaze down, god-like, on the insect figures striving to reach the top—on the whimpering horses and the cursing men and on the women bent double beneath man-sized loads.

This fevered scene was enacted against a massive backdrop: the cloud-plumed mountains in the foreground, the rolling hills in the distance, and far below—as if in another world—the bright shine of the ocean and the tiny outlines of shuttling boats still disgorging endlessly more human cargo.

And hanging over the whole like a pall was the sickly stench of carrion drifting with the wind.

CHAPTER THREE

The Trail to Sheep Camp

ALL THAT WINTER MEN STRUGGLED, MOSTLY IN VAIN, TO REACH THE KLONDIKE GOLDFIELDS. SOME WENT OVER THE GLACIERS THAT LAY ON THE SOUTHERN COAST OF ALASKA. SOME TRIED TO GO UP THE YUKON RIVER FROM ITS MOUTH ON THE BERING SEA. OTHERS LEFT FROM ASHCROFT IN SOUTHERN BRITISH COLUMBIA AND PLUNGED NORTH THROUGH THE HEART OF THE PROVINCE WITHOUT SUCCESS. HUNDREDS TRIED TO GO NORTH FROM EDMONTON AND CROSS THE MACKENZIE MOUNTAINS, EVEN AS FAR AS THE ARCTIC CIRCLE. FEW MADE IT.

The great irony of the stampede was that what seemed to be the toughest trail was actually the easiest. This was the Chilkoot Pass—the little notch in the Coastal Mountains through which a long line of stampeders poured all during the winter of 1897–98. You can travel the Chilkoot Pass today. The worn trail left by the gold seekers is still visible. You might even find a souvenir—a pair of ladies' slippers, for instance, hidden in the mosses. And you can certainly see the tangled cable that is all that is left of the tramways that once operated twenty-four hours a day.

For many people, the whole story of the Klondike Gold Rush is summed up in the scene of the long line of people trying to climb the pass. That human chain, hanging across the snowy face of the mountains, is a spectacle that has become a symbol for the Klondike stampede.

Who would have thought that this wall of glittering white, with the final slope so steep that no animal could cross it, would turn out to be the most successful way to reach the goldfields? Who would have thought that, in spite of its steps of solid ice, its howling winds, its crushing fall of snow, and its terrifying avalanches, the Chilkoot was to be the route by which the majority of the stampeders would reach their goal? But that's how it turned out.

The trail through the Chilkoot was higher than the White Pass by more than six hundred feet (180 m), and only human beings could successfully defy its dizzy grade. But twenty-two thousand men and women, each burdened by a ton of supplies, finally made it to the other side.

The gateway to the Chilkoot was Dyea—a little town almost identical to Skagway, with its jungle of frame saloons, false-fronted hotels, log cafés, gambling houses, stores, and real estate offices bound together by a stiff mortar of flapping tents. Dyea existed for little more than a year. The building of the railways through the White Pass in 1898 made it obsolete. But in that fevered winter, a stream of humanity gushed through the town's narrow streets day and night, so that the air was never still from animal cries and human curses.

Only the Natives remained silent. Of all the thousands who attacked the Chilkoot that winter, none profited more than they. The Tlingit tribes were quickly put to work as packers. So were the Chilkoots, who guarded the pass, and their brothers, the Chilkats, from the western arm of the Lynn Canal and the Stikines from Wrangell, Alaska. They trudged over the mountains, squat, swarthy, quiet men, with a tumpline taut around their flat foreheads and a stout stick in one hand as they balanced a pack on their massive shoulders.

They were shrewd bargainers. They worked for the highest bidder and ran their own informal union. They wouldn't work on Sundays, for all were strict Presbyterians. As the rush increased, they raised their fees. Sometimes they'd throw a pack into the snow and go to work for a man who offered more money. Sometimes they'd stop in the middle of the trail and strike for higher wages. They wouldn't take paper money because they had once been cheated with old bills. As a result, they quickly took the gold and silver out of circulation. They treated all the stampeders with contempt, and with good reason. In that mad army of amateurs, they were the only professionals—the elite of the stampede.

Just as at Skagway, the first men to reach Dyea found that their outfits had to be taken by boat from steamer to shore. There they were dumped on the tidal beach, and when the tide rose tragic scenes often followed.

It was absolutely necessary for each man to move his gear above the high-tide mark before the saltwater ruined everything. Grown men sat down and cried when they failed to beat the tide. Their limited amount of money had been spent to buy their goods and to get them this far. Now their flour, sugar, oatmeal, baking powder, soda, salt, yeastcakes, dried potatoes, and dried fruit were under saltwater and ruined. There was no time or money to replace them. Their chances of getting to the goldfields were gone.

The new arrivals used dogs, horses, and even oxen to push or pull their outfits across the glistening sands. When the wharves were finally built, they were so icy any man stepping from ship to dockside often slid into the sea and had to be fished out with his clothes frozen solid. And when warehouses were built, they were jammed from dawn to dusk with crowds of men, all demanding their goods, so the owners sometimes had to brandish pistols to stop a riot.

And here, for a few months, the horse was king. Pack animals were so scarce that even the poor ones sold for six or seven hundred dollars.

And here, for a few months, the horse was king. Pack animals were so scarce that even the poor ones sold for six or seven hundred dollars. And though the cost of feed was high—it ran as much as $150 a ton—each animal could earn forty dollars a day in packing fees before it collapsed.

Like so many routes to the Klondike, the first few kilometres of the Dyea Trail were deceptively easy. A pleasant wagon road rambled along through meadow and forest, crossing and recrossing the gravelly river that wound through clumps of cottonwood, spruce, birch, and willow.

Then, piece by piece, the tell-tale symbols of the stampede appeared—a litter of goods thrown away by men who had already begun to lighten their burdens. Here were trunks of every description, many filled with jewellery and trinkets and framed pictures that didn't have any value for those seeking gold. Trunks were useless; each stampeder soon learned the only possible containers for his outfit were stout canvas bags fifty inches (1.3 m) long.

After everything had been discarded, the weary Klondikers, on leaving the river, kicked off their heavy rubber boots and left them behind too. Two Alaskans grabbed this mountain of footwear, took it back to Juneau, and sold it to the newer arrivals, so that hundreds of pairs came back over the passes time after time.

Five miles (8 km) from Dyea, the trail reached Finnegan's Point, a huddle of tents surrounded by a core of blacksmith's shops, a saloon, and a restaurant. From that point, the trail led directly toward the canyon of the Dyea River, two miles (3 km) long and fifty feet (17 m) wide, cluttered with boulders, torn-up trees, and masses of tangled roots. Through this slushy thoroughfare a steady stream of panting men trudged on.

After the canyon, the grade began to rise slowly until Sheep Camp was reached at the base of the mountains. This was the last point on the trail where it was possible to cut timber or firewood. Everything beyond was naked rock and boulder, covered during the winter in a coating of ice and smothered in a blanket of snow.

The camp lay in a deep basin that seemed to have been scooped by a giant paw out of the mountains. In one of these, a small notch could be glimpsed—that was the Chilkoot. On most days, the peaks were shrouded in a gloomy fog. When the sun came out and the sky cleared, the pale rays glinted on the evil masses of glaciers that hung from the rim of the mountain wall. The summit was only four miles (6.5 km) distant, but it was a long way up—3,500 feet (170 m) above the town of Dyea.

There were seldom fewer than fifteen hundred people in Sheep Camp. The tents and shacks were wedged so closely together it was hard to squeeze between them. At times it looked like a giant dry goods store. Outside one supply store was a ragged curtain of pots and pails and tall rubber boots, while heaped against the front and almost obscuring the doorway were stacks of kitchen ware, stoves, barrels, and coils of rope. Private post offices in tents offered to send mail to Dyea for ten cents a letter. Canvas shops offered groceries, hay, rifles, and laundry service. The biggest store of all— a log building with a slat and tarpaper roof—offered everything from drugs and medicine to candy and stationery.

The professional packers had a club, a shack known as the Packer's Rest. In addition there were fifteen "hotels," none more pretentious than a hut. The best known was the Palmer House, which fed five hundred people a day and slept forty each night, jamming them so tightly together on the plank floor it was not possible to walk through the building after nine o'clock at night. But it did have running water: a brook rippled through one corner of the building.

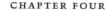

CHAPTER FOUR

The Chilkoot Lock-Step

FROM SHEEP CAMP, THE TRAIL ROSE SHARPLY UNTIL IT REACHED AN INCLINE OF MORE THAN THIRTY-FIVE DEGREES. THAT MEANT A MAN COULD DROP TO HIS HANDS AND KNEES AND STILL SEEM PARTLY UPRIGHT. THERE WERE ONLY TWO POINTS ON THIS FOUR-MILE (6.5-KM) STRETCH WHERE ANYBODY COULD REST. THE FIRST LAY UNDERNEATH A HUGE OVERHANGING BOULDER THAT GAVE SOME SHELTER AND WAS KNOWN AS THE STONE HOUSE. THE SECOND WAS A FLAT LEDGE A FEW CITY BLOCKS SQUARE AT THE VERY BASE OF THE STEEPEST ASCENT. THAT WAS CALLED THE SCALES, BECAUSE EVERYTHING THERE HAD TO BE WEIGHED AGAIN, AND THE PACKER'S RATES INCREASED TO A DOLLAR A POUND. NO LOADED ANIMAL COULD GO FARTHER THAN THE SCALES. EVEN SLEDS AND DOGS HAD TO BE PACKED OVER ON MEN'S BACKS. HERE THOUSANDS OF TONS OF GOLD, HALF HIDDEN BY THE CEASELESSLY FALLING SNOW, WERE PILED WAITING FOR THEIR OWNERS TO GET STRENGTH FOR THE FINAL CLIMB.

All winter long, from Sheep Camp to the summit, for four weary miles, the endless line of men stretched up the slope—a human chain hanging from the summit and draped across the mountain slope. From first light to last, the line was never broken. The men who formed it inched slowly upward in an odd rhythmic motion that came to be called the Chilkoot Lock-Step. And here, as on the White Pass, each man became a robot, nothing more than a link in the chain. Even separate sounds were merged into the single groan that rose from the slow-moving mass and echoed like a hum through the bowl of the mountains.

Blizzards and gales made the slope impassable for days. Accidents caused the line to move by fits and starts. A single trip across the pass was no great hardship, but the gold seekers had to endure it again and again.

It took the average man three months or more to shuttle his goods over the pass.

As the winter progressed, some men began to hack steps out of the ice wall above the Scales. The first stairs were chopped out of the last 150 feet (50 m) of the climb. There the going was so steep one stampeder compared it to scaling the walls of a house. Two partners cut the steps out with axes in a single night and collected more than eighty dollars a day in tolls.

More steps were cut and more tolls were charged until there were fifteen hundred steps cut in the mountain slope. There was a rope to hang onto and little shelves where you could step out of line and rest your pack. But few stepped out, because a man might have to wait all day before slipping back into place. Each paid his toll in the morning to climb the "Golden Stairs," as the stampeders called them. It took six hours to climb a thousand feet (300 m) loaded down with a fifty-pound (23-kg) pack—and fifty pounds was as much as any man could handle.

The professional packers, however, could manage one hundred pounds (45 kg), and some carried even more. One Indian packer reached the summit with a 350-pound (160-kg) barrel on his back. A Swede crawled up on his hands and knees with three huge six-by-four (15 cm x 10 cm) timbers strapped to him. An Iowa farm boy, on a bet, took a 125-pound (60-kg) plough up the slope.

The new arrivals quickly learned their ton of supplies had to be packed in such a way it could be divided into fifty- or hundred-pound portions. The first eggs survived the haul in special canvas cases. Flour was poured out of light sacks into heavier canvas sacks and sewed so tightly that water couldn't soak in. The two prized cargoes were whisky and silk—one for the Klondike dance halls, the other for the dance-hall girls. The whisky posed a difficult problem since it had to be smuggled across the Canadian border. All kinds of clever tricks were used to get liquor past the Canadian customs house—kerosene cans with hidden compartments, false-bottomed egg crates, and bales of hay concealing small barrels of liquor.

Whisky and silk, steamboats and pianos, live chickens and stuffed turkeys, timber and glassware, bacon and beans, all went over on men's backs. If the man was too poor to hire a packer, he climbed the pass forty times before he got his outfit across.

When he dropped his day's load on the summit and marked it with a pole, he turned back down again, for there was no shelter at the top. That was a swift return. He simply tucked his boots beneath him and tobogganed down the slope on his rump, gouging deep chutes in the snow and hitting the bottom in a matter of minutes.

By December 1897, the first crude tramway had been opened. This was merely an endless rope wound around an upright wheel and turned by a horse moving in a circle. Later on more and better tramways were built, so that by May there were five operating. By the spring of 1898, it was possible for a man's goods to be transported by aerial tramway all the way from Canyon City to the summit of the pass. The tramway was run by steam and was fourteen miles (22.5 km) long. The cars, each loaded with three hundred pounds (135 kg), were dispatched at the rate of one a minute, day and night, so that by spring freight was being dumped on the summit of the Chilkoot Pass at the rate of nine tons (8 tonnes) an hour.

On the top of the pass, a silent city took shape. The "buildings" were towering piles of freight, the "streets" the spaces between. The blizzard that rarely stopped covered these goods soon after they were dropped, so the owners had to leave poles or long-handled shovels to mark their goods. Even these didn't always work because almost seventy feet (20 m) of snow fell on the summit in the Chilkoot that winter. Before spring two "cities" of goods had been buried and couldn't be retrieved until the thaw.

The pass at this point was a trench a hundred yards (90 m) wide through which a spray of snow whirled. On either side the mountains rose for another five hundred feet (150 m), their tops hidden by clouds and blowing snow. The piles of freight provided the only shelter. Firewood cost a dollar a pound because it had to be hauled seven miles (11 km) by sled from the timberline on the Canadian side. Those who could afford to pay $2.50 for a stale doughnut and a weak cup of coffee gulped it down and were away because no one wished to stay long on the pass.

Only the Mounted Police held fast to their post. The presence of these men in their huge buffalo coats, with the brass buttons of the force, marked the summit as the international border. The sight of a tattered Union Jack fluttering in the storm, and the blurred lines of a sentry with a machine gun always on duty, were the first indications to the stampeders they had reached Canadian territory. Here every man had to pay duty on the outfit he had hauled across from the Alaskan side.

At night, when the summit was silent and empty, when the climbers had retreated to Sheep Camp on the south or moved on down to Crater Lake on the north, the police held their ground in a tiny hovel perched in the shadow of the overpowering mountains. The snow came down so thickly (six feet [2 m] in a single night) that Bobby Bilcher, the officer in charge, had to post a sentry to shovel it away to prevent the sleeping men from being smothered. One storm raged for two months. All movement stopped. But the police hung on, their hut dripping like a shower bath as the snow was melted by its warmth.

> *The snow came down so thickly (six feet [2 m] in a single night) that Bobby Bilcher, the officer in charge, had to post a sentry to shovel it away to prevent the sleeping men from being smothered.*

On one occasion, they were driven from their post by the gale. They fled into the lee of the mountains and pitched their tents on the ice of Crater Lake—a cupful of frozen water in an old volcanic hollow just below the peak of the pass. Here they crouched while the water rose six inches (15 cm) above the ice, soaking their bedding. Unable to move their tents, they pulled their sleds inside and slept on top of them. When the wind dropped, they went back to their perch on the mountain.

The Mounted Police checked twenty-two thousand men across the pass that winter—Scots and Canadians, Yanks and Greeks, Swedes and Australians, Japanese and Kanakas. And there were women too—stocky dance-hall girls, heading for Dawson, their charms concealed beneath heavy clothing … lithe Indian girls carrying seventy-five pounds (35 kg) on their backs … an old German woman, almost seventy, in a full dress and a lace gown … and on the lower slopes a middle-aged woman, all alone, who tugged a hand sled onto which a glowing stove was fashioned, so that whenever she stopped she was able to warm her hands and enjoy a hot meal.

Jack Crawford, an old frontiersman, trudging back to the summit from Lake Lindemann below the pass, met "a handsome girl, straight as an arrow, blue eyes, curly blonde hair, dressed in boy's clothes—blue shirt, no coat, with a belt, with a .44 Colt pistol strapped around her waist." Her brother-in-law walked ahead of her carrying only a guitar.

Mixed in with the gold seekers were fake stampeders sent up from Skagway to fleece the stampeders. The head of this gang of criminals was the notorious "Soapy Smith," a confidence man originally from Denver, who had earned his name from selling cakes of soap for five dollars apiece on the pretense that they contained folding money.

Smith's men mingled with the endless line of plodding figures, tugging sleds behind them or carrying packs that seemed to be bulging with Klondike gear but were actually stuffed with feathers or shavings. The sleds were also specially built dummies designed for fast travelling and a quick getaway. The canvas lashed over them concealed a hollow shell from which protruded the occasional axe handle, at the proper angle—all for effect.

It was hard for many of the weary climbers to resist these crooked gamblers. The confidence men built fires for them to warm themselves by, and they put up tents to keep out the winds, and they constructed little seats or ledges for the tired packers to rest on. For a tired man toiling up the straight and narrow path of the Chilkoot, such temptations could not but appear inviting. On a single mile of trail, one observer counted four shell games in operation, each surrounded by an eager knot of players. But no one who played with one of Soapy Smith's con men could ever find the pea under the shell—and thus collect his reward.

Every variety of the human species seemed to be in the pass that year. On one hand, there was an English nobleman, dressed in tweeds, with a valet who fed him morsels of food while he lay beneath a net to protect his skin from insects. On the other was the famous Wilson Mizner, wit and gambler, who later became well known as a Broadway playwright and as the owner of Hollywood's Brown Derby Restaurant.

Like Soapy Smith and his men, Mizner wasn't so much interested in finding a gold mine as he was in finding a man who had already found one. Many of those who crossed the pass with him had the same idea, though their methods were more legitimate. A newsboy struggled up the slope with a sackful of old newspapers, which he hoped to sell at high prices to miners starved for information. Another man managed to lug a grindstone over the summit—he'd figured that by spring most of the picks in the Klondike would need to be sharpened. Frank Cushing of Buffalo took ten thousand bottles of mosquito lotion across the slopes. He'd bought them for twenty cents and hoped to sell them in Dawson for ten dollars each to prospectors maddened by the Yukon mosquitoes. While floating down the Yukon, however, he tested the lotion on himself, and it raised such painful blisters that he decided to dump his cargo in the river.

Some showed a profit before they reached the goldfields. One woman paid her way by giving impromptu concerts on a banjo as she went along. Another, a famous western scout named Arizona Charlie Meadows, carried a portable bar that he set up on every possible occasion, raising the prices of the drinks as he climbed higher and higher.

The singleness of purpose with which these men and women flung themselves at the mountain, time and time again, was extraordinary. It was as if each was pulled by invisible strings from which he couldn't free himself. The worst hardships, the most racking tragedies, often failed to dampen their fanaticism. A man lay on the trail for all of one day in agony from a broken leg, seemingly unseen. Hundreds passed him by, their eyes fixed firmly on the road ahead. At last a professional packer, who carried heavier loads and walked farther than any, came by, picked up the sufferer, and trudged all the way to Dyea with his 180-pound (80-kg) burden.

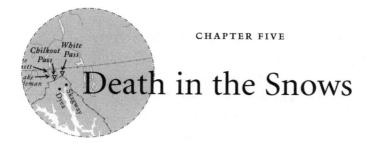

CHAPTER FIVE

Death in the Snows

THERE WERE TWO MAJOR TRAGEDIES IN THE CHILKOOT THAT WINTER. THE FIRST OCCURRED IN SEPTEMBER OF 1897, WHEN A HUGE GLACIER THAT HUNG LIKE A MONSTER OVER THE PASS CRASHED DOWN UPON THE CLIMBERS. DURING THE SUMMER, THE WARM WEATHER AND HEAVY RAINS HAD CAUSED A LAKE TO FORM WITHIN THE HEART OF THIS ICEFIELD. THE AUTUMN WINDS WHISTLING THROUGH THE MOUNTAINS TORE HALF AN ACRE (0.4 HECTARES) FROM ITS EDGE.

With a noise like a thousand cannons, a wall of water descended upon the pass. The roaring waters picked up the Stone House as if it were a pebble and moved it a quarter of a mile (400 m) down the valley, smashing forty tents to pieces, including Arizona Charlie Meadows's entire gambling casino and liquor supply. But there were only three deaths.

The second tragedy, on April 3, 1898, was far worse. For two months, a storm had been raging, making travel impossible on most days. For two weeks, the snow had fallen without stopping. Then, on April 2, the blizzard increased in intensity. Six feet (2 m) of wet snow fell, so that the peaks and glaciers were top heavy with its weight. Now the pass was at its most treacherous. The few who dared to climb it did so only in the cool of the evening. The Indians and the packers refused to go up at all.

But in spite of their warnings, large numbers who had been waiting for weeks took advantage of a lull in the storm to make for the summit. The first hint of tragedy came early on April 3. A bent old man, groaning and waving his arms, hammered on the door of a restaurant owned by two partners, Joppe and Mueller, at the Scales. They woke from their Sunday rest to hear that several people had been buried alive by a snowslide up the trail. They aroused a dozen others and dug frantically through ten feet (3 m) of snow and managed to rescue all but three of the victims. Now everybody was thoroughly alarmed, and a headlong race began for Sheep Camp two miles (3 km) below.

But higher in the mountains the rumble of avalanches could be heard. Downward the fleeing men and women scrambled, staying close together in single file while clinging to a rope that had been strung along the way. At noon it happened. One of the survivors, a man from Maine named J. A. Rines, described his own feelings: "All of a sudden I heard a loud report and instantly began to feel myself moving slowly down the hill and, looking around, saw many others suddenly fall down, some with their feet in the air, their heads buried out of sight in the snow."

Rines braced himself, kept to his feet, and let himself be carried along. He was caught up in the snow and buried instantly thirty feet (9 m) deep.

Others had similar experiences. Some grasped the rope that had been used to haul freight to the summit. Some, finding themselves buried to their hips by the weight of the loose snow, struggled only to be smothered by the main force of the avalanche that followed. Mueller, the café owner from the Scales, felt himself held as fast as if he were in a plaster cast.

The avalanche had tumbled from a peak twenty-five hundred feet (760 m) above the trail just above the Stone House. It covered ten acres (4 hectares) to a depth of thirty feet (9.1m). Within twenty minutes, a thousand men from Sheep Camp were on the spot digging to locate the victims.

The scene was weird and terrible. Small air holes sometimes appeared in the snow to mark the spot where a man or woman had been buried. Somewhere beneath them the searchers could hear the muffled cries of the victims. Those who still lived could hear one another talking. Conversations were carried on between them. Relatives above called out their last goodbyes to those buried below. One old man could be heard praying and cursing until his voice was stilled. But even the strongest couldn't move a muscle, because the snow was packed so tightly around them.

As the hours wore on, those who hadn't been rescued were slowly becoming unconscious from the lack of air. When their corpses were lifted out in the days that followed, many were still in a running position, as if forever fleeing the onrushing avalanche.

More than sixty died. A handful were rescued alive. Some had been three hours under the snow. Four died later, but others, including Mueller and his partner, Joppe, made extraordinary recoveries.

When Joppe was lifted from his frozen tomb, apparently dead, his sweetheart, Vernie Woodward, was beside herself. She'd been packing in the pass since the previous summer like a man. But now she flung herself upon her lover's limp figure, begging him to return to her, working his arms and legs, rubbing his back, breathing warm air into his lungs, crying and praying by turns. She kept at this for three hours, and then, to her amazement, he suddenly opened his eyes and spoke her name. It was as if a dead man had come alive again.

There were other strange rescues. One woman was hauled from the snow where she had been buried head down, hysterical, but living. An ox was found after two days contentedly chewing his cud in a natural stable of a snow cave that he tramped out himself when the avalanche buried him.

For days after the tragedy, sled after sled loaded with corpses moved down the trail to a mass morgue. And here Soapy Smith's criminals were waiting. Indeed, Smith had himself appointed coroner. Near the site of the tragedy he set up a tent to which corpses were brought for identification—and here each body was stripped expertly of rings, jewellery, cash, and other valuables.

Some of the bodies of the victims were buried in a little hollow in the mountains not far from the scene of the disaster. But, even as the service was being held, the long line of men resumed its slow trek across the mountains. The sun increased as the days lengthened. The snow grew softer and started to slide from the high peaks. The wildflowers spattered the mountainside, while the sedges and grasses began to creep over the debris of the previous winter's rush.

The hollow where the bodies rested became a lake. When summer arrived, the last stragglers following in the wake of the main wave of stampeders came upon the grisly spectacle of dozens of bloated corpses floating on the surface of the water. The following winter a railway was pushed through the neighbouring White Pass, and the mountains that had once resounded to the groans and shouts of thousands became as silent as the graves of those who had perished beneath the snows.

CHAPTER SIX

The Ordeal of the Sawpits

ALL WINTER THE TWIN LINES OF HUMANITY FLOWED THROUGH THE TWO GAPS IN THE COASTAL MOUNTAINS UNTIL, BY SPRING, THE SHORES OF THE SLENDER LAKES FEEDING THE YUKON RIVER WERE BLACK WITH PEOPLE. THE TWO TRAILS FROM DYEA AND SKAGWAY, RUNNING ALMOST PARALLEL, ENDED AT ADJOINING LAKES. THE DYEA TRAIL ENDED AT LAKE LINDEMANN AND THE SKAGWAY TRAIL AT THE LARGER LAKE BENNETT A FEW KILOMETRES BELOW.

A boulder-filled canyon connected the two lakes. Those who portaged past it could not fail to read a lesson from the grave of John A. Matthews, a twenty-six-year-old Idaho farmer, who'd come this way the previous June. Twice Matthews had attempted to navigate the canyon, and twice he had foundered with his entire outfit. "My God," he cried out in despair after the second mishap, "what will become of Jane and the babies?" and he pulled a pistol from his pocket and put a bullet through his brain.

The Chilkoot climbers, on reaching Lake Lindemann, proceeded at once to build boats along its shores. Others kept moving on until they reached Lake Bennett. Still more pushed even farther on until by spring more than thirty thousand men were strung out for six miles (10 km) from Lake Lindemann to Lake Tagish at the headwaters of the Yukon River, hard at work building a fleet of more than seven thousand boats.

On the snow-covered shores of Lake Bennett, the greatest tent city in the world was springing up. They encircled the lake in a white cloud—every size and shape of tent, from little pups to huge circus marquees. There were tents for everything—for baths, haircuts, real estate offices. There were tent hotels, tent saloons, tent cafés, tent post offices, tent casinos.

In between the tents was a mass of goods—sleds stacked up against mounds of supplies, crates of food and tinned goods, furniture and stoves, mining equipment and tethered animals, everything from oxen to chickens. And everywhere were half-built boats and mounting piles of logs and lumber. From the hills above, the lakeshore looked like a vast lumberyard. Planks were stacked like cordwood in towering heaps or strewn like toothpicks among the rocks. Boats of every size, shape, and description lay bottom-up in various stages of construction.

A few years earlier this green lake, one of the most beautiful in all of the North, had been as silent as a tomb. Now the frosted mountains that enclosed it looked down upon an incredible spectacle. As spring crept closer, the rumble of avalanches mingled with the screech of the new sawmills, the crash of toppling timber, the rasp of saw and plane, the pounding of mallets, the tap-tapping of a thousand hammers, the arguments of embittered partners, the neighing of horses, the bleating of goats, and the howling of dogs.

The ordeal of the pass was not yet over. Facing each stampeder was a supreme test of the stampede—the whipsawing of green logs into dressed lumber. This was the cruelest toil of all, because its effects were mental as well as physical. All along the lakeshore, in raised platforms known as "sawpits," tempers boiled and exploded. Friendships that had stood the strain of the climb over the mountains snapped under the tension of the jag-toothed whipsaw.

It worked like this: to make the rough planks, the peeled logs were laid on the top of a scaffolding, and a line was chalked down the side. One man stood upon the platform and held a six-foot (1.8-m) saw vertically against the end of the log while his partner underneath grasped the lower handle. Together they were supposed to guide it along the line for the full length of the log, but it demanded an act of faith for each to believe the other was doing his full share of the work.

The cutting was done on the downward stroke only. The man above guided the saw and pulled it up, and then the man below, watching the chalk line, hauled it down again, letting its great hooked teeth bite into the green lumber. As they did that, he got a shower of sawdust in his eyes. While he swore in his rage at the man above, he himself received a bitter tongue-lashing for hanging on too tightly.

This back-breaking work caused the end of hundreds of friendships. For instance, there were two bank clerks who had come over the Chilkoot that winter. They had been friends from childhood, had gone to school together, and had worked side by side in the same bank as youths. Rather than be parted from each other, they had married sisters. But the effect of the whip-sawing turned them into enemies so fierce that, when they decided to divide their outfits, they insisted on cutting everything exactly in half: instead of dividing twenty sacks of flour into two piles of ten sacks each, they insisted on sawing each sack in two. And then they set off, each with his twenty broken halves, the flour spilling away from the torn and useless containers.

The Mounted Police did their best to maintain order in the milling throng. Down from the mountains came Sam Steele, the Lion of the Yukon. He'd had a brilliant career: he had joined the army at the age of fifteen, and as one of the original Mounties he had helped to negotiate with Sitting Bull after the Custer massacre. He'd helped police the building of the Canadian Pacific Railway and led the pursuit of Big Bear during the Saskatchewan rebellion. He was a big man of magnificent physique, tall, powerful, deep chested, and massive shouldered, and he intended to run the stampede like a military manoeuvre. It was largely due to him and his men that there were so few tragedies along the route the Mounties policed.

Because of Steele's iron rule, there was little of the lawlessness that had turned Skagway on the American side into a hell on Earth under Soapy Smith. It was said that a miner could lay a sack of nuggets on the trail on the Canadian side and return in two weeks to find it untouched. One day a man sent up to manage one of the banks in Dawson confided to Steele that he was afraid for the safety of the bank notes entrusted to his care. The policeman took the package and shoved it carelessly under his own bunk, assuring the uneasy banker that it would be quite safe.

On rare occasions, one or another of Soapy Smith's Skagway gang tried, without success, to cross the border and operate in Canada. One member of the gang walked into the police post on the White Pass summit in the early spring and asked what was needed to enter into the Canadian Yukon. A constable told him he would need a year's outfit.

"Well, supposing I don't want to comply with your regulations," the con man said. "Suppose I decide to shoot my way into the country—what then?"

The constable opened a drawer in his desk, pulled out a pistol, and laid it down. "There is a gun," he said. "Go ahead and start shooting. That's the easiest way to find out what will happen." The visitor retreated to Skagway.

Here the difference between the two national characters—American and Canadian—stood out in sharp contrast. The Americans didn't really want interference from the police or the authorities. That is why the U.S. army didn't move in on Soapy Smith. The Americans wanted to run things their own way, organizing committees and electing their own kind on the spot to enforce the law. The Canadians preferred the red-coated father figures enforcing the law from the top down rather than from the grassroots up. The Mounted Police were government appointed; the American sheriffs were elected by the people. That's how Soapy Smith—a known criminal— became marshal of the Independence Day parade the following year. And when, a few days later, he met his death, it was at the hands of a man elected by a committee of citizens to finish him off.

At the lake, Sam Steele now instituted a new rule. Every boat must carry a serial number painted on its bow. Steele's men went from boat to boat, recording the numbers, the names of the occupants, and the addresses of their next of kin. These lists were sent to police posts strung out along the river. If a boat failed to check in at each within a reasonable time, the Mounties went searching for it. As a result of this foresight, an undisciplined armada of more than seven thousand boats was safely convoyed through more than five hundred miles (800 km) of unknown water.

As the boat builders worked away on the shores of the mountain lakes, Steele's men moved among them, advising on methods of construction and urging the amateur carpenters to "build strong—don't start out in a floating coffin." They settled disputes, helped angry partners divide their outfits, acted as general administrators, and settled the estates of those who died, selling those articles that weren't worth shipping home and sending the money to the next of kin. And when real estate speculators tried to seize the land around the lakes and charge the stampeders a fee for its use, the police sent them packing.

By spring the police had collected $150,000 in customs duties. They had not only saved the lives of scores of amateur gold seekers, but they had actually made the great stampede pay off in favour of the Canadian taxpayers.

CHAPTER SEVEN

Drifting down to Dawson

O<small>N</small> M<small>AY</small> 29, <small>WITH A CREAK AND RUMBLE, THE ICE BEGAN TO MOVE IN THE</small> <small>LOWER LAKES, AND THE GREAT BOAT RACE TO</small> D<small>AWSON</small> C<small>ITY WAS ON</small>. D<small>URING</small> <small>THAT FIRST DAY, EIGHT HUNDRED CRAFT SET SAIL FOR THE</small> K<small>LONDIKE, WITH</small> <small>EVERY MAN BENDING TO THE OARS IN AN ATTEMPT TO MAINTAIN A LEAD ON</small> <small>THOSE BEHIND</small>. O<small>NE OR TWO WHO LOOKED BACK SPOTTED A SOLITARY FIGURE</small> <small>STANDING ON A SMALL HILL BEHIND THE POLICE POST</small>. I<small>T WAS</small> S<small>AM</small> S<small>TEELE, LIKE</small> <small>A MOTHER HEN, WATCHING HIS BROOD DEPART</small>. T<small>HE POLICEMAN'S BROW WAS</small> <small>CREASED WITH WORRY, FOR HE KNEW THAT THE BOATMEN HAD NO MORE EXPE-</small> <small>RIENCE WITH RIVER NAVIGATION THAN THEY HAD IN BOAT BUILDING</small>.

Within forty-eight hours, all the lakes were clear of ice, and the whole freakish flotilla of 7,124 boats, loaded with thirty million pounds (13,500,000 kg) of solid food, was in motion. Out onto the mint-green water the ungainly armada lazily drifted. Then a slender breeze rippled down the mountain passageway and caught the sails. A tremor of excitement could be felt in each man's heart as it quickened with the speed of his craft. Off they sailed like miniature galleons, seeking the treasure that lay beyond the horizon's rim, the strangest fleet ever to navigate freshwater.

Here were twenty-ton (18-tonne) scows crammed with oxen, horses, and dogs, one-man rafts made of three logs hastily bound together, light Peterborough canoes packed over the passes on men's shoulders, and strange oblong vessels that looked like—and sometimes were—floating packing boxes.

Here were slim bateaux brought in sections from the outside and canoes made from hollow logs with sticks for oarlocks and paddles hand-whittled from tree trunks. Here were skiffs and cockleshells, outriggers and junks, catamarans and kayaks, arks and catboats and wherries. Here were boats with wedge bottoms, boats with flat bottoms, and boats with curved bottoms; boats shaped like triangles and boats shaped like circles; boats that looked like coffins and boats that *were* coffins.

Here were enormous rafts with hay and horses aboard, propelled by mighty sweeps, and here were others built from a single log with only a mackinaw coat for a sail. Here was a craft modelled after a Mississippi side-wheeler with two side paddlewheels operated by hand cranks, twisting and turning awkwardly in a zigzag movement down the lake. And here was a boat with two women who had sewn their undergarments together and suspended them between a pair of oars to make a sail.

From each mast fluttered a makeshift flag, usually a bandana or a towel. And on each bow was daubed the name of a wife, a sweetheart, a hometown, a good luck slogan, or a memory—*Yellow Garter, Seven Come Eleven, San Francisco, Golden Horseshoe.*

As the bright sub-Arctic evening fell, the breeze dropped, the sails went limp, and every boat drifted to a stop. The sun was still high in the sky and, softened by the haze, seemed to bathe the water in a golden mist.

Now a feeling of strange contentment spread across the gold seekers as each individual settled back in the stern of his craft and, often for the first time, contemplated the scene around him. This was a sight that no one had seen before: thousands of boats becalmed on the blue-green waters of a mountain lake. No one would ever see it again.

Few made any attempt to move that first night. One or two broke into song or were joined by others until, in the larger boats and scows, quartets could be heard singing in harmony. The Klondike was more than five hundred miles (800 km) distant, but, as everyone could see, it was a boat race all the way.

On leaving the mountain lakes, each boat had to run the gauntlet of Miles Canyon and the rapids beyond before the river proper could be reached. Everybody had heard about this canyon, but few knew exactly where it was. Then they saw, at a turn of the river, a piece of red calico and a board on whose rough surface the single word *cannon* had been scrawled. In the distance, the travellers could hear the roar of tumbling waters.

Before them lay the gorge—a narrow cleft in the wall of black rock with a whirlpool at its centre. Beyond that lurked two sets of rapids. As the river descended into the canyon, it narrowed to one-third its size, so the water was forced to a crest four feet (1.2 m) high. From this funnel of foam, small jets erupted, and the boats sweeping between the rock walls were forced to teeter upon it as on a tightrope while the man at the helm tried to get around the obstacles that blocked the way—the huge intertwining drifts of timber, the jagged reefs of boulders and sandbars, the twisted roots of trees, and the sharp little rock teeth that tore the bottoms from the scows and barges.

The walls rose a hundred feet (30 m) from the foaming crest. The whirlpool in the centre was so swift and fierce that, back in 1895, two Swedes carried into the canyon by accident were spun for six hours in a circle before escaping. But this wasn't the end of the hazard. After broadening out to form the whirlpool, the canyon narrowed again to a mere thirty feet (9 m), so that the water spurted from it into the rapids as though it were gushing from a hydrant.

Into the gloomy gorge the first stampeders plunged almost without stopping, for they were at the head of the fleet and eager to hold on to their position. Most had never handled a boat before, but that didn't stop them. In the first few days, 150 boats were wrecked, and five men drowned. Now the others hesitated to chance the waters and hung back until several thousand craft were crowded together at the bottleneck of the canyon in a bewildering traffic jam. At this point, Sam Steele appeared on the scene.

A picture of utter chaos greeted him along the banks of the rapids. At the head of the gorge was a throng of men, some putting up tents, others just sitting glumly on the banks staring at the waters. All were trying to decide whether to chance the rapids or whether to shoulder their packs once more and shuffle their ton of goods around it.

Five miles (8 km) downstream was another dishevelled mass of people. Many had lost their outfits. Others had lost portions. Large numbers were crying and wringing their hands in despair. Their goods, stretched across the shattered bottoms of their upturned boats, lay drying out in the sun.

Steele gathered these people around him like errant children and laid down the law, which he invented on the spot. He placed one Mountie, Corporal Dixon, an expert riverman, in charge of the operation. He wouldn't allow any women or children to be taken in the boats. No boat could go through the canyon until the corporal was satisfied that it had sufficient freeboard to get it over the waves in safety. No boat would be allowed to pass with people in it unless it was steered by a competent man—and of that Corporal Dixon would be the judge.

Many of the Americans complained bitterly at this interference in their private affairs. In keeping with the American tradition of individualism—a tradition that went back to the Boston Tea Party and the American Revolution—they wanted the right to drown themselves if they wished. The Mounties wouldn't let them.

Steele announced a fine of one hundred dollars would be charged to anyone who broke the rules. As a result, the wrecks in the canyons came to an end. The Yukon River had become as safe as a mill pond, thanks to the Mounted Police. In all that vast army of thirty thousand that floated down to Dawson that year, only twenty-three were drowned, thanks to the Mounties who shepherded the stampeders from checkpoint to checkpoint along the way.

By mid-June small steamers were being taken through the gorge. Captain Goddard, having assembled one of the little steamboats that he and his wife had brought across the mountains, took it through under its own power.

Meanwhile, the swift journey down the Yukon to the goldfields took on all the elements of a race. Two large boats containing the personnel, equipment, and hard cash of two leading banks were eager to be the first to obtain the bulk of the mining business. Two newspapers in boats were also racing for Dawson, each eager to be the first to publish a paper in the City of Gold. Other boats contained luxuries that the owners hoped to sell at sky-high prices to the starving and isolated mining camp. Many were loaded with eggs, while others contained recent newspapers. One man was taking in fifteen hundred pairs of boots, another boat was stocked with tinned milk, a third carried a case of live chickens that the owner had managed to pack intact across the Chilkoot. And one man had a scowload of cats and kittens—which he hoped to sell to miners dying for some kind of companionship.

Hegg, the photographer who had moved his portable darkroom across the passes with a goat-drawn sled, was now in the forefront of the race in a poling boat that bore the words *Views of the Klondike*. He was preparing a photographic record of the entire stampede, and his pictures are still to be seen in books about the experience.

Below the rapids for hundreds of kilometres, the swift-flowing waters were speckled with boats. There were half a dozen to be seen around every bend. In the broad terraced valley of the Yukon, once so silent, empty, and unknown, no one was ever free of the sight of other people. There were no further obstacles of importance. Though the Five Finger Rapids looked formidable, few found them really troublesome, and almost every boat got through without incident.

As the main fleet slipped down the river, other flotillas joined it. Men frozen in during the winter along the upper Yukon were on the move. Some had made boats out of their sleds. One youth was seen sitting on his Yukon sled with his dogs around him, having lashed two logs to the sides to serve as floats. A contingent of about 150 boats had moved directly behind the crumbling ice long before the upper lakes gave way, and these were the first to reach the goldfields.

> As the main fleet slipped down the river, other flotillas joined it. Men frozen in during the winter along the upper Yukon were on the move. Some had made boats out of their sleds.

Other boats poured down from the Teslin River loaded with men who had negotiated the trails through central British Columbia. Others slipped down the Pelly and the Stewart—great tributaries of the main river, bringing those stampeders who had come overland from British Columbia and Edmonton.

Twilight and darkness were now banished by the sun, which now dropped below the horizon shortly after midnight and rose again at two in the morning. At the peak of the day, the temperatures rose to the nineties (30° C), and the merciless light beat harshly on the blistered faces of the boatmen. In the steaming forests, mosquitoes, gnats, and black flies buzzed and hummed in clouds as thick as wood smoke—driving the newcomers half crazy. Without the protection of a fine-meshed net, sleep was not possible. The mosquitoes were so fat they seemed more like blowflies. And if a man so much as opened his mouth, he sucked in hordes.

Now the tensions, which had subsided momentarily on the calm lake, sprang up again, and bitter feuds arose once more between friends who had survived previous battles. A person sitting on a boat and watching the banks roll past him could watch in fascination the little human scenes that took place along the river:

- two men caught on the rocks in the middle of the river, and unaware of their surroundings, fighting with their fists in white-hot anger;
- two more, on a lonely beach not far from the mouth of the Teslin River, solemnly sawing their boat down the middle;
- ten men at the little community of Big Salmon dividing up everything ten ways onto ten blankets, including an enormous scow that was torn up to build ten smaller scows so that each could go his separate way in peace.

Once again the Mounties were called in to settle these disputes. Two men who tried vainly to divide up a single frying pan were at each other's throat until a policeman arrived and solved the situation by throwing it into the river.

The names along the river suggested the bitterness that sprang up in these last few miles before the goldfields. There was a Split Up Island and a Split Up City in the Yukon that summer. Split Up City lay at the mouth of the Stewart River, where the Yukon splays out into a confusing tangle of channels and islands, where a boat can be lost for hours or even days. The choice of a wrong channel led to endless battles, and the halves of boats lying all along this section of the river were evidence of what happened during bitter arguments.

From that point, it was only a few hours' run to the Klondike. The stampeders pushed eagerly on, travelling without sleep during nights as bright as days. The tension rose as the miles ticked by. Each boat kept close to the right bank in case by error it should be swept past the city—for no one quite knew where the city was. Then, at last, each in turn swung around a rocky bluff and saw spread before him a sight he would always remember.

Roaring into the Yukon from the right was the Klondike River, about which everybody had heard so much. Beyond the river rose a tapering mountain with a great scar of a slide slashed across its face. At its feet, spilling into the surrounding hills and all along the swampy flats and between the trees, and across the junction of the two rivers, were thousands of tents, shacks, cabins, caches, warehouses, half-built hotels, false-faced saloons, screeching sawmills, markets, shops, and houses of pleasure.

Here in the midst of the wilderness—a thousand miles from nowhere—a great city was being built. It seemed slightly unreal in the June heat, bathed in a halo of sunlight, blurred slightly at the edges by the mists that steamed from the marshes. The stampeders caught their breath, half expecting the whole phantom community to vanish. This was the goal they had set themselves. This was the finish of the long trail north. This was where their rainbow had its end. They turned their boats toward the shore, a shore already thickly hedged by scores of other craft, and landed, still in a daze yet inwardly triumphant at having at last set foot upon the threshold of the golden city.

CHAPTER EIGHT

The Test

It would be nice to report that, after so much hardship and so much back-breaking work, these stampeders found the gold they sought so eagerly. But that wasn't to be. Only a handful got rich from the Klondike's gold. Most of the ground had been staked already by the early birds. There was very little left for those who had started out the previous fall with such high hopes.

And yet it didn't really seem to matter to most of the stampeders. Only a few of them even bothered to go out to the fabulous creeks and look over the ground that had been staked. And only a few of them bothered to look for gold in other creeks and other river valleys. Instead they wandered back and forth, like men in a dream, along Dawson's Front Street, which wound past the grey Yukon River.

They weren't downhearted. In fact, all the evidence suggests they were elated. They had left their homes, their families, and their jobs in search of—what? *Gold*? No; that was only an excuse. What they were really seeking was adventure—the chance to test themselves against natural barriers, to find themselves, to see if they could really achieve what they set out to do.

And, having achieved it—having reached their goal, when others faltered and fled—they were strangely content. That summer they began to sell the ton of goods that the police had insisted they bring with them. The sandspit along the riverbank became a vast bazaar where you could buy anything in the world, from pink lemonade to dancing slippers. And having sold their goods, for whatever they could get, they took the money, bought a steamboat ticket, climbed aboard one of the scores of sternwheelers then plying the Yukon River, sat up on the decks, and watched the forest unroll.

Each man had done something that very few people could do today.

He'd hauled a ton of goods over a mountain of ice. He'd built a boat with his own hands. He'd navigated five hundred miles of river and rapids. He'd taken part in one of the great adventures of his day, and he had survived. He hadn't found any gold, but he had certainly found himself. That was treasure enough to satisfy any man.

INDEX

Lunch on the Yukon Trail, Dyea Valley, Alaska, circa 1897.

(P87-667, ALASKA STATE LIBRARY, WINTER & POND PHOTOGRAPH COLLECTION)

TRAILS OF '98

CONTENTS

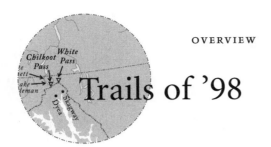

Trails of '98

IN 1896 THE CANADIAN NORTH WAS A VIRTUALLY UNKNOWN REALM. IN THE YUKON TERRITORY, A FEW WHITE PROSPECTORS SEARCHED FOR GOLD AND, ON FORTYMILE RIVER NEAR THE ALASKA BORDER, ACTUALLY FOUND SOME. WHEN THE BIG GOLD STRIKE WAS MADE IN THE KLONDIKE VALLEY IN AUGUST, THESE MEN WERE THE FIRST ON THE SCENE.

But the rest of the world knew nothing about the Klondike gold. A little community called Dawson was growing up on the frozen swampland where the Klondike flows into the Yukon—but nobody in the outside world had heard of it.

So remote was the Yukon valley that nearly a year went by before the word of the gold strike reached civilization. Two little ships loaded with prospectors and gold arrived in San Francisco and Seattle on July 17 and 19 of 1897, and suddenly the word *Klondike* was on everybody's lips. Tens of thousands of men and women decided to set out for the Canadian North, without any idea where the Klondike was. Many thought it was part of Alaska.

The main routes led up the Pacific coast, along the panhandle of Alaska, and over the Coastal Mountains by way of two passes—the White and the Chilkoot. On margins of the lakes that lay on the far side, tens of thousands built boats and, when spring came, headed downriver to the goldfields.

Everybody who came this way had to cross an international border. Canadians paid duty on their goods when they entered Alaska. Americans paid duty when they entered Canada.

That is one reason why thousands more sought out other ways to reach the goldfields—hoping that, by taking a so-called all-American route or an all-Canadian route, they wouldn't have to deal with customs agents.

There were other reasons. One route, the so-called all-water route up the Yukon River from the Bering Sea, appeared remarkably easy. The fare was expensive, but it looked like a boat ride all the way.

Businessmen in Canadian cities such as Edmonton touted "all-Canadian" routes, apparently for patriotic reasons but really because they wanted the business. They too suggested that *their* route to the Klondike was easier than any of the others.

There was, in truth, no easy route. Most of the promises made were false. Many of those who planned to strike it rich were two years on the trail.

Few of these found gold, but their struggles and hardships did have a positive result. The tens of thousands of sweating men and women who laboured through the ghostly forests and up the freezing rivers, from Valdez to the Liard, from Ashcroft to the Rat River, from St. Michael to Great Slave Lake, did what no concentrated government effort could have achieved.

They opened up the Canadian Northwest, and the evidence of their passing is everywhere today.

CHAPTER ONE

Opening the Northwest

ON NEW YEAR'S EVE, 1897, SIX YOUNG ENGLISHMEN SAT AT MIDNIGHT SUP-
PER IN A LOG CABIN THEY HAD BUILT ON THE SHORES OF GREAT SLAVE LAKE IN
THE NORTH-WEST TERRITORY OF CANADA.

If anybody had told them six months before that the new year would
find them imprisoned by winter on the shores of a frozen inland sea as big
as Belgium, nine hundred miles (1,440 km) north of the nearest town, they
would have thought him mad.

And yet here, with the grey-green forest stretching endlessly around
them, they could no longer move forward or backward. They were trying to
reach the fabulous Klondike goldfields, and they had another two thousand
miles (3,200 km) of hard travel facing them. But until spring came they
could not move.

Six months before, they had learned of the gold strike on an unknown
river named "Klondike" flowing into the Yukon. Like thousands of others,
they were heading for that distant spot. It wasn't as easy as they thought it
would be.

One of them, a Cambridge University law graduate named William
Ford Langworthy, began to scribble some notes in his diary.

"I wonder whether Dolly and the others are at St. Moritz dancing the
old year out as we did in 1897?" he wrote. "This world is a farce ... Of all the
places in the world this is the last I thought I'd be on New Year's Day ... I
did not imagine how lonely one can feel until today, when six thousand
miles [9,600 km] from home and friends. I hope to goodness we 'strike it
rich' within a couple of years ..."

All over the northwest corner of the continent, in an unexplored wilderness almost a million and a half square miles (3,840,000 sq. km) in size—

half as big again as the subcontinent of India—thousands of others were thinking similar thoughts.

An artist from Boston found himself trapped for nine months in an Inuit village on the upper delta of the Yukon. A schoolmaster from Edinburgh found himself living on wild berries on the banks of a frozen river two thousand miles (3,200 km) to the southeast near the same river's headwaters. A ventriloquist from Chicago found himself in a huddle of tents far to the north on the banks of the Rat River in the tundra country north of the Arctic Circle.

There was a touch of madness in the men who followed the gold rush trails. What on Earth was a little circus doing heading for the gold rush? And yet on the Ashcroft Trail through the wild interior of British Columbia, there it was—complete with a tightrope dancer and music box, a striped marquee tent, performing dogs, and even a trained horse.

What were four other young English aristocrats doing in a log cabin on the Kowak River along the Arctic Circle, five hundred miles (800 km) northeast of Dawson? There they continued to act as they would in England. They even trained a Native as a valet to black their boots and serve them coffee and cigars while they lay in bed till noon, amusing themselves by shooting at stray mice and knot holes in the log walls.

Gold in fabulous quantities had been discovered in the Klondike valley in August 1896. The news didn't reach the outside world until July of 1897— that's how remote the Yukon was from civilization. Tens of thousands of men and women—and even some children—headed north almost immediately, determined to find gold and make themselves rich. They had no idea that both Alaska and the entire Canadian northwest was empty of both people and supplies. A few white prospectors worked along the Yukon River; a few thousand native Indians fished and hunted. There were hardly any settlements and no stores to speak of. Even in Dawson, the only real town, there was little anyone could buy in the "starvation winter," as it was called. Every morsel of food, every tool and piece of equipment, every bit of clothing had to be hauled in by boat, by pack animals, or on the backs of those struggling to reach their Mecca.

Now, in the midwinter of 1897–98, the stampede—as some called it— ground to a halt. From the Cariboo to the Arctic, from the Mackenzie to the

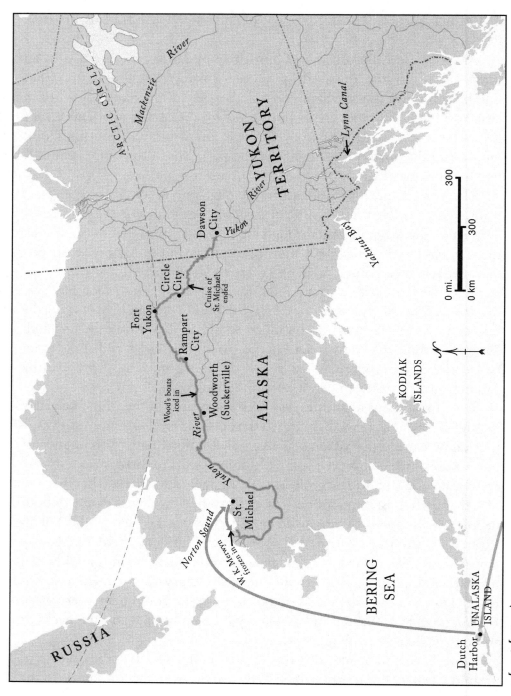

The Rich Man's Route

Bering Sea, from the Rockies to the Pacific, thousands of men like William Langworthy sat huddled in lonely cabins waiting for spring.

There is no single "Trail of '98." There were dozens. The stampeders advanced on the Klondike like a great army executing a giant pincer movement. Those who took part in it poured in from every point of the compass.

The main force, planning a frontal assault, collected in the teeming anthills of the Chilkoot Passes. Far to the west, smaller groups were trying to get over the pitted glaciers that sprawl across the mountainous southern coastline of Alaska. But the great left arm of the pincer was advancing up the Yukon from the Bering Sea by steamboat.

A central column was forcing its way through the heart of British Columbia. This was joined by a second, moving by steamboat, dog team, and on foot up the Stikine River from the Pacific coast.

The great right arm of the pincer was launched from Edmonton. From this point, it fanned out—dozens of groups of men plodding their way through the Peace

There is no single "Trail of '98." There were dozens. The stampeders advanced on the Klondike like a great army executing a giant pincer movement.

River country or struggling through the canyons and rapids of the Liard or pouring down the Mackenzie to the Arctic Circle and filtering over the continental backbone at a dozen different points, almost to the edge of the Arctic Ocean itself.

Thus, in that strangest of all winters, the once empty northwest was swarming with stampeders. They were everywhere—on the Aleutian Islands of Alaska, at Fort Chipewyan on Lake Athabasca more than two thousand miles (3,200 km) to the east, at Old Crow on the Porcupine, 250 miles (400 km) north of Dawson, and on Disenchantment Bay, three hundred miles (480 km) due south.

Some were dragging their sleds up the Gravel River across the Mackenzie Mountains—the great barrier that separates the Northwest Territories of Canada from the Yukon. Others were moving up the Dalton Trail from Haynes on the seacoast that now forms a branch of the Alaska Highway. Some were deep in the south Nahanni valley in the Northwest Territories, with its caves and its canyons.

Relics of their passing remain today in the form of crumbling cabins or rotting grave markers on a silent riverbank or in a lonely forest. But the great legacy was less obvious but more enduring. In a very real sense, they broke down the barrier of the frontier and opened up the northwest.

CHAPTER TWO

The Rich Man's Route

FOR ANYONE WITH MONEY, IT WAS NO PROBLEM TO REACH THE KLONDIKE GOLDFIELDS—OR SO IT SEEMED. ALL YOU DID WAS BUY A TICKET ON A STEAM-SHIP HEADING UP THE COAST OF BRITISH COLUMBIA AND AROUND THE GREAT PENINSULA OF ALASKA TO THE MOUTH OF THE YUKON RIVER. THERE YOU TRANSFERRED TO A STERNWHEEL STEAMBOAT—BUYING ANOTHER TICKET—AND WENT SEVENTEEN HUNDRED MILES (2,720 KM) UPRIVER TO DAWSON.

But, as thousands were to discover, this easiest route of all—the so-called rich man's route—wasn't as easy as it seemed. It was the long way around—three thousand miles (4,800 km) from Seattle, Washington, or Victoria, British Columbia, to St. Michael at the mouth of the Yukon and seventeen hundred more upstream to Dawson. In theory no one needed to walk a foot. It was a boat ride all the way.

And yet those who chose to buy their way around the Alaskan peninsula did not understand the shortness of the navigation season on the Yukon. Eighteen hundred stampeders tried to take the all-water route in the fall of 1897. Only forty-three reached the Klondike before winter set in. Of these, thirty-five had to turn back because in the last frantic moments they had flung all their possessions aside and then found that there was nothing to eat in Dawson.

No one who left the United States or Canada after August 1 reached the Klondike by the all-water route that year. When the early freeze-up came, some twenty-five hundred persons were stranded along the seventeen hundred miles of river between the mouth of the Yukon and Dawson City. At least one-quarter of these had no money left. None would reach Dawson until the following July, and some would never reach it.

One of these was W. D. Wood, the mayor of Seattle, Washington, who quit his job as soon as he heard of the gold strike and chartered a ship to go to the Yukon. He left on August 16 and reached St. Michael on August 29. It was only here on this bleak, volcanic beach that the passengers realized, for the first time, that a steamboat would have to be built before they could embark for the Klondike. A hundred tents were pitched and a mess set up to feed the horde in a style that one described as "worse than a cheap Japanese restaurant."

Now for the first time it became clear that this voyage was no luxury cruise. The passengers would have to work hard unloading the cargo and pitching their tents and helping to build the steamer on which they had so trustingly bought their passage.

There was chaos, confusion, distrust, and discontent. Wood tried to abandon his party, but the passengers held him as a sort of hostage. It took three weeks to build the steamer, which was christened *Seattle No. 1* but unofficially dubbed *The Mukluk* because it looked like an Inuit sealskin boot.

A smaller vessel, the *May West*, was being built at the same time, touching off a race to see which ship would be finished first. The *May West* won by a day, but it didn't make any difference. Halfway up the river, both boats were frozen in for the season. Dawson was eight hundred miles (1,280 km) and nine months away.

A cluster of shacks and cabins sprang up around these two steamers. The town was officially called Woodworth in honour of Mayor Wood and Captain Worth of the *May West*. The passengers called it Suckerville. They held indignation meetings and tried to get the mayor to sell them supplies at Seattle prices—supplies that he had hoped to sell in Dawson at a handsome profit.

Wood was now heartily sick of the word *Klondike*. He must have wished he had never quit as mayor of Seattle. As soon as the chance came, he escaped and made his way on foot back to St. Michael on Norton Sound near the mouth of the Yukon. The trip was a hard one but was better than listening to the passengers' complaints. The rest stayed on until spring. By that time, two of the women passengers had married two of the men. They were the only ones who gained any reward from the adventure.

At three o'clock in the morning on June 25, 1898, bitter and discouraged, they finally trudged down the gangplank at Dawson in their tattered clothing, patched with old flour sacks. It had taken 314 days for them to reach the Klondike by the all-water route. Those who could afford it immediately bought a ticket home.

While Wood's little community was being established, another boom-town, known as Rampart City, was taking form a hundred miles (160 km) farther up the river at the mouth of Minook Creek. Here too was gold. In 1896 a Russian named Minook had scooped three thousand dollars from a hole eight feet (2.4 m) square and fifteen feet (4.6 m) deep. Now, in 1897, with steamboats frozen in all along the river, Rampart was expanding. Its population was close to a thousand. Its poorest cabins were selling for eight hundred dollars, while lots went for twelve hundred.

Early in September a curious craft, with an equally curious crew, chugged into Rampart. This was the tiny sternwheeler *St. Michael*. She was manned entirely by amateurs who knew nothing about steamboats—a lawyer, a doctor, several clerks, some salesmen, and one lone tramp printer.

They were part of a large number of stampeders who had been dumped near the Yukon delta after a harrowing trip north aboard the sea-going vessel *Cleveland*. Each would-be prospector had brought along a ton (907 kg) of goods—everything from gold pans and pick axes to soup cubes. Now they learned that the transportation company would allow them to take no more than 150 pounds (68 kg) upriver to Dawson.

What to do? Nobody wanted to dump everything on the bleak shores of Alaska. Finally, sixty members of the expedition got together, formed a company, and bought the *St. Michael* from a nearby Jesuit mission entirely for the purpose of moving their personal freight to the Klondike. They elected a crew and headed upriver, leaving the rest of the passengers to take another sternwheeler, the *John J. Healy*.

By the time the *St. Michael* reached Rampart, fourteen stockholders had had enough. They'd been in trouble all the way along the Yukon with their little boat. They removed their share of the cargo and went prospecting on Minook Creek, where one of them immediately froze to death. The remainder insisted on going on.

They had no fuel because the transportation companies had bought up all the cordwood on the river. But then, by one of those strange happenings that marked so many Klondike expeditions, they discovered a seam of coal in the banks of the river! That kept them going in spite of two boiler explosions and a fire.

On September 19, this unhappy little steamboat met the *John J. Healy*, which was coming back downstream. The *Healy* had failed to get across the Yukon flats in the heart of Alaska. On board were the remainder of the *Cleveland*'s passengers. Six of the stockholders of the *St. Michael* insisted on rejoining their comrades and heading back up the river again in the teeth of the oncoming winter. Twelve more had been set ashore by the *Healy* at Fort Yukon. When the *St. Michael* reached this river port, they climbed aboard the *St. Michael* as well.

Now heavy with passengers and freight, the tiny steamboat pushed on. At the end of the month, it reached Circle City, the oldest of the Alaska gold camps. Most of those on the boat had lost their enthusiasm, but there were nineteen left who insisted on going forward.

At this point, the situation on the river was completely confused. Half the population of Dawson was trying desperately to get away because there was no food in the town. The ice-choked waters were thick with boats fleeing from the Klondike goldfields. These boats met other boats jammed with men and women equally desperate to *reach* the goldfields at any cost. Many of them were so heavily laden with shovels, gold scales, food and clothing, bedding, and whisky, and other paraphernalia, they could make little headway against the current.

The little *St. Michael* was so badly overloaded that when she backed out onto the river she couldn't move an inch against the speed of the current. There she stood, motionless, her ancient engines throbbing and shuddering to no effect. The captain refused to go farther unless half the passengers got off. Nobody wanted to do that, and so the captain quit in disgust, and the passengers elected a new one.

It took the new captain four hours to move the vessel a mile (1.6 km). The engineer quit, and a new one was elected. He placed the safety valve on the boiler twenty pounds (1.4 kg per sq. cm) higher than his predecessor. A steam connection began to leak. An amateur fireman cried out "Save yourselves! The boiler's bursting!" Everybody clambered for the rails while the new captain, trying to reach shore, rammed the boat into a sandbar. And that was the end of the cruise of the *St. Michael*.

CHAPTER THREE

An Incredible Voyage

OF ALL THE JOURNEYS BY THE ALL-WATER ROUTE, THE STRANGEST WAS THAT TAKEN IN THE FALL OF 1897 BY THE *ELIZA ANDERSON*. THE OLDEST VESSEL ON THE PACIFIC COAST, THE *ELIZA ANDERSON* WAS AN ANCIENT SIDEWHEELER, BUILT FORTY YEARS BEFORE AND LONG SINCE SENT TO THE BONEYARD. FOR YEARS SHE HAD BEEN TIED UP AT A BANK IN SEATTLE HARBOUR WHERE SHE SERVED AS A FLOATING GAMBLING HALL. BUT THE NEWS OF THE KLONDIKE BROUGHT HER OUT OF RETIREMENT.

The *Anderson* was hastily fitted out for the three-thousand-mile (4,800-km) ocean voyage to the Bering Sea. Her owners were so eager to squeeze the last ounce of profit from the expedition that duplicate tickets were sold for passage aboard her. That trick so enraged her passengers they tried to hurl the purser into the sea. They were only prevented from doing that by the skipper, a tough sea dog named Tom Powers who stood for no nonsense.

The *Anderson* seemed to lack every item necessary for a sea voyage. She had no propeller, no up-to-date boilers, no water condensers, no steam hoisting tackle, no electric power, no refrigeration, and incredibly no ship's compass.

This broken-down vessel was the flagship of a weird fleet of five craft that set out from Seattle on August 10, 1897, to the cheers of five thousand well-wishers. The limping sidewheeler led off the pack. Her decks were jammed with tables and chairs, collapsible silk tents and canvas beds, sleeping bags, tin and granite pots, pans, cups, dishes, and stoves, assorted sleds of curious shapes, and mounds of clothing and provisions.

Just behind her, puffing furiously, came an ocean-going tug, the *Richard Holyoke*. She had three queer craft in tow. The first was a coal barge—a former Russian man-o'-war, the *Politofsky*, built in Sitka back in 1866. Once she had been the flagship and pride of the Russian Pacific fleet, but now, with her superstructure long since ripped away, she was nothing more than a weather-beaten derelict hulk, black with coal dust.

The second ship behind the tug looked like a replica of Noah's Ark. This was the *W. K. Merwyn*, a seventeen-year-old sternwheeler that had been used as a hay and grain carrier but was now intended for traffic on the Yukon River. The plan was to abandon the *Anderson* at the mouth of the Yukon and transfer the passengers to the *Merwyn* for the river trip to the Klondike. Her smokestack and paddlewheel had been removed for safety and stowed on her main deck. The boat was now encased in a wooden jacket from stem to stern. Inside this grotesque craft boxed like rats in a cage were sixteen passengers, the overflow from the *Anderson*.

All that kept the *Merwyn* on a steady keel was a cargo of tinned goods and supplies, which were lashed to the main deck and acted as a sort of counterweight.

The final craft in the flotilla, also towed behind the tug and looking out

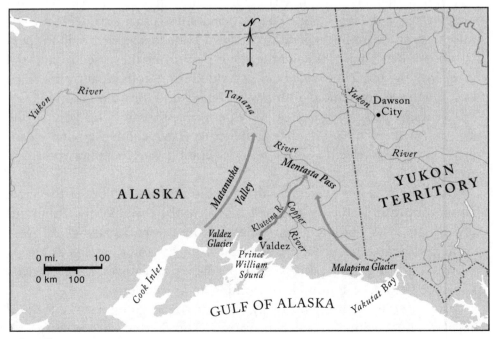

The All-American Route

of place, was a sleek pleasure yacht, the *Bryant*. This was owned by an adventurous Seattle clubman, Jack Hansen. Hansen had tried to buy passage aboard the *Anderson*, but even the duplicate tickets had been sold. So he and three friends hooked their yacht behind the *Holyoke*.

The trip up the coast was a nightmare. At Comox on the east coast of Vancouver Island, the inexperienced seamen loaded the coal unequally into the bunkers of the *Eliza Anderson*. As a result, the ship listed to starboard. Her rudder went out of action, and she drifted broadside into a three-masted clipper, *Glory of the Seas*, shattering a large section of the *Anderson*'s side-wheel paddlebox.

That and other mishaps kept the passengers in a continual uproar. Everyone wanted the vessel to turn back. Captain Powers refused, roaring he would sail his boat "come hell or high water." By the time the *Anderson* and her sister vessels had reached Kodiak Island off the south coast of Alaska, five passengers were ready to give up. They fled the ship, and nobody could lure them back.

Now the *Anderson* struck out for Dutch Harbour, the bleak port on the island of Unalaska at the very tip of the Alaskan peninsula where the Aleutian Islands have their beginning. Soon she was wallowing in a raging storm, her engines straining to keep her on course. And at this crucial moment, the ship ran out of coal. It turned out the lazier members of the crew had hidden half the coal sacks at Kodiak so nobody would notice they had not loaded the full amount.

The escorting tug and coal barge had vanished in the driving rain, and the *Anderson* was foundering. The passengers were ordered to tear the wooden bunkers apart and use the heavy planks for fuel. When these had been burned, the large wooden water tubs were ripped apart and flung into the furnace. The ship's furniture followed. Finally, the stateroom partitions were taken down and tossed in, until the *Anderson* was little more than a hollow shell tossing fitfully in the north Pacific.

By this time, the passengers were all writing farewell notes and stuffing them into bottles. There were plenty of bottles because most of the whisky had been drunk in an attempt to raise their spirits. By the time the storm reached its height, the life rafts and boats had been swept overboard, and the vessel was out of control. The captain gave the order to abandon ship.

At this point, fate intervened in an extraordinary way. A six-foot stranger, with a wild mop of greyish-white hair, a hawk nose, and a flowing white beard, appeared suddenly out of the storm. Dressed in oilskins and rubber boots, he strode into the pilot house, seized the wheel, got the vessel under control, and steered her into a quiet cove on Kodiak Island where she was anchored protected from the raging winds. That done, the mystery man vanished as suddenly as he had appeared.

To the terrified passengers, he must have seemed a god or a demon from another world. Actually, he was a stowaway, a Norwegian who lived on the island with his brother and was trying to get free passage to Unalaska.

Now, in harbour, the *Anderson* experienced a second fantastic piece of luck. The passengers discovered an abandoned cannery loaded with coal. And so, with more fuel aboard, the ancient sidewheeler staggered on along the coast of the peninsula toward the tundra of Unalaska.

She stumbled into Dutch Harbour, swivelled sideways, and smashed into the docks. The ship and passengers were still shuddering from this blow when a pipe in the boiler room burst, sending great clouds of scalding steam in all directions.

In spite of this, Captain Powers roared he would sail on for St. Michael. The numbed passengers had had enough. Twenty-eight immediately booked passage for home. The remainder, still intent on getting to the goldfields, chartered a whaling schooner to take them 750 miles (1,200 km) across the Bering Sea to their destination.

The whaler deposited them on the bare mud shores of the old Russian port, where, to the surprise of all, the rest of the original fleet was awaiting them. Most now expected that the worst part of the long journey was over and that the remainder of the trip up the Yukon River to Dawson would be swift and gentle. Few realized that the Klondike was seventeen hundred miles (2,720 km) and, for them, ten months away.

It turned out that the *W. K. Merwyn* wasn't big enough to take them all. And so they got a makeshift scow with a bunkhouse built on top to be pushed ahead of the vessel.

The *Merwyn*'s voyage began on the morning of October 10. She was hardly into the web of the delta when the river froze around her. The steamboat settled in for the winter while the scow was towed to an Inuit village.

Now it slowly dawned on the passengers they'd have to stay here for eight months.

They reacted in various ways to this dismal news. One, an artist, became so morbid that he wandered aimlessly about in the snow until he died. Another, a dog driver named Jack Carr, simply traded his outfit for a team of huskies and mushed off through sixteen hundred miles (2,560 km) of wilderness to Dawson, setting a new long-distance record.

The remainder of the party simply sat and rotted until spring. Most had been so shattered by the voyage up the coast that this latest episode only served to depress them further.

They hibernated in the fog-shrouded banks of the river, and when the ice broke they set off for the goldfields. The urge to reach the Klondike had become a habit more than an obsession. When, at last, on June 30, they walked glumly down the gangplank at Dawson, most of them turned right around and went home again.

By the fall of 1898, only three members of this expedition were left in the goldfields. Several had died of scurvy, one had hanged himself, dysentery had killed another. The rest worked their way or paid their way to the outside world.

Only two actually dug for gold. One of these, oddly enough, had started out with less than any of the others. Indeed, he'd thrown his last ten cents into Elliott Bay out of Seattle leaving for the North with only the clothing he wore. His name was Thomas Wiedemann, and he eventually returned to his home richer by five thousand dollars—a handsome sum in those days when a working man made less than five hundred dollars a year.

CHAPTER FOUR

The Valdez Trail

WHILE STEAMBOATS LOADED WITH GOLD SEEKERS TRIED VAINLY TO REACH THE
KLONDIKE BY THE ALL-WATER ROUTE, THOUSANDS MORE STAMPEDERS ATTACKED
ALASKA FROM THE SOUTH. AN OUTPOURING OF GUIDEBOOKS HAD ALREADY
ADVERTISED THIS ROUTE, WHICH WAS SUPPOSED TO LEAD THE PROSPECTORS INTO
THE HEART OF GOLDEN ALASKA WITHOUT DEALING WITH CANADIAN CUSTOMS.

It was rumoured that a Russian trail led into the interior from Port
Valdez on the sea, and that's where many gold seekers headed. Pamphlets,
put out by transportation companies to lure prospectors north, gave detailed
information on what to do and where to go. Most were unreliable. But the
stampeders didn't know that. All that fall and winter chartered
vessels were dumping their human cargoes all along the shores of the Gulf
of Alaska.

This great gulf is almost a thousand miles (1,600 km) wide, bordered on
the west by the thin finger of the Aleutian Island chain and on the east by the
island-studded coast of North America. It is encircled by some of the finest
scenery on the continent.

Here are massive mountain battlements, topped by sprawling glaciers;
canyons and valleys choked by moving rivers of rumpled ice; and peaks that
tower over all others on the continent. But, as the stampeders were to discover, the very nature of this scenery made entry into the interior almost
impossible.

There are three main indentations in the gulf. On the west lies Cook
Inlet, at whose head the modern city of Anchorage now stands. In the centre is Prince William Sound, one of whose fiords leads to the present town
of Valdez. On the extreme east lies Yakutat Bay, where the huge Malaspina
Glacier flows down to the sea.

Most of the boats went to Prince William Sound and the Port of Valdez. Here a great icefield barred the way between the coastal strip and the interior. But once this brooding mass was crossed, a series of valleys took the stampeders to the Copper River, which pointed the way across a mountain divide to the majestic Tanana River. The Tanana led to the Yukon, and, as everyone knew, the Yukon led to the end of the rainbow.

Some thirty-five hundred men and women tried to cross the Valdez Glacier in the winter of 1897–98. They began to arrive early in the fall, but the six-foot-deep (1.8 m) snow made travel impossible. The real movement began in February. The first big steamers left the Pacific Northwest for Valdez with six hundred passengers lured on by tales of "nuggets as big as bird's eggs" in the land beyond the glacier.

The weather was so wicked in the gulf that most of the horses, mules, burros, and dogs aboard had to be shot before the ship arrived. The mules couldn't be used anyway; their feet were so small they broke through the crust of the snow on the trail. But range horses from Montana and Wyoming that had sold for fifteen dollars in Seattle now brought as much as five hundred.

The new arrivals saw that they would have to drag their loaded sleds across three hundred yards (274 m) of coarse sand and six miles (9.6 km) of snow-covered flatland before they reached the lip of the glacier. The ice then rose in a series of benches so steep that a block and tackle was required to hoist goods over them. The glacier itself, glittering and flashing like a sapphire in the sunlight, rose up toward the mountain barrier until it reached a mile (1.6 km) into the sky.

To the men from the industrial cities, it must have seemed a nightmare. The slope to the summit was twenty miles (32 km) long. A nine-mile (14.4- km) descent led to the interior lakes and the streams and then to the Copper River. Most of the men who faced this monstrous glacial cone had never been in such country before. They wandered out on to the chill, white breast of the ice sheet, and others followed sheep-like in their wake. The wavering trail they established led over the most difficult section of all.

Once they were caught on this glistening expanse of creaking ice, the stampeders began to suffer the tortures of snow blindness. Their eyes seemed to fill with red-hot sand. The white world around them changed to

crimson. The blindness struck when they least expected it. They didn't realize that, when the sun was hidden behind the fleecy clouds, its rays could do
more harm than any direct glare.

There were other torments—the eternal strain of crawling across the ice
on steel-shod boots, the loss of sleep brought on by the need to move only
at night when the crust was firm, the constant nausea of having to eat raw
or half-cooked food, the fierce glacial reflection that turned faces lobster red.

Quarrels sprang up. Men found themselves burdened by a snow-blind
partner and often dissolved the union in the middle of the trail. One old
expert, Captain W. R. Abercrombie of the Second U.S. Infantry, watched
friends of long years' standing become the most bitter of enemies.

Quarrels sprang up. Men found themselves burdened by a snow-blind partner and often dissolved the union in the middle of the trail. One old expert, Captain W. R. Abercrombie of the Second U.S. Infantry, watched friends of long years' standing become the most bitter of enemies.

When two partners split up, they cut everything in half—even if that meant destroying all
their goods. Some of the stories of these
breakups are mind-boggling. In one instance,
three partners broke up a small grindstone into
three equal pieces. Another trio split their two
pairs of oars: each took one oar, and they
destroyed the fourth so no one could have it.

Most of the stampeders crossed the ice
between March and June of 1898. At the end of
April, a four-day blizzard covered the ice with
five feet (1.5 m) of snow. On May 1, the snow
turned to rain. Avalanches began to hurtle down the sides of the ice sheet,
burying men and equipment. One slide buried more than two dozen people. They were located by their muffled cries under twenty-five feet (7.6 m)
of snow, and all but two were saved. But their goods were never recovered.

By this time, the constant thawing and freezing made it impossible to
cross the glacier during the day. By 9:00 PM, it was strong enough to bear a
man's weight. By 1:00 AM, it would take a horse. All the dark night the eight-
een-inch (0.5-m) trail was thick with people—those on foot arguing and
quarrelling with those on horseback, for each interfered with the movement
of the other.

By the end of June, the water poured from the face of the glacier in a steady cascade. Men were trapped for days on the ice. They couldn't move forward, and they couldn't go back. They were forced to throw away all they owned.

Warm, moist air poured into the funnel of Port Valdez from Prince William Sound and struck the air blowing through the pass, falling to the ground as snow, sleet, and rain. A dense white fog steamed from the surface, turning bacon into masses of mould and sacks of sugar into sticky tubes of syrup.

The effect was weird and terrifying. The ghostly fog-shrouded ice sheet, sprawling down from the hidden mountains, would crack like a pistol shot as it settled. The vibrations rumbled down through the valley, causing men to halt in their tracks and horses to snort in terror.

After the tremors, and with a deafening roar, thousands of tons of ice, torn from one of the hundreds of smaller glaciers hanging from the mountains, would crash down on the main body. At the same time, bits and pieces would bound off the canyon walls in a series of overlapping echoes that took minutes to die to a whisper in the valleys below.

In the final climb to the peak of the glacier, the stampeders struggled up a twenty-degree slope. Even after twenty yards (18 m) of movement, the energy of even the strongest man was exhausted. The wind whistled down with hurricane force through the pass. The snow froze on men and beast as fast as it struck them, coating all in a ghostly armour.

By August the glacier was impassable. Only one man dared to cross its slushy, steaming face, and that was the army captain, Abercrombie. He made it after twenty-nine hours of continuous toil, without rest or shelter. On the far side in the valley of the Kluteena River—which flows northeast into the Copper River—he found the remnants of the mob building their boats and pushing off down the river, still intent on reaching the Klondike.

The first three miles (4.8 km) of the Kluteena were gentle. The rest was horror. The boatmen rounded the bend and came face to face with chaos.

Roaring like a wounded animal, the river plunged in leaps and bounds over sandbar and boulder for twenty-five miles (40 km). Drift piles blocked the main channel. Snags, like skeleton fingers, reached out from the bank and the river bottom to pluck at the whirling craft. Here the river was strewn with wrecked boats, provisions, clothing, and equipment.

On June 1, one observer counted thirty-six rafts wrecked and abandoned. One man in four was ruined on the Kluteena and left to wander aimlessly along its banks without food, spare clothes, or shelter. Some made one or two trips successfully, then were wrecked in the next attempt. Hundreds lost all stomach for the Klondike and turned back, using any excuse that came to mind.

Of the more than three thousand who landed at Valdez, only two hundred successfully defied the Kluteena. By October they'd reached the Copper River and were dragging their boats upriver by towlines or struggling to pole them against the current. The route, long and weary, led to the Mentasta Pass, the high point of land that overlooked a wilderness of scraggly spruce and birch.

Standing on this height of land, a man could see the great blue valley of the Tanana in the distance. Beyond that somewhere lay the headwaters of the Fortymile River, and beyond the Fortymile lay the Klondike. But it's doubtful if half of one percent of all who crossed the Valdez Glacier that year ever achieved this final objective.

The great majority turned back before another winter set in, terrified that their retreat across the ice might be cut off by melting snow. Thoroughly demoralized, they blundered back, cursing transportation companies and government alike. Each had arrived convinced that he could pan a fortune and be home in time to eat Christmas dinner. Each tasted the bitterness of disappointment.

In this ragtag and bobtail crew were two strapping young Virginians, weak from illness brought on by gorging themselves on uncooked beans. They still clung to a bundle of heavy canvas grain sacks, each of several bushels' capacity, which they had brought north with them. The sacks had been intended as containers for the nuggets they expected to find, lying like apples in an orchard on the shores of Alaska's rivers. Now the bags were useless, but they couldn't let them go.

At Valdez the mail was piling up. There was nowhere farther for it to go. A new postmaster, faced with a mountain of letters and parcels, simply quit and fled home.

In August the government began to issue rations to more than three hundred who had lost everything in the Kluteena rapids. The whaling company that had urged them on to the Klondike was forced now to carry a hundred of them home free of charge. Another 180 paid second-class fares to Seattle or Juneau.

The Christian Endeavour Society built a relief station on the glacier to pick up those men who were too exhausted to come back. By this time, some were tumbling into open crevasses to be rescued only at great risk. Snowslides were making the trail impossible. On November 7, the gale-force wind lifted one guide clear off the ice and carried him several yards. A week later a party on the summit was forced to claw a cave in the snow with their snowshoes. They crouched there for four days and nights, living on meat capsules.

As the winter of 1898–99 progressed, men began to go mad on the ice. All seemed terrified by the vision of a glacial demon who, they said, haunt-ed the crevices. Every man firmly believed in this hallucination.

By the spring of 1899, Valdez presented a pitiful sight. All winter long men had died, one by one, of scurvy. Captain Abercrombie, the army man, couldn't recognize the people he had known the year before—they looked like scarecrow figures, with their hair hanging like string to their shoulders, their faces masked in matted beards, each man scabrous and frost-bitten.

Demoralized and wasted, they staggered about in faded mackinaw suits stripped to rags, their footwear made from the tops of rubber boots attached to strips of gunny sacking. All winter long they had existed like sar-dines, jammed twenty to a cabin in a twelve-by-fifteen foot (3.6-by-4.6 m) space, where wet and steaming clothing hung from the rafters emitting a poisonous stench that sickened even the healthiest.

These were the dregs from the proud expeditions that almost two years before had arrived at the glacier to dig the Klondike's gold. In Valdez alone, the taxpayers of the United States had spent $3,700,000 vainly trying to establish an all-American route to the interior of Alaska.

Two similar all-American trails proved equally hopeless. One led inland from Cook Inlet some distance west of the Valdez area. A lieutenant of the Fourth Infantry, J. C. Castner, had the bad luck to lead a military expedition through this so-called trail up the valley of the Matanuska and over the divide to the Tanana. By the time they reached the Tanana valley, he and his men were near starvation, their clothing in tatters, their feet torn and bleeding. Castner wrote that "my men often said it would be impossible to make others understand what we suffered those days, no tongue or pen could do the case justice."

Yet these hardships pale in comparison with those suffered by the unfortunate handful of men who decided to cross the terrifying Malaspina Glacier, in the vain hope of reaching the Klondike.

CHAPTER FIVE

Death on the Malaspina

THE MALASPINA GLACIER LIES AT THE HEAD OF YAKUTAT BAY NEAR THE SOUTHERN BORDER OF THE YUKON TERRITORY. ALL THE STORIES OF HARDSHIP AND DEATH ON THE SOUTHERN COAST OF ALASKA SEEM LIKE PLEASANT SUNDAY OUTINGS COMPARED TO THE HARDSHIPS ENDURED BY THOSE WHO CROSSED THAT TERRIBLE ICE SHEET IN THE STAMPEDE WINTER.

Only a few parties dared to trespass into that tortured land of enormous ice masses, treacherous canyons and crevasses, unexplored precipices, and mountains four miles (6.4 km) high.

Here was an unreal world of shimmering ice—a meeting place of glaciers that hung by the dozens from the mountain walls. The greatest of all was the mighty Malaspina, the father of glaciers. Down from the mountains it poured in an immense fan shape—an icy desert fifteen hundred miles square (3,840 sq. km), the largest glacier of its kind on the continent. Its six tentacles squeezed back into the black valleys that lay between the crags of the St. Elias Mountains.

We don't know how many crossed the glacier in that stampede winter. But there are records of four parties—about a hundred men in all—who landed at its edge on the ill-fated and condemned brigantine, *Blakely*, in the spring of 1898.

Forty-one of these died trying to reach the Klondike. Many more were disabled for life. They took various routes across the ice, some heading for the Tanana River, others striking directly north into the area now crossed by the Alaska Highway, toward Dawson City. All who survived rued the day they had heard the word *Klondike*.

The worst experience was that of the party of Arthur Arnold Dietz, a

God-fearing young man who advertised in the New York *Herald* in January 1898 for a partner or two to form a mining company. By February he had eighteen recruits. The group met faithfully each Sunday to plan the trip and make themselves familiar with Arctic conditions. Here was a fair cross-section of the Klondike stampeders—moderately well-educated, middle-class, white-collar workers mainly: a doctor, a policeman, a mineralogist, a tin smith, an engineer, a clerk.

In April this group of city-bred adventurers found themselves dumped on the shores of Yakutat Bay, their machinery and equipment coated with rust and all their food, except for their flour and meat, spoiled by saltwater.

Nevertheless, they started off across the glacier on a trip that few men had dared to make before—nineteen citizens from New York City, whose main exercise until this moment had been a stroll in the country or a Sunday jaunt on a bicycle.

The setting was unearthly. The ice itself was clear as crystal, slippery as glass, and lovely to gaze upon, being navy blue in colour. But it was treacherous. Its surface was like a washboard, split by blue-black crevasses, some of them easily seen, others clogged with snow that was sometimes hard-packed and able to bear their weight but otherwise soft as feather down.

This monotonous expanse faded away off to the distant mountains. Its surface was broken only by colossal piles of stones deposited thousands of years before or by stark ridges of ebony rock that rose like islands from the angry ocean of turbulent ice.

Rarely could the Dietz party pitch a tent because of the storms that whirled across the glacier's face. Instead they slept in the lee of their supplies, waking each morning beneath a two-foot (0.61-m) blanket of snow. Fissures barred their way, forcing them to detour for miles. Snow blindness plagued them into rubbing their eyes so furiously that the lashes were worn away. Even the dogs went half blind.

After the first week, no man could speak to his neighbour. They travelled without a word and, when they stopped to rest, were too weary to utter a groan. In the words of Dietz himself, they very much "resembled a party of deaf mutes."

It took them three months to cross the Malaspina, and in all that time they were never free of the sight of the hummocky ice stretching in an endless expanse into the storm. On those days when the sun's pale halo pierced the haze, they could see the mountains in the distance—the sharp peaks of the St. Elias range, highest on the continent. Between these massive pinnacles, the glacier squeezed like toothpaste, the ice crushed together to form hillocks between which ran deep and jagged fissures.

Before the mountains were reached, these narrow canyons in the ice claimed three of the party.

After three months, the men who had started out were unrecognizable. Some had lost twenty-five pounds (11.3 kg). Their sunken faces were matted by unkempt beards. They left the icefield behind and plunged into a different world, struggling through mountain precipices as wild as a jungle. The brambles here were almost impassable. The ground was so thick with decayed vegetation it made passage as difficult as wading through deep snow. And yet they managed somehow to drag across the glacier an eight-hundred-pound (363-kg) motor. They were forced to abandon it in the forests.

Before they reached the headwaters of the Tanana, another man had died of fever. Finally, in September, they could go no farther. They knew they were trapped until spring, and so they hastily built a hovel of logs and prepared to sit out the long winter.

They were all partially insane by this time. The boredom was so maddening that three, casting aside all caution, insisted on trying to reach Dawson overland. They took some provisions, pushed off into the wild, and were never seen again.

The remainder sat in the cabin, huddled together for warmth. They had nothing to do but wait and read, over and over again by the firelight, the single Bible that was their only book. The fire was never allowed to die out, but the interior of the shack was still so cold the ice formed within two feet (0.6 m) of the fireplace. They lay in their sleeping bags like grubs in cocoons for twenty hours at a time, coming out only once a day to cook a hasty meal, often eating their meat raw to save fire.

As the days and months slipped by, the men forgot what day it was. They repeated poems, songs, and hymns over and over again to relieve their boredom. Each confessed details of his past life merely to make conversation—details, in Dietz's words, "that could not have been wrung from him by the most severe third degree methods under ordinary conditions."

They lay so long on their backs that they became sore and rheumatic. Soon their beards were a foot in length. They recited their family trees and memorized tables of weights and measures. They carved up the cabin walls into grotesque shapes to reduce the monotony. Yet none of these trials was enough to destroy their urge to look for gold.

The need to find it became an obsession. Without it the whole ghastly nightmare would have lost its meaning. The mineralogist in the party tried to explain it was useless to seek gold in this frozen forest. In spite of that, when spring came they sank a shaft and with their ebbing strength built a windlass and went through the pantomime of mining.

Now, to their horror, they found themselves again face to face with the glacier. Try as they would they had not been able to avoid it. It lurked at the forest rim like a monster, waiting for them.

Of course they found nothing but gravel, but that didn't stop them. Three of the party set off to the base of the distant mountains, again seeking gold, and there an avalanche buried them forever.

Now the expedition was down to nine people. Their only desire was to escape, but no man wished to recross the terrible glacier. When the warm weather arrived, they decided to follow instead the pathway of the Tanana River. Before they set out, another man died of scurvy, and they were down to eight.

They stumbled through the forests, numbed by a spring blizzard until they had to club each other with their fists to restore circulation. Their clothes were in tatters, their socks reduced to masses of filthy wool, their moccasins in shreds, their feet swathed in rags. And here they were discovered by a group of Indians who sold them seal coats and fur mukluks. Half conscious, they plunged on.

Now, to their horror, they found themselves again face to face with the glacier. Try as they would they had not been able to avoid it. It lurked at the forest rim like a monster, waiting for them.

The second trek across the ice sheet was far worse than the first. With the coming of spring, the expanse seemed even more of a tortured mass, splintered by spider's webs of crevasses. The snow was frozen so hard it cut like sharp sand. One man's feet swelled to twice their normal size before he died.

The storms were so fierce that the seven survivors could see nothing farther than ten feet (3 m). They couldn't build a fire or cook any food. The flour supply vanished after six weeks, and they lived on raw beans and smoked fish given to them by the Natives they had met. When these were gone, they killed and ate their dogs. Only then did the storm clear, and in the distance a wavering line of blue appeared.

It was the Pacific Ocean. Now completely demented, they reached the beach. Here they killed and ate the last of their dogs and collapsed on the cold sands, where the U.S. revenue cutter *Wolcott* found them. Four were alive but didn't know who they were or where they were. The other three were dead in their sleeping bags.

When the four survivors were brought to civilization, one newspaper reported that they had arrived with half a million dollars in gold dust. How bitterly ironic that must have seemed to them! In fact Alaska's only legacy was a physical infirmity that plagued them all their lives. Two were made near-sighted by the glare on the ice. The other two were totally blind.

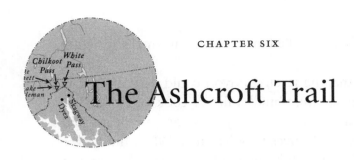

CHAPTER SIX

The Ashcroft Trail

LIKE THE AMERICANS WHO WANTED TO AVOID CUSTOMS PAYMENTS, MANY CANADIANS WANTED TO CHOOSE THE "ALL-CANADIAN ROUTES" TO THE KLONDIKE — ROUTES THAT DIDN'T CROSS INTERNATIONAL BORDERS.

Businessmen in Canadian cities played on this attitude. It was wiser and cheaper, they claimed, to stay on British soil for the entire journey. Pamphlets issued in favour of these trails were so alluring, in fact, that many Americans chose them rather than those that led through Alaska.

One such route was known as the Ashcroft Trail or sometimes "The Spectral Trail." It ran north for one thousand miles (1,600 km) through the tangled interior of British Columbia, beginning at the town of Ashcroft on the Thompson River—which was reached from Vancouver 125 miles (200 km) to the southwest. It worked its way through the Fraser River country and the old Cariboo mining district and from there followed the route of the Collins Overland Telegraph toward Teslin Lake on the headwaters of the Yukon River.

There were still some faint traces of the route cut in the black pines in 1869 by the men of Western Union, who had hoped to link Europe and America with a telegraph cable that would run across Alaska into Russia. This astonishing project was abandoned when the *Great Eastern*—then the largest ship in the world—laid a cable across the Atlantic at about the same time. But the stampeders could still see the rusted and twisted wire lying along the route. One Native-built suspension bridge was made from this wire. Rotting telegraph poles complete with insulators still poked up from the forests.

At least fifteen hundred men and some three thousand horses tried this route, but only a few reached their goal. Before the summer of '98 arrived, the trail was a thousand-mile rut, with no food for the horses except poisonous weeds. Clouds of flies and mosquitoes tormented the pack animals as they stumbled through the black bogs. Many stampeders gave up the attempt before they reached the Skeena River.

But there were others who pushed on north. They made their horses swim over the great olive-green river to enter a dark and desolate land—where fallen logs and slippery roots blocked the trail, where greasy slate slopes had to be scaled, where the lifeless forests were empty of grass, where horses sank belly deep in mud holes, where the rain fell ceaselessly, churning the soil into a deep jelly, and the only vegetation seemed to be the prickly and evil devil's clubs.

The route grew more eerie. Along its length, dead horses lay beneath clumps of northern spruce, from whose branches the pale mosses hung in ghostly cascades. From the hilltops, the men who trudged north could see the endless waves of evergreens rolling off into the horizon under the drizzling skies. The forests were so dense that only an occasional patch of weak light made its way through them. And on most days the sun didn't shine. There was still no grass for the horses, only leaves and fireweed, skunk cabbages and Indiana rhubarb, nettles and poisonweed.

The names along the way told their own story: Poison Mountain, Reduction Camp, Starvation Camp, and Groundhog Mountain. "As most travellers had only laid in grub for two hundred miles (320 km), many of them were glad to eat groundhog," one Chilcoten rancher, Norman Lee, wrote in his diary.

Lee was one of several who attempted to drive cattle north to the Klondike along the Ashcroft Trail—"a sea of mud such as I have never seen before." By the time they reached Groundhog Mountain, Lee and his party had discarded every pound of unnecessary equipment. The entire trail was littered with discarded shotguns and shovels, picks and tents, and even gold pans. Lee saw a first-rate saddle lying amid the coils of rope, the boxes of candles and matches, and the rusting mining equipment against which the limping pack animals stumbled.

His own cattle were lame, and some were dead from eating poisonous weeds. All were reduced to bone and gristle from the lack of feed. Horses died daily from hunger and overwork and lameness caused by the mud. Lee noted that it was scarcely possible to travel a hundred yards (91 m) without finding a dead or abandoned horse.

All along this sinister pathway, mingling with the Indian carvings on the trees, and the strange telegraph wire and insulators, were notes of despair and defiance left by those who had gone before. "Where the hell are we?" somebody had written on one tree. On Groundhog Mountain, a farmer's son standing in the rain and mud scribbled a cheerful piece of doggerel on the side of a spruce tree:

There is a land of pure delight
Where grass grows belly-high;
Where horses don't sink out of sight;
We'll reach it by and by.

Another blazed a hemlock and, with a knife and indelible pencil, produced an eight-verse poem illustrated by cartoons and entitled "The Poor Man's Trail." It vigorously attacked newspaper editors, swindlers, steamboat owners, and others who had advertised this all-Canadian route to the Klondike.

One man tried to cross the Skeena River in an Indian dugout with a collie dog and five pack horses swimming behind him. He lost them all in the torrent and lamented his bad luck in a pencilled message written on a blazed tree. Another pegged a wallet to a tree with the words "A thousand miles to nowhere." Inside were money and letters of farewell to a relative in Ohio. The wallet passed through many hands and was finally delivered intact.

And still, in the midst of all this suffering and frustration, these men too could not get the idea of gold out their minds. It was the Grail that drove them on, deeper and deeper into the labyrinth of the North.

Of all the stories told of the Ashcroft Trail, none is sadder than that of the old man trudging along all by himself with a pack on his back and asking, over and over again, "Where is the gold?" He kept asking it as he moved on. "I'm not a bit worried," he told a group of Natives, "but I wonder how far I am from the gold diggings." When he reached the Stikine River and was told the Klondike was still another thousand miles (1,600 km) away, he blew out his brains.

By the time they reached the Stikine, the hundreds who had managed to

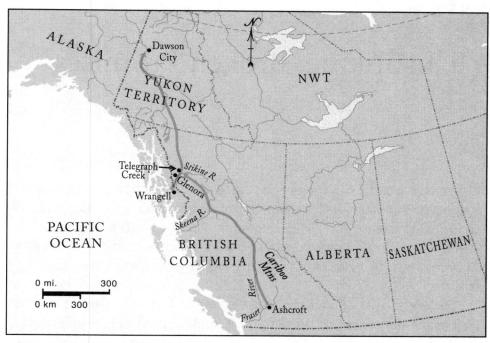

The Ashcroft and Stikine Trails

make it this far were despondent. A few, like the old man, committed sui-cide. One German hanged himself from the cross-tree of his tent and left behind a scribbled note, "Bury me here where I failed."

Others, swallowing defeat, headed down the river to the coast and booked steamship passage home. But some refused to be beaten and continued to push north. And these were joined by a second force of stampeders working their way inland from the Pacific coast.

CHAPTER SEVEN

The Stikine: Broken Promises

WHILE ONE CONTINGENT WAS FORCING A PASSAGE THROUGH THE DRIPPING FORESTS OF THE BRITISH COLUMBIA INTERIOR, ANOTHER WAS MAKING ITS WAY ALONG THE SLUSHY ICE OF THE STIKINE RIVER, ANOTHER OF THE "ALL-CANADIAN ROUTES." THE TWO TRAILS CAME TOGETHER AT THE RIVER TOWN OF GLENORA, WHICH IN MARCH OF 1898 WAS SWOLLEN WITH FIVE THOUSAND PERSONS.

The merchants of Victoria and Vancouver had advertised the Stikine Trail as the only practical route to the Klondike. A pamphlet published by the British Columbia Board of Trade said that the trail "avoids the dangers and hardships on the passes and the Whitehorse and other rapids." Another advantage, it said, was that "the prospector on leaving the steamer, finds himself in the heart of a gold country practically unexplored."

The theory was that the Stikine River, which leads through the narrow Alaska Panhandle, could be used to get around the U.S. customs. The merchants of the Canadian coastal towns were locked in a desperate tug of war with their Seattle rivals for the Klondike trade. They had put pressure on the Canadian government to help them out by improving this route. As a result, the Minister of the Interior, Clifford Sifton, announced that a wagon road, a railway, and a steamboat line would be built along the Stikine.

Surveys were made, material was delivered, and twelve miles (19 km) of track were actually built. Thousands of tickets were sold, but the railway remained a dream. Thousands of gold seekers moved up the river, only to find there was no railroad and a trail so rutted and lacking in feed that few horses could make it.

All winter and spring they dragged their sleds up the frozen Stikine. At the mouth, like a bright festering sore, was the Alaskan city of Wrangell.

Woe to any stampeder who paused here! Confidence men from Skagway were waiting for him with their fake information offices and their phony poker games. Robberies were frequent, and guns popped in the streets all night. No one was safe—not even in the court of law. In February a whisky dealer on trial for bootlegging got so mad at the evidence of a prosecution witness that he shot him as he testified.

Once again those familiar scenes of chaos that marked all the stampede routes for the Klondike—tents in clusters, snow-covered mountains of goods, yapping sled dogs, and brawling men—were repeated along the broad mouth of the Stikine.

The wet slush that coated the river like soft plaster made travel impossible until two in the morning. Then the stampeders took advantage of the crust that formed in the cool of the night. But as spring advanced and the slush increased, they began to throw away their goods. Soon this trail, like all the others to the Yukon, was littered with the garbage of the stampede.

The going became so difficult it sometimes took a week to move nine miles (14.4 km). And it was back-breaking work. "Imagine pulling a hand sleigh loaded with grub through a foot or more of slush, temperature of said slush being at freezing point, often up to the middle in ice water, and a keen Northeast wind rushing down the river to meet you." That's how one man described the problems.

The surface was so treacherous by April that men began to break through the ice and drown. All of a sudden the load would drop without warning through the rotten ice. The river opened, and seventeen steamboats went into operation—but the water was so shallow that many got stuck on shoals and sandbars.

At Glenora, as at Valdez, the mail was piling up. When the postmaster couldn't handle the flood of letters, he simply burned several sacks. He had to be spirited out of town in a Native canoe before the stampeders could lynch him.

For a good many men, this was the end of the trail. One well-equipped party had come all the way from Fargo, North Dakota. They had planned to establish a freighting, mining, and merchandising business in the Klondike. They purchased a huge tent and enough supplies to stock a general store as well as feed a herd of horses. The expedition split into two parties. One took the tent and provisions up the Stikine to Glenora. The remainder went overland from Ashcroft with the horses.

The horses were all lost in the swamps, and when the overlanders arrived in Glenora they found the rest of the expedition trapped by winter. They had no hope of reaching the goldfields. But all was not lost. They set up the big tent, whipsawed some lumber for shelves, used the sawdust as floor covering, and began selling off the stock to hungry stampeders at high prices. Farther along the trail, the prices were even higher. Salt, which had sold in Victoria for half a cent a pound (0.45 kg), actually went as high as sixty cents.

Farther up the Stikine was a second frantic community—the one-time trading post of Telegraph Creek. This had been a waypoint on the incomplete telegraph line to Russia. From here the wagon road was supposed to lead overland to Teslin Lake 156 miles (250 km) away. But there was, in truth, no road.

By spring the whole country was a great marsh, and half of those who had come this far began to turn back. The rest pushed on. The route to Teslin became black with people and animals of all descriptions:

Goats harnessed like dogs, munching on the bushes as they passed. Dogs with haversacks strapped to their backs like pack animals.

Weird vehicles based on the wheel and axle principle that jerked over rock and hillock before collapsing.

A cow hitched to a sled by a man who milked it every night.

A man from Los Angeles hauling in the traces like an animal with his fourteen-year-old son straining barefoot beside him and a boy of ten pushing behind.

A Mounted Policeman's widow with a loaded gun, seeking not gold but the man who had killed her husband.

An Idaho lumberman and his wife, wearing a short skirt and high rubber boots and singing in a clear soprano as she trudged along.

A double murder on the trail—one man axed to death and another shot, a third in flight pursued by the police.

An English opera singer singing Gilbert and Sullivan in a high tenor.

Piles of useless equipment strewn along the wayside—sacks of sugar, discarded clothing, and the wreckage of broken sleds.

And at one spot, a heap of dog food five feet (1.5 m) high, piled like cordwood and abandoned.

Here, in the midst of all this hurly-burly, was the strangest sight of all: 203 uniformed soldiers in scarlet jackets and white helmets marching as best they could in close order. They had the help of Hudson's Bay packers and mules. They trudged in step through the mud holes and over the rocks and stumps, performing parade-square drill, spearing fish with their bayonets, and dragging their Maxim machine guns along with them.

This was the Yukon Field Force made up of officers and men from the Royal Canadian Rifles, the Royal Canadian Dragoons, and the Royal Canadian Artillery. They'd been sent north to reinforce the Mounted Police by a government that feared that the flow of foreigners might cause a revolution that could grab the North away from Canada.

CHAPTER EIGHT

Edmonton: The Overland Routes

WHILE THOUSANDS WERE TRYING TO REACH THE KLONDIKE BY VARIOUS ROUTES, THE MERCHANTS OF EDMONTON WERE DOING THEIR BEST TO CONVINCE THE WORLD THAT THEIR CITY WAS THE GATEWAY TO THE ONLY TRAILS OF '98 THAT MADE SENSE.

But, as hundreds were to discover, some of these trails were among the least sensible. Fifty-seven years later one of those who tried to reach the Klondike by this method wrote that "I can't imagine how sane men could have chosen the Edmonton route to the goldfields."

Yet to many it appeared that this was the best way to go. Edmonton advertised that it was "the back door to the Yukon." Maps and pamphlets distributed by the merchants made the trip sound no worse than a Boy Scout hike.

To everyone who inquired, the Board of Trade answered that "the trail was good all winter" and that "the Klondike could be reached with horses in ninety days."

That was a bald lie.

In fact there was scarcely any trail at all. But, as one editor was to write, to question the Edmonton route was "regarded as a species of treason." Hadn't the noted woodsman and outdoor illustrator, Arthur Heming, declared that the trail was "the inside track"? And that the Klondike could be reached from Edmonton in six weeks by canoe or dog team?

"All you need is a good constitution, some experience in boating and camping, and one hundred and fifty dollars," Heming wrote. He added that, if the "stampeders are lucky enough to make their pile in the Klondike, they can come back by dog-sled in the winter."

Those words were widely published. Because of them, dozens were to lose their lives, including the former mayor of Heming's hometown, Hamilton, Ontario, who trusted Heming to organize his expedition. In March 1899, not far from the Arctic Circle, the ex-mayor died slowly of scurvy.

Heming didn't accompany that party. In fact he had never been over the track himself. He knew of it only through reports of the Hudson's Bay Company. But the Hudson's Bay traders had travelled light in canoes and with dog teams, guided by relays of Indians and voyageurs. They didn't have to carry much equipment because they used letters of credit in various Hudson's Bay posts on the way. They had little in common with the amateurs, dragging their sleds and their tons of goods down the Mackenzie River.

A good deal of confusion about this "backdoor route" came from the fact that there was no single trail leading to the goldfields from Edmonton. That term, "Edmonton route," seemed to suggest a well-travelled, carefully marked pathway leading from the banks of the North Saskatchewan to the mouth of the Klondike. But actually the country to the north and to the west was a bewildering tangle of branching trails. None was well marked.

The combinations were almost numberless. Most people, when they described the Edmonton route, were talking of the various trails that led to the Yukon by way of the Peace River country and the Liard River. The distance from Edmonton to Dawson was about fifteen hundred miles (2,400 km).

The other main route, known as the "water route," led down the Mackenzie River and branched off at various points to cross the divide that separates the Yukon and the Mackenzie valleys. The distance by these routes was about twenty-five hundred miles (4,000 km).

Again, these distances were deceptive. The longer route was passable for about two-thirds of the men and women who attempted it. The overland route, on the other hand, was simply appalling.

It's been estimated that 766 men, nine women, and four thousand horses set out for the Klondike by one or other of the overland trails. Of these, only 160 men finished the journey. No woman was able to complete it, and every horse died on the trail.

A good many stampeders who set out from Edmonton spent two winters on the trail. By the time most of them reached the Klondike, Dawson City was already fading away. A sign on a tree on one of the trails suggested its hardship. It read: "Hell can't be worse than this trail. I'll chance it." The man who scribbled those words killed himself in despair.

In 1897 Edmonton was a small agricultural village of about twelve hundred persons. It consisted of a steamboat dock, some log booms, two sawmills, a brick plant, the remains of the Hudson's Bay fort, and a five-block business section straggling along Jasper Avenue with a hotel at one end and a trading post at the other.

The gold rush burst like a cyclone upon this backwater. Thousands of men suddenly jammed the streets. The flats along the river blossomed with tents. Sleds loaded with supplies clogged the roads.

The zaniest pieces of equipment since the days of the Ark rolled through town. In fact there actually was an ark, a curious boat of galvanized iron intended for use in all seasons, with a keel for river travel and runners for snow. And there was a forty-foot-long (12-m) cigar-shaped "boat sled" with a wheel beneath it that did duty as a rudder in the winter because the vessel was supposed to be amphibious. There was also a contraption, built like a lawn mower, with a sixteen-foot (5-m) axle sticking out from each side. The interior was loaded with supplies and the exterior covered in sheet steel.

A man known as Texas Smith had a device designed to cross muskeg, snow, mud, and mountains. Its wheels were wooden wine barrels. At the top was a sleeping platform. Smith called it "The Duck" and set off across the prairie. After the first mile (1.6 km), the hoops came loose from the barrels. After three or four miles (4.8 to 6.4 km), the whole contrivance collapsed.

George Glover of Chicago arrived with an ambitious steam sleigh. It was complete with locomotive and cars loaded with freight. These were supposed to go through mountain passes and cross gorges and canyons by means of a huge driving wheel—a four-hundred-pound (181-kg) steel drum with projected spikes for traction.

Glover called it the "I Will." A crowd gathered to watch it set off. Black smoke belched from its funnels. Steam hissed from its boiler. Then, as the wheel started to turn, the whole machine began to shudder and groan. With each turn of the driving wheel, the device clawed itself deeper and deeper into the earth, hurling clouds of snow and flinging pieces of frozen mud into the faces of the spectators. Thus, firmly embedded in the snow, the "I Will" just wouldn't.

The stampeders were as strange as the machines that didn't work. One of the most colourful was Viscount Avonmore, whom the Natives called Lord "Have One More." He came with a group of old British army pals, along with servants, grooms, a hundred horses, and ten thousand pounds (4,536 kg) of supplies, ranging from tinned turkey to folding tables. It was said he had a hundredweight (45 kg) of toilet tissue and seventy-five cases of vintage champagne with him. But the wine was allowed to freeze and had to be auctioned off at twenty-five cents a case.

The expedition failed after a series of mishaps. One man died of pneumonia. Another sprained an ankle and had scarcely recovered when he stumbled across a sleigh and cracked his ribs. Another fell off a sled and broke his arm. A fourth was kicked by a horse and suffered a fractured shoulder blade. A fifth froze his feet, went out to Vancouver, and died there. Squabbles caused this party to split up, and none of its members reached the goldfields.

The general direction of the pack horse trails led northwest to the Rockies where the Peace River starts and then north to the Liard and across the mountain divide to the headwaters of the Pelly, which flowed into the Yukon. Most of those who travelled these routes took two years' supplies, which were carried on the backs of eight to ten animals.

There were several ways of reaching the Peace River country. The most southerly route led directly across brush and muskeg through swamps and over deadfalls to Fort St. John. Its worst section was called "Dog Eating Prairie" because for decades starving Native people had been forced to eat their animals there.

More stampeders, however, headed for Peace River Crossing, 320 miles (512 km) from Edmonton. The best route took them by boat down the Athabasca and up the Lesser Slave Rivers and then across the seventy-five-mile (120-km) expanse of Lesser Slave Lake. After that they travelled overland by way of a seventy-five-mile portage that led them to the banks of the Peace.

Later on, when the lakes and rivers were frozen, most parties crossed the Swan Hills by way of the so-called Chalmers Trail, which had been hacked out for 120 miles (192 km) as a result of pressure from the Edmonton merchants. It ran between Fort Assiniboine and Lesser Slave Lake, but by the time it was finished it was an almost impossible pathway, littered with broken boxes, smashed sleighs, discarded harnesses, and the carcasses of horses.

Once again, tree after tree was blazed so that disappointed gold seekers could scrawl out their feelings about the Edmonton route. "Due north to Dawson: starvation and death; due south, home sweet home and a warm bed," one such inscription read.

Of the four thousand horses that died or were shot on the overland routes, two thousand died on the Swan Hills. There was no feed for them in this country. At some points, the maddened animals gnawed the bark from trees and staggered on.

With the trail blocked by stranded parties, those who followed were forced to detour. Now they hacked new trails out of the forest as they passed on toward the Swan River. By spring the Chalmers Trail had become a two-way route, with those in the rear crying "Forward" and those in front shouting "Back!" Close to a hundred gave up before reaching Peace River Crossing and trudged back to Edmonton, only to find that the newspapers were still boosting the so-called backdoor route to the goldfields.

For the hardy few who pressed on after the Peace was reached, there was no trail at all. Four main routes led out of either Fort St. John or Peace River Crossing to the Liard River. Each was four hundred miles (640 km) long. A Canadian guidebook told of a road all the way to Fort Selkirk, where the Pelly flows into the Yukon. That was pure fiction.

The Edmonton town council hired a man to open a trail from Peace River Crossing to the Pelly. The only evidence of his work was occasional slashes on trees—nothing more. Few stampeders were able to make the thousand-mile (1,600-km) trek from Peace River Crossing to the junction of the Pelly and Yukon. Some turned back, while others chose an alternative route down the Peace River and Great Slave Lake and then down the great Mackenzie to the Arctic.

Those who did continue on found themselves in a savage land of muskeg, bogs, and deadfalls, where acre upon acre of dead spruce lay fallen crosswise, the trunks so close together that it was impossible for the horses to avoid scraping their legs to shreds on the rough bark. It was said that one could trace the trail of the horses over the deadfalls by blood alone.

At the very top of British Columbia, the Liard River was reached. Up this wild watercourse, with its hot springs, its canyons, its whirlpools, and its rapids, the remaining stampeders forced their way in homemade boats. They went through Hell's Gate and the Grand Canyon, on through the Rapids of the Drowned, where boats capsized and men vanished into the foam. On they went past banks so steep that there was no footing at water level, and they could pull their craft from the cliff tops only by means of hundred-foot (30.5-m) tow lines. On they went through Devil's Portage, where the river, twisting through a horseshoe gorge, could no longer be navigated. Everything had to be dragged for eight miles (13 km) over a mountain.

Those who finally reached Liard Post on the Yukon border were exhausted. The route now led up the tributaries of the Liard toward the mountain divide that blocks it from the Pelly. Only the hardiest dared face that hazard. Dozens more turned back to civilization, striking through BC to Glenora and the seacoast.

By the spring of 1899, men were still stumbling through the forests trying to escape from the trap. Some, disabled by sickness, frostbite, and hunger, were imprisoned in little cabins along the banks of the Liard and its tributary, the Dease. When a local trading company outfitted a relief expedition to try to save this human wreckage, about sixty suffering stampeders were gathered up and taken to Telegraph Creek. Some were so ill or so lame they had to be lifted on and off the pack horses and the scows. Of the thirty-five deaths on the overland trails out of Edmonton in the stampede years, twenty-six occurred in the Liard-Cassiar area. Most were from scurvy.

Of every five men who set out for the Klondike by these overland routes, only one reached his goal. The one party that did get through was composed not of gold seekers but of North-West Mounted Policemen. This patrol, headed by Inspector J. D. Moodie, was ordered to make a report on the best routes to follow across the Rockies and through northern BC to the goldfields. Its job was to supply the government with all reliable information that anybody leaving Edmonton would need. The idea was that the stampede would go on for years. However, by the time Moodie reached his objective, it was all over.

Moodie started out in September 1897. It took him and his party about fourteen months to cover the sixteen hundred miles (2,560 km) from Edmonton to Fort Selkirk on the Yukon. He and his men chopped their way through the wilderness, paddled, climbed, waded, and trudged—their clothes in tatters, their horses half dead, their packers constantly deserting, their constitution weakened by illness.

In one instance, Moodie and his men had to pack their way through three hundred miles (480 km) of fallen timber. At one point, a forest fire almost wiped them out. Only an eleventh-hour change of wind saved them from roasting to death.

Their ponies devoured poisonous weeds and died on the spot. One guide went mad and vanished. Snow threatened to halt the party for an entire winter, but Moodie fought on through the drifted mountain passes, killing his pack horses to feed his sled dogs and hiring more teams as he went along.

His superiors thought he was lost. He was out of touch with the world for months. But in the end, he crossed the mountains by himself and reached the Pelly. Down that great turbulent river he raced in a canvas canoe, until the sharp-edged ice floes tore into the sides and ruined it. He built himself a raft. It was too bulky, and the ice in the channel blocked his way. He spent $450 to buy a Peterborough canoe from another stampeder and kept going—half starved, half frozen, his underclothing caked to his body, and his uniform in rags.

The current grew fiercer. The ice began to suck him under. He tossed the canoe aside, put on snowshoes, and kept on over the ice-coated boulders and through the fast-forming drifts. He didn't stop for sleep. When at last he arrived at Fort Selkirk, dazed with fatigue, Inspector Moodie had been on the move without rest for forty-eight hours. The date was October 24, 1898.

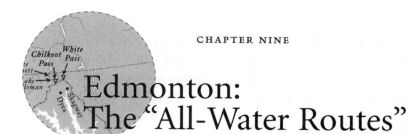

CHAPTER NINE

Edmonton:
The "All-Water Routes"

THE ALTERNATIVE ROUTE FROM EDMONTON—THE SO-CALLED ALL-WATER ROUTE—LED STRAIGHT DOWN THE MACKENZIE RIVER SYSTEM TOWARD THE ARCTIC CIRCLE. THE TRAILS FANNED OFF TOWARD THE WEST OVER THE MOUN-TAIN DIVIDES LIKE THE BRANCHES OF A TREE, WITH THE MACKENZIE AS ITS TRUNK. THOUGH ALL THESE WATER ROUTES ARE FAR LONGER THAN THE TRAILS THROUGH THE PEACE COUNTRY—LONGER BY AS MUCH AS A THOUSAND MILES (1,600 KM)—A GREATER NUMBER OF STAMPEDERS REACHED THE KLONDIKE THIS WAY.

That seemed to be the rule during the Klondike stampede. Many a gold seeker learned to his regret that the shortest path to the treasure was not necessarily the easiest. Simple routes in the end turned out to be more com-plicated than those that seemed difficult on paper. Of an estimated 855 who took the water route to the gold country, some 565 actually reached it. But it took a long time—eighteen months or more. One couple actually conceived and gave birth to a child somewhere between Edmonton and Dawson.

Those who used this route moved overland from Edmonton a hundred miles (160 km) toward Athabasca Landing. Along that well-travelled path, where the tall pines often shut out the sun, a river of humanity flowed in two directions, shuttling freight, machinery, animals, trail outfits, and even steamboats from the railhead across bench lands and sloughs to the banks of the Athabasca.

Here, as elsewhere, the international character of the stampede could be glimpsed. One man, a cowboy from the Alberta foothills named Jim Wallwork, actually hauled his steamboat with him. She was the *Daisy Belle*, a North Saskatchewan sternwheeler that he and his partner had bought in

Edmonton and that they confidently expected would take them to Dawson.

For Otto Sommer of Chicago, this was a honeymoon trip, although a difficult one. It had been forced upon him when his girlfriend refused to let him go alone to the Klondike. He solved the problem by marrying her and taking her with him.

For Frank Hoffman, a recent immigrant from Germany, the pitfalls of the trail held no terrors. He was a veteran of the Franco-Prussian War, and even the fact that his wife was pregnant didn't stop him.

There were embezzlers on the Athabasca Trail, and there were paupers who fared no better and no worse than the wealthy boat owners or the honest trail breakers. Somewhere in the crowd was the Edmonton agent of a New York insurance company who had made off with his clients' funds. And moving along the same route was a Massachusetts carpenter who arrived in Edmonton with less than five dollars in his pocket and was working his way north in stages by plying his trade.

There was a Dutchman who stood six foot seven (2 m) in his stocking feet and a French-Canadian who was only four foot six (1.4 m)—the smallest stampeder on record. And there was one black man on the trail, very much in demand because he entertained his companions with Negro melodies.

By the spring of 1898, the Hudson's Bay settlement of Athabasca Landing had swollen to ten times its original size. Tents bleached the riverbank for two miles (3.2 km). Between these tents, half-formed pathways had been chopped out of timber, bearing crude signs. On either side were campgrounds known as East and West Chicago, so named because the men from that city outnumbered their fellows four to one.

On the north side of the river along a winding trail were camped several parties of boat builders from Ontario. Southeast of the Hudson's Bay post lay a line of shacks known as Bohemian Row, the first thing in the village to resemble a street. Here—where, people said, ten languages were spoken—the tenants included an artist, two miners, three carpenters, two ex-tramps, an actor, a Boston policeman, a one-time temperance lecturer, a banjo-playing Englishman, and a butcher.

Every type of craft was being built—from ungainly scows to sixty-foot (18.3-m) steamboats. In late May, the entire flotilla of more than one hundred craft began to float north. Within two months, it had lost its bunched-up character and was scattered for thirteen hundred miles (2,080 km) along the Mackenzie River system.

A hundred and ten miles (176 km) of rapids faced the boatmen on the Athabasca River. They churned around the great boulders of the Pelican Rapids, where the spray was flung twenty feet (6 m) in the air. They forced their way through Boiler Rapids, Strong Rapids, Crooked Rapids, and Grand Rapids until they reached the Big Cascade, where the current raced over a ledge of rock at twenty-five miles (40 km) an hour.

Boats were mired, crushed, abandoned on sandbars, and wrecked on rocks. One man was drowned; many turned back. The rest surged on down the broadening river, past the oozing and mysterious tar sands, and over the hard portage of the Slave River, whose rapids were so fierce that white pelicans bred in masses on the island in the centre, out of reach of predators. Finally, they burst out onto the leaden expanse of Great Slave Lake, where the storms were as fierce as those on the ocean and the tossing waters vanished over the rim of the horizon.

Once they had crossed this dismaying inland sea, the stampeders found themselves swept into the Mackenzie River proper—the great waterway that led to the Arctic. Out of the mountains from the west and into the mile-wide (1.6-km) river poured the turbulent Liard. About eighty men turned up this stream to fight their way through the canyons and rapids in the hope of joining those who had come overland from the Peace.

The remainder continued on down the main river, where hidden seams of coal smoked and smouldered perpetually, where great blue ice lenses lay exposed on the tottering clay banks, where ghost-like thickets of scorched aspens and "drunken" forests of spindly spruce reeled at awkward angles in the permanently frozen soil, where Indian children ran naked and babbling around the sandy shoreline and Native women like Oriental idols sat unsmiling on high green cliffs.

Halfway down the Mackenzie, not far from the site of Old Fort Norman, a second group split off from the main body and turned west to tackle the mountains by way of the Gravel River, (today known as the Keele). Through this gaunt mountain country no white man had yet travelled. Now a thin, human seepage was trickling in. Some ninety-five men assaulted the divide.

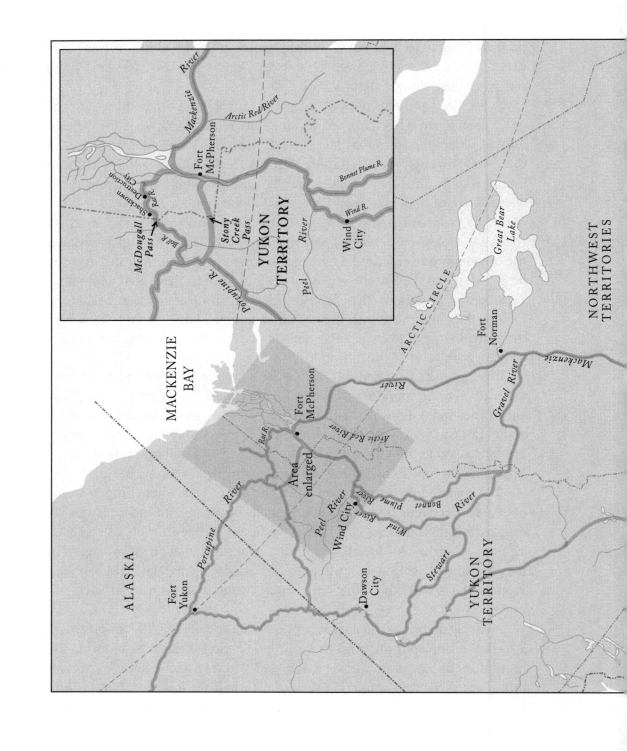

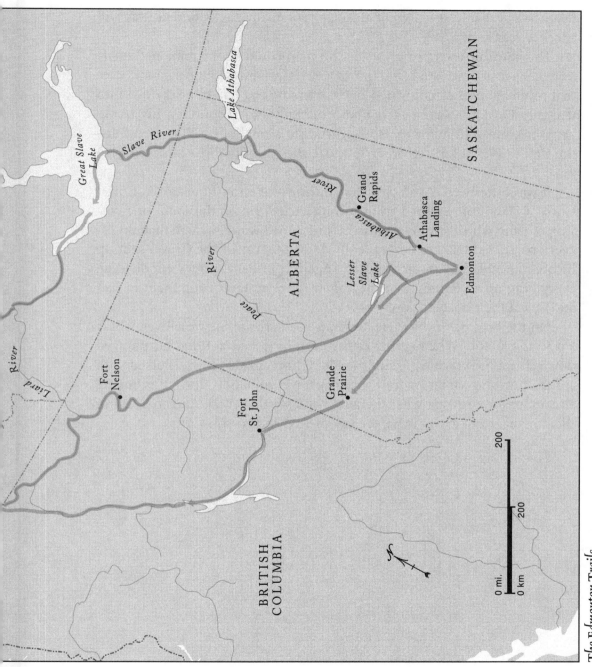

The Edmonton Trails

Of these, probably seventy got through. For many the Klondike was still another year away.

The hardships were so great that no man could say he remained unaffected. Since no one could haul more than 150 pounds (68 kg) at a time over that seven-thousand-foot (2,134-m) barrier, the trip had to be divided into ten-mile (16-km) stages, each man doubling and redoubling his tracks between camps. In many cases, men trudged a total of twenty-seven hundred miles (4,320 km) in order to move their outfits three hundred (480 km).

It was bitterly cold—so cold that, during one noon-hour break, Ernest Corp of Hamilton watched an inch-long icicle form on the spout of a coffee pot from which steam was also hissing. Small wonder, then, that almost every party that tried to cross the divide by the way of the Gravel split up before the goldfields were reached. Again, partners were seen dividing everything up so bitterly that they often chopped their equipment in half and sawed their boats in two.

On the far side of the divide was the rock-strewn Stewart River, which led to the Yukon. When spring came, those who had got that far plunged down its unknown canyons and rapids in homemade scows, caulked with spruce gum and winter underwear. They travelled blindly down this boiling stream, never knowing what the next bend would reveal. And so a few of them managed to arrive in September of 1899 in Dawson City.

Crossing the Great Divide

THOSE WHO CROSSED OVER THE MACKENZIE MOUNTAINS BY WAY OF THE GRAVEL RIVER REPRESENTED A MERE EDDY IN THE MAIN CURRENT OF THE STAMPEDE POURING DOWN THE MACKENZIE. MOST PEOPLE KEPT DRIFTING DEEPER AND DEEPER INTO THE NORTH—BORNE ALONG WITHOUT EFFORT ON THE TAWNY BREAST OF THE MOTHER STREAM.

On they floated, into the land of the Dogrib Indians, who pitched their ragged tents on islands for fear of an invisible enemy stalking the forest glades. On they went past the yawning mouth of the Great Bear River, pouring its cobalt waters out of another freshwater ocean on the Arctic Circle— on and on past blue-green forests and rust-red ponds, salt sinkholes, dried-up channels, yellow with weeds, and ribbed cliffs jutting blackly a quarter-mile (400 m) above the water's crest.

They lounged in their boats with nothing to do but relax against the rudder bar, until the silt-laden water suddenly splayed out into the web of the delta within hailing distance of the Arctic Ocean. At this point, the long, eleven-hundred-mile (1,760-km) slide from Great Slave Lake was at an end.

Now the boats had to quit the Mackenzie and turn up its two most northern tributaries—the Arctic Red River and the Peel, whose headwaters stretched back like slender blood vessels into the maze of the Mackenzie and Richardson Mountains.

This was sullen country, the bald, windswept land of the Crooked-Eye Indians, who lived in hide teepees and believed in a ghostly cannibal, black-faced and yellow-eyed, who gobbled women and children. Across this drab landscape, with its lifeless muskeg, broken only by the occasional stunted spruce and a few thin groves of skeletal willows, the winter snows shifted ceaselessly.

Long before the main body of the stampeders reached the mountain divide, the snow was upon them. Some turned off the Peel and headed west up its tributary, the Rat, hoping to cross the mountains and drift down the Bell and the Porcupine into Alaska to reach the Yukon River. Others pushed farther up the Peel, heading for other tributaries—the Wind, or the Bonnet Plume, which led to passes in the mountains directly north and east of Dawson City.

But sooner or later the mountains had to be faced. In the late fall of 1898, as the land froze under the white hand of winter, the men from the cities, the farms, the offices, and the factories began to attack this barrier, dragging scows and boats up and over the divides by the process called "tracking."

Tracking is the crudest and most exhausting form of towing. Each man, with a canvas sling over his shoulder, helped haul the boat behind him, trudging thigh-deep through the freezing waters, leaping from rock to rock in the shallow, frothing streams, struggling along the edges through tangled willows and over cliffs, or crawling on hands and knees along the slimy banks.

Winter set in, and the snow fell, and the winds shrieked down the canyons that marked the entrances to the passes. The trackers began to wheeze and cough with bronchitis. They were seldom dry. Their legs were masses of boils because of the cold water. Their flesh was rubbery from scurvy, for it was six months since they had enjoyed a balanced diet. Faced with shoals and savage currents, by jagged rocks and ferocious boulders, by gloomy canyons and dizzy banks, they forced their way on until the ice blocked the river and all movement ceased.

Now, all over the Canadian northwest along the Edmonton trails, little settlements sprang up from Great Slave Lake to the Arctic Circle, from the Peace River to the mountains of the Pelly. Some were mere huddles of shacks. Some had names, like Wind City on the Wind River, a tributary of the Peel, or Shacktown and Destruction City on the Rat. Everywhere in the Canadian northwest scores of stampeders settled down for the long wait till spring.

Many of the seventy men camped at Wind City suffered horribly from scurvy. When gangrene set in, as it did in one or two cases, their toes were cut off with hacksaws. When men died, as two or three did, their bodies were stuffed down empty mine shafts that some had dug in the wistful hope there might be gold there in the land of little sticks. The others whiled away the winter's night with chess, checkers, and euchre, with dances and lectures on scientific and literary subjects. Wind City residents passed a code of municipal laws so the winter might pass "pleasantly and profitably away."

Destruction City was located at the start of a fierce series of rapids on the Rat that marked the ascent to McDougall Pass. Here the riverbed rose so steeply—twelve hundred feet (366 m) in thirty-five miles (56 km)—that it was impossible to haul a large craft farther. Men were forced to chop their boats down to manageable size, and so the banks were marked by a confusion of wreckage that gave the settlement its name.

The only way to cross the pass that fall was to travel as lightly and as fast as possible. A French-Canadian from Ottawa, J. E. des Lauriers, was one of those who threw away almost everything he owned in order to get to the Klondike. He left his entire outfit on the banks of the Rat at Destruction City, taking only a sack of flour, a side of bacon, a rifle, and a small boat. Thus, travelling lightly, he actually reached Dawson.

Others couldn't get through. Between fifty and a hundred wintered in the immediate area of Destruction City, crouching in tents or cabins, or huddled in caves scooped out of the banks, surrounded by piles of goods that had been tossed aside. Here was everything a man needed, except for footwear—that had all been torn to shreds on the rocks of the river. And yet, in the midst of plenty, men sickened and sometimes died because they didn't eat the proper food.

Elsie Craig, who wintered there, kept a death roll that reflected the international character of the camp. On November 20, a man from Chicago died of scurvy. On December 13, a Frenchman died of scurvy. In January, two Dutchmen died of scurvy. And over this doomed camp there fluttered bravely several homemade Red Ensigns and Stars and Stripes, made out of flour sacking and red calico.

Many of those who found themselves trapped in Destruction City had already spent one winter imprisoned in the North. These were bitterly disillusioned. One party of thirteen from Chicago was there because they'd answered a newspaper ad and paid five hundred dollars each to a trickster with the curious name of Lambertus Warmolts, who pretended to be a veteran of the Mackenzie country. He guaranteed to deliver them to the Klondike in just six weeks. But when they reached Slave Lake, Warmolts vanished with all the money, leaving all his victims stranded until spring. Yet they would not turn back, so great was their desire to reach the goldfields. Now here they were, rotting from scurvy on the banks of the Rat, with another winter facing them. A few did manage to reach Dawson in August of 1899.

Of those who left Edmonton in 1897 and 1898 and pursued the various routes to the Klondike, only three found any gold at all. Indeed, many who trickled into Dawson, ragged and destitute, didn't even bother to go out to the goldfields but turned back to civilization a few days after arriving.

William Ford Langworthy, the Cambridge law graduate who celebrated New Year's Eve, 1897, so nostalgically on the shores of Great Slave Lake, was one of these. His diary scarcely mentions Dawson. His later entries never refer to gold but only reflect the strange exhaustion that fell over those who finally succeeded in reaching the end of the trail.

To these gold no longer meant very much. Survival had taken its place. Otto Sommer, who had turned his Klondike expedition into a honeymoon trip, got no farther than Grand Rapids on the Athabasca before turning back in despair. Frank Hoffman, the veteran of the Franco-Prussian War, was drowned in Great Slave Lake. His wife went on without him, lost her newborn baby somewhere en route, and wintered at Shacktown. A. D. Stewart, the Hamilton mayor who had come down the river on the *Golden Hope*, died by inches on the Peel.

But there were some who beat the odds. Jim Wallwork, the cowboy, actually dragged his steamboat *Daisy Belle* over the summit, from Shacktown to the Bell River, aided by thirty Indian sled dogs. The little craft finally reached the Yukon and there, unable to face the swift current, gave up the ghost. Wallwork transferred the eight-horsepower engine and the boiler to a York boat and continued upstream to Dawson. No doubt it was enough for him that he made it. For those who set out for the Klondike to seek their fortunes counted themselves truly fortunate if they reached their goal.

There were others who never found what they were seeking—such as the two partners who were discovered in a cabin on the Porcupine River. They had come almost three thousand miles (4,800 km), fighting the rapids and scaling the mountains, and hacking their way through the forests, but when they were found they were frozen rock solid beside a stew kettle hanging over a long-dead fire. The pot contained a pair of partly cooked moccasins embedded in a cake of ice. The rest was ashes.

Index

Two men of the Klondike display gold nuggets.

(P20-041, ALASKA STATE LIBRARY, ALASKA
PURCHASE CENTENNIAL COMMISSION PHOTOGRAPH COLLECTION)

CITY OF GOLD

CONTENTS

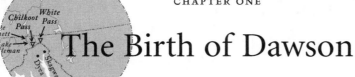

CHAPTER ONE

The Birth of Dawson

IT WAS THE WORST POSSIBLE SITE FOR A CITY.

Who in his right mind would lay out streets and avenues on a flat piece of frozen swamp, so close to the river's edge that the spring floods swept over it?

Covered by a coarse mattress of willows and alders, infested by mosquitoes, a breeding place for typhus and malaria, it would have been avoided by any modern city planner.

But gold camps are not chosen for their setting. They exist solely because of the gold.

And the gold lay just a few miles up the Klondike River from its junction with the Yukon. There, where the rivers joined and where Indians still dried their salmon catches, Dawson was born. Once George Carmack struck it rich on Bonanza Creek on August 16, 1896, it was inevitable that this sprawling wedge of flatland, nestling below the Klondike hills, would become a vibrant community.

Joe Ladue was its founder. He'd been operating a trading post a day's journey up the Yukon when he heard about Carmack's strike. Joe wasn't interested in looking for gold. He had the most valuable piece of equipment on the river—a sawmill. He rafted it down and laid out the beginnings of a new community.

Joe Ladue knew that dressed lumber would be badly needed—not only for buildings but also to make the sluice boxes down which the pay dirt is washed to separate it from the heavier gold. That would be the basis of his fortune.

They called the new community Dawson, after Dr. George Dawson, the director of the Geological Survey of Canada. The Americans, who formed nine-tenths of the population, called it "Dawson City," not because of its size but because it was the centre of a mining district, like Carson City, Virginia City, and Dodge City in the American West and Circle City in Alaska. The name stuck.

The town began to grow almost immediately, even before it was surveyed. The news of Carmack's strike spread up and down the Yukon like a great stage whisper. Everywhere, men dropped their shovels and headed for Dawson, until the entire river from St. Michael at its mouth on the Bering Sea to its headwaters, 2,200 miles (3,500 km) away in British Columbia, was stripped of men.

They came by boat and raft, drifting down from the headwater lakes or poling upstream from Fortymile and Circle. By early September 1896, when the birches and aspens were turning the colour of gold, and the buckbrush above the treeline took on a purple hue, the City of Gold came into being.

In its first winter, Dawson City was a tent town, stretched along the margin of the Yukon near the Klondike's mouth. By January there were only five houses in Dawson, one of them belonging to Joe Ladue. The tents, like dirty white sails, were scattered in ragged order between the trees and the frozen swampland.

The accepted standards of wealth vanished. There was a desperate shortage of almost everything a man needed. There was only one commodity not in short supply— gold. Gold was cheap; it was salt that was expensive—so scarce it was worth its weight in gold.

No one in the outside world yet knew of the existence of Dawson or the gold that nourished it. But as the town grew up around Ladue's sawmill and saloon, a change began to work among those prospectors who for years had had nothing to call their own. The accepted standards of wealth vanished. There was a desperate shortage of almost everything a man needed. There was only one commodity not in short supply—gold. Gold was cheap; it was salt that was expensive—so scarce it was worth its weight in gold.

No other community had a greater percentage of potential millionaires, but its citizens were living under conditions of dreadful squalor. Food became so scarce the most expensive dogs had to be killed because their owners couldn't feed them. Fortunately, a raft load of beef cattle saved the camp from starvation. A Juneau butcher brought the beef into town and sold the lot for sixteen thousand dollars. Within a year, he was worth $200,000.

It is important to realize that there were no shops, as we know them, in the Yukon or Alaska at this time. Two trading companies—Alaska Commercial and North American Trading and Transportation—supplied the miners' needs. Each operated a small steamer on the river—the *Alice* for the AC Company, the *Portus B. Weare* for the NATT. They carried basic essentials only—flour, tea, and beans, shovels, picks, and wheelbarrows. With more prospectors pouring into the new town of Dawson, that supply could not last.

Dawson operated on the law of supply and demand. It cost one man two hundred dollars just to have the tip of his finger amputated. A small keg of bent and blackened nails salvaged from a fire went for eight hundred dollars. There was no writing paper and nothing to read. The only eggs came from two hens owned by a policeman's wife; they cost a dollar apiece. Laundry was so expensive most men wore their shirts as long as possible and then threw them away.

A night on the town, which meant a night in Joe Ladue's saloon, could cost at least fifty dollars. But nobody cared—they could dig it out of the ground whenever they wanted. One man went to work in the morning and came back at night with fourteen hundred dollars in gold. He ordered two whiskies, toasted his former self in the one, making believe his former self was drinking the other, then stuck two cigars in his mouth and smoked them together.

Each man's life was changed by the gold strike. On the day he reached the pay streak and saw he was rich, he became a different person. Some men could no longer eat or sleep at the thought of mining so much gold. One, who had washed out thirty thousand dollars, became so obsessed by the fear of being robbed that he suffered a mental collapse and shot himself.

Dawson grew slowly all that winter of 1897 as the news spread through Alaska and sifted as far south as Juneau on the Panhandle. All winter long a thin trickle of men had been climbing the Chilkoot Pass. About one thousand men at the headwaters of the Yukon waited for the spring thaw. They hadn't even heard of the Klondike but were heading for an older gold camp—Circle City—in the heart of Alaska.

At noon on May 14, the ice in front of Dawson broke, and the whole mass began to move slowly off toward the sea. For two days, a solid flow of ice cakes, some the size of houses, drifted past the town. On May 16, the river was open. The first small vessels to arrive belonged to men who had wintered somewhere along the river. The main body of boats was only a few days behind.

The newcomers, sweeping around a bend, came unexpectedly upon two tent cities scattered raggedly along both sides of the Klondike at the point where it joined the Yukon. The first—on the south side—was officially known as Klondike City but better known as "Lousetown." It was the site of the old Indian salmon camp. On the north bank of the Klondike was Dawson City proper. Within twenty-four hours, some two hundred boats had landed with the first news from the outside world.

Soon boats of every size and shape were pouring into Dawson day and night. In Harry Ash's Northern Saloon, the sawdust on the plank floor glittered with fine gold. There was no paper money in Dawson. All business was transacted in gold. When a teenage boy, Monte Snow, walked into the saloon, Ash offered him twenty-five dollars for all the gold he could pan from the sawdust. In two hours, young Monte (whose father ran a theatrical troupe) took out $278 in fine dust. It had all sifted out of miners' pokes when they were slapped onto the bar.

By June Ash was taking in three thousand dollars a day. On the night that he opened his saloon in a permanent log building, he took in thirty thousand, perhaps because he had the only piano in Dawson. The previous fall he had written to an old friend in Juneau, Billy Huson, to bring a piano into Circle City, and all that winter Huson and his wife had been lugging the instrument over the Chilkoot in bits and pieces, the sounding-board carefully wrapped in wool yarn for protection. It was a tiny upright, made in Hong Kong for the steamer trade, and within a month every dance-hall girl in town had scratched her name on its surface with hatpins. As for the wool yarn, Mrs. Huson knitted it into sweaters, which sold for a handsome profit. Within three months of the opening, Ash was able to leave town with $100,000.

By the end of summer, there were ten saloons in Dawson, none taking in less than three hundred dollars a night. Some were only tents; others were more substantial. Money meant nothing. Log cabins sold for as much as two hundred dollars a square foot (0.09 sq. m) of floor space. Bacon and tea cost seven to eight times their outside values. Dance-hall girls were paid a hundred dollars a night; town lots were selling for as high as twelve thousand dollars—this at a time when $1.25 a day was the going wage in the outside world for a common labourer.

By summer the population was nearing thirty-five hundred. The ring of hammer and axe was heard all over town. Buildings were sprouting up in helter-skelter fashion. The muddy roadways were covered with chips and sawdust.

Early in June, with the river finally free of ice and the first mosquitoes buzzing over the meltwater in the ponds and sloughs, a shrill whistle galvanized the town into action. A few minutes later the Alaska Commercial Company's little sternwheeler, *Alice*, puffed into shore. The entire populace rushed down to greet her, for she was loaded with equal quantities of liquor and food.

The town went on a spree, which continued when, two days later, the *Portus B. Weare*, owned by the NATT Company, arrived. When these two boats left on the return voyage with their load of wealthy miners, they would carry the news of the great gold strike to the outside world.

CHAPTER TWO

Starvation Winter

THE NEWS BROKE IN SAN FRANCISCO AND SEATTLE IN LATE JULY OF 1897, ALMOST A YEAR AFTER THE BIG STRIKE. BY AUGUST SHIPS CRAMMED WITH PROSPECTIVE GOLD SEEKERS WERE HEADING NORTH FROM THE WEST COAST PORTS. ONLY A FEW HUNDRED MANAGED TO GET THROUGH THE PASSES THAT FALL TO REACH THE CITY OF GOLD. AS THEIR BOATS NUDGED INTO THE FOG-SHROUDED BANKS AMIDST CAKES OF FLOATING ICE, THE PEOPLE ONSHORE SHOUTED AT THEM: "THERE'S NO GRUB IN DAWSON. IF YOU HAVEN'T AN OUT-FIT, FOR GOD'S SAKE TURN BACK!"

Inspector Charles Constantine, the head of the North-West Mounted Police, realized that the town was facing starvation. As early as August 11, he had sent a blunt letter to Ottawa saying that "the outlook for grub is not assuring for the number of people here—about four thousand crazy or lazy men ... "

The two trading companies began to measure the shortage of food against the new crowds with growing dismay. Both the Alaska Commercial Company and the North American Trading and Transportation Company proceeded to give out supplies in small amounts. Prospectors lined up fifty feet (15 m) deep, pleading for a chance to buy, but only one man was allowed in at a time. Each was able to buy a few days' supplies before being sent on his way. A man could have half a million dollars in gold—as many did—and still be able to purchase no more than a few pounds of beans.

As more and more boats drifted in, the air of panic began to settle over the town. Five steamboats were supposed to be heading for Dawson, but they hadn't arrived. Where were they? In September Captain J. E. Hansen, the Alaska Commercial Company's assistant superintendent, headed downstream to find them. He came upon them near Fort Yukon, Alaska, 350 miles (560 km) below Dawson in the shallow and desolate maze of the Yukon flats. All were marooned in low water. Realizing now that Dawson faced famine, Hansen headed back at breakneck speed to warn the town.

On September 26, his canoe was spotted, and a cry rippled across the town: "A boat! A boat from the north!" Four thousand men and women streamed down to the waterfront thinking that a steamer with provisions had arrived. As the canoe touched shore and Hansen's tall figure leaped from it, a deadly calm settled over the crowd. He raised his hand in silence and cried out:

"Men of Dawson! There will be no riverboats until spring … I advise all of you who are out of provisions, or who haven't enough to carry you through the winter, to make a dash for the outside. There is no time to lose!"

A dreadful silence greeted these words. Most of those on shore had risked everything to reach the Klondike in the first wave. They had won that race, apparently only to lose the prize. Some screamed out their disappointment. One or two actually fainted. Then the mob broke into smaller mobs who threatened to seize the warehouses.

The restaurants closed as the news spread and the miners poured in from the gold creeks. For hundreds there was no sleep that night, as partners pooled what they owned and drew lots to decide who would stay and who would flee. Within a few hours, fifty open boats had pushed off for Fort Yukon. Another hundred were getting ready to leave.

Now those who had been frantic to reach the Klondike were just as frantic to flee. There were desperate scenes on the lower river. At Circle City, Alaska, two of the NATT's steamboats were subjected to an armed holdup. A committee of six climbed aboard and offered to pay the company's price for enough provisions to last the winter. When they were refused, fifty men with rifles and shotguns emerged from the bushes. They unloaded their cargo, checked it carefully, and paid for it as it was removed. A few days later a second sternwheeler was attacked and was forced to leave the community twenty-five tons (22 tonnes) lighter.

In Dawson, as winter came on, men took to the hills to search for rabbits. Others tried to catch fish through holes chopped in the ice. A few even went into the distant mountains hoping to shoot some big game.

In front of the town, the ice slipped by in a rustling mass.

Then on September 28, to everybody's surprise, the NATT Company's steamboat, *Portus B. Weare,* puffed into town. John J. Healy, the manager of the Dawson Trading Post, boarded the company's ship and was greeted by Eli Weare, the president. Healy asked how much cargo was on board. Weare replied, proudly, that it was loaded with all the whisky that could be floated across the flats. That drove Healy into a fury, for he had given direct orders to load the boats with food and clothing only. He seized Weare by the throat and almost choked him to death.

Two days later, when the second steamboat arrived, also half empty, the Mounted Police realized that a thousand persons would have to be evacuated from the town. With luck they might reach Fort Yukon, where the other steamboats, loaded with provisions, were stranded.

Inspector Constantine posted a notice on Front Street. "Starvation now stares everyone in the face who was hoping and waiting for outside relief …" The Collector of Customs and the Gold Commissioner addressed street-corner meetings urging people to escape. Hansen, of the AC Company, ran up and down Front Street from group to group, calling out, "Go! Go! Flee for your lives!" Only Healy remained calm. A tough old frontiersman, he refused to be panicked. He called Hansen a hysterical cheechako (newcomer) and said there was food enough in Dawson for all. "There'll be no starvation," he kept saying. "Some may go hungry, but no one will starve."

In spite of that, he allowed anybody who wanted to take passage on the *Weare* to go to Fort Yukon for a token fifty dollars. Constantine allowed free passage on the *Bella* and five days' allowance of food to anybody who would leave town. One hundred and sixty accepted that offer. And so they crowded up the gangplank like defeated soldiers, men who had hoped to become rich by being the early birds in the Klondike. All that fall the exodus continued.

Scores attempted to go back up the frozen river to the passes. As they stumbled on, they threw away their sleds and their food, their clothing and even their shoes. Half a dozen died on this journey. Others returned to Dawson.

The town settled down to its second winter in which poverty, famine, and sickness were fortune's bedfellows. In Bill McPhee's Pioneer Saloon, homeless men slept on benches and tables. But there was gold everywhere —buckskin sacks of it, known as "pokes," stacked like cordwood behind the bar at the Yukon Hotel. Above this glittering hoard, the guests were herded into double-decked bunks beneath bare rafters to sleep in their work clothes, with only filthy blankets over them and a nail for a coat hanger. A crack in the wall served as ventilation, a bit of candle stuck into the logs as light; a red-hot sheet-iron stove supplied an uneven heat.

Gold, which could buy so little, slipped from hand to hand at the gambling tables. One man lost eighteen thousand dollars in a day and a half. Another lost a thousand in five minutes and cheerfully bought liquor and cigars for all.

What would gold buy in Dawson that winter? It would buy a meal of beans, two apples, bread, and coffee for five dollars in a restaurant before the restaurants closed. It would buy dried potatoes at a dollar a pound or rancid flour at three. It would buy a one-minute waltz with a girl in a silk dress at a dollar a waltz. One man wanted so badly to dance he bought seven hundred dollars' worth of dance tickets in advance and danced all week, while a violin scraped and a piano rattled.

Then, on Thanksgiving night, with the temperature at fifty-eight below Fahrenheit ($-50°$ C), a dance-hall girl threw a flaming lamp at a rival, and most of Front Street went up in smoke. Pete McDonald's saloon burned down at a cost of $100,000, but Pete built a new one, aptly named the Phoenix because it rose from the ashes. He had no whisky glasses left because they'd been cornered by speculators who were charging five to ten dollars each for them. He made his own drinking cups of copper and tin, and so the dance whirled on.

CHAPTER THREE

The Saint of Dawson

THE STARVATION THAT HANSEN AND CONSTANTINE PREDICTED LOOMED CLOS-
ER. BY CHRISTMAS 1897, THE STOCK OF SUPPLIES WAS RUNNING LOW, AND THE
LAST RESTAURANT HAD CLOSED ITS DOORS. THE POLICE WERE ON REDUCED
RATIONS. THEY WOULDN'T ARREST ANYBODY UNLESS HE BROUGHT HIS OWN
FOOD WITH HIM.

You couldn't escape from Dawson, because the town was isolated from
the world. An occasional dog driver could be found who would try to make
the trip to Skagway, but the fee was one thousand dollars, and the passengers had to run behind the sled, rather than ride on it. Few took advantage
of that.

As the cold came down, the food diminished, the days shortened, and
the sun vanished entirely. The community slowed to a standstill. Like the
hibernating bears, they lay in their bunks till noon and wolfed their food,
half cooked and cold.

It cost as much to die as to live. Two men died on Clarence Berry's claim
that winter, and the price of their funeral was astronomical. It cost two
thousand dollars to hire a team of six malamutes to take the bodies into
town. The nails for the coffins cost $8.50 a pound (0.45 kg), and the lumber
cost forty cents a foot (0.3 m). Two workmen took six days to hack the
graves out of the frozen ground and were paid two hundred dollars in
wages.

By mid-January flour was so scarce the hunters had to trade an entire
mountain sheep to get a sack of it. In April a few hardy souls took advantage of the improving weather to mush in from Dyea and Skagway on the
Alaska coast with articles for sale. They didn't bring staples such as flour,
meat, or butter but, with a rare understanding of human nature, brought
luxuries. One man arrived with a lady's hat made of black ostrich feathers,

which was snapped up at once for $280. Another brought in several tins of oysters and a turkey, ready cooked and dressed. Oyster stew went on sale at fifteen dollars a bowl. The turkey was put on display at the Pioneer Saloon and was raffled off for $174.

As Healy had predicted, no man starved—perhaps because so many had fled the town in the late fall. The real victims were the Native peoples. On the Porcupine River north of Fort Yukon, Indian women and children were dying on the trail. Once they had been the best customers of the trading companies. Now they were forgotten.

Hunger's companion was scurvy. The need for a new hospital became apparent, and the man to supply it was Father William Judge, a Jesuit missionary in Alaska. A one-time apprentice in a Baltimore planing mill, he had, for the last dozen years, been a servant of the Lord in the North. He had no interest in gold and no desire for material wealth. An emaciated man with a skull-like face, high cheekbones, and huge, cavernous eyes, he looked out at the world from small, gold-rimmed glasses.

He had made the long trek to Dawson from Circle City in the fall of 1896, dragging his own sled, which he had loaded with medicine and drugs rather than food. Ill nourished, he trudged along in harness with his single dog in order to preserve the animal's strength. He knew the new camp would soon be facing plague, and he was determined to build a hospital as swiftly as possible. They called him "the Saint of Dawson."

Since he had arrived, he had never ceased working. The task of building a hospital, a church, and a staff residence was enough to tax the energies of a much more powerful man. Yet, in spite of his thin and wasted body, the priest seemed able to perform superhuman tasks. He was his own architect, contractor, and workman. He did every job, including cooking for those who helped him. He roamed the hills collecting dried grasses to fill the mattresses and herbs to amplify his small medical stock. He invented a mixture of muslin, glue, and white lead, which took the place of plaster. He made the furniture himself, using rough boards placed on stumps for pews in his church. He tacked heavy muslin onto frames in place of stained glass windows.

And he suffered bitter disappointments. His church was scarcely completed after months of careful work before fire destroyed it. Everything was reduced to ashes, including the altar, which he had carved so painstakingly with a common penknife, the hand-hewn furniture, and even the vestments for the choir.

Without complaint he began once again the back-breaking task of rebuilding from the ground up. In this he was aided by a collection taken up by both Protestants and Catholics. Once the church was rebuilt, the priest refused to collect a penny of pew rent or to take up collections at any of his services—a sobering decision in a community where on every other occasion gold was tossed to the winds.

The townspeople helped to raise the thirty-five thousand dollars needed to complete the hospital. Women roamed the mining areas passing the hat. Others held bazaars and dances. In return, Father Judge took into his hospital all who required aid. By March there were forty-five scurvy cases alone, jamming the wards and even the hallways.

Meanwhile, the news of Dawson's starvation winter had seeped out into the outside world. The United States Congress had voted $200,000 to buy a reindeer herd, which they believed could be shipped north in time to save Dawson from starvation. The herd of 539 animals was bought in Norway, shipped to New York, then shuttled across the continent by train to Seattle. It was taken north by steamer to Haines Mission at the end of the Dalton Trail on the Lynn Canal. Forty-three Laplanders, ten Finns, and fifteen Norwegians, especially trained for the job, became herdsmen.

In May 1898, the reindeer finally reached Haines. Nine months later they were still struggling along the trail toward Dawson. By that time, the herd had been reduced to a few. They died by the score. Wolves killed some. The Indians shot more. Some strangled in their harnesses. Others collapsed from lack of reindeer moss. By the end, the herders themselves were reduced to picking up raw beans spilled on the trail by the gold seekers.

After a trek of 750 miles (1,200 km), the expedition staggered into Dawson to the amusement of the townspeople. The date by then was January 27, 1899, and the herd was reduced to 114 animals, about one-fifth of its original size. Thus, in that starvation winter, the real victims of starvation had been the wretched reindeer themselves. It was the Klondike Relief Expedition itself that required the most relief.

CHAPTER FOUR

Stampede Summer

ALL DURING THE WINTER OF 1897–98, TENS OF THOUSANDS OF MEN AND WOMEN HAD BEEN TOILING UP THE PASSES FROM SKAGWAY AND DYEA AT THE HEAD OF THE LYNN CANAL. ON THE OTHER SIDE OF THE MOUNTAIN BARRIER, THEY BUILT MORE THAN SEVEN THOUSAND HOMEMADE BOATS. AND WHEN THE ICE FINALLY BROKE IN MAY, THE ENTIRE FLOTILLA BEGAN THE LONG JOURNEY THROUGH THE HEADWATER LAKES AND DOWN THE YUKON RIVER TO THE CITY OF GOLD.

Dawson was waiting, but for what it did not quite know. A few dog drivers, who had pierced the winter wall of isolation, brought back exciting tales of an army of gold seekers camped on the upper lakes. Everyone sensed the stampede was reaching some sort of climax, but no one realized how big it was.

The snow was melting on the mountains at an alarming rate, and frothing little streams were pouring down the sides into the Yukon River. Nature was filling up the river as if with a thousand pumps. Some of the Indians recalled that these flats had been flooded twenty years before and that they had paddled their canoes across the very spot where the new dance halls were being erected. Now everybody realized that Dawson had been built in the wrong place—but how could it have been built elsewhere?

Inspector Constantine walked the riverbank at night, watching the ice stealthily rising, his brow creased with worry. A wave of panic was sweeping across the community. A bad flood could tear this city apart and send horses, tents, dogs, and men hurtling down the ice-choked river.

On May 8, at 4:00 AM, the ice broke with a crackling roar, and the river became a hissing mass of floes. Huge grime-encrusted cakes were squeezed out of the channel and flung high onto the shore. As the townspeople watched

166

in horror and fascination, the river crept upward toward the bank. But there was no time for panic because, even as the water started to spill into the city, the cry "Cheechako!" went ringing through the hills. (Cheechako was the Native word for "greenhorn"). The first boat had already arrived amid the floating ice.

With the water lapping at their boots, several hundreds trotted along the bank, following the craft for about a mile (1.6 km) before it could be beached. There were five men with dogs and sleds aboard. They had only come from the Stewart River a hundred miles (160 km) away and had no news. The crowd melted away.

Then a second cry went up. A green Peterborough canoe slid in between the ice cakes, and again the town rallied. The new arrivals were also old-timers, but they'd actually been at Lake Bennett earlier that winter and had dragged their canoe down the frozen Yukon until the ice broke.

All during the month of May, while the water rose slowly upon the town, boats in twos and threes slipped in from various wintering points between Bennett and Dawson. But everybody knew the main rush was yet to come. The Mounted Police at Tagish on the upper Yukon had already checked three thousand boats through, and more were pouring in every hour.

The early birds made money. Someone brought eggs that were worth as much as gold. Others also brought news: the United States had declared war on Spain! One man arrived with an ancient newspaper soaked in bacon grease. He sold it for fifteen dollars.

More boats trickled in. A man arrived with fifteen hundred pairs of boots and sold them all at fifteen dollars a pair. A man with a load of tinned milk sold it for a dollar a tin. Another made a clear profit of five thousand dollars on women's hats and dresses. One man brought in a scowload of kittens. He got an ounce (28 g) of gold per kitten from lonely miners craving the companionship of a pet.

A sharp-eyed newspaper editor named Gene Allen arrived in town over the ice, stubbornly determined to be the first to produce a newspaper. He had no printing press but launched it as a bulletin. The *Klondike Nugget* appeared on May 27, typed on a machine borrowed from a correspondent of the *New York Times*. And thus, although the *Midnight Sun* was to be the first to get its printing press into operation, Allen could always say that he had launched the first newspaper in the Klondike.

The following day, May 28, most of Dawson's business section found itself under five feet (1.5 m) of water, with cabins near the river already afloat and the townspeople fleeing to the hills. Nobody could move except by boat. But the town didn't float away. The water dropped on June 5, leaving behind an ocean of mud so deep that horses couldn't move through it.

Dawson continued to wait for the great flotilla to arrive from Lake Bennett. A day passed. Two days passed. No sign yet. And then suddenly, on June 8, the river became alive with boats. They poured in day and night without a break, like a parade, until there was no space along the shore. The boats were tied to each other six feet (1.8 m) deep for nearly two miles (3.2 km), so that Dawson's waterfront looked like a Chinese seaport.

Five thousand men, women, and children crowded together to welcome her as she puffed into the bank. "Has she whisky aboard?" came the cry.

And then the first steamboat arrived from the opposite direction. Five thousand men, women, and children crowded together to welcome her as she puffed into the bank. "Has she whisky aboard?" came the cry. She had sixteen barrels, and it went on sale at once in the bars at a dollar a drink.

Meanwhile, a late edition of the Seattle *Post-Intelligencer* had been brought in. A struggle ensued for its ownership. A miner from Hunker Creek got it for fifty dollars and paid a lawyer to read it aloud at the Pioneer's Hall. A crowd followed him down the street as he read them snatches from the headlines. Here was heard the first news of U.S. Admiral George Dewey's victory at Manila over the Spanish fleet in the Spanish-American War. Hundreds cheerfully paid a dollar each to hear that news.

Day after day, for more than a month, the international parade of boats continued. They brought hay and horses, goats and cattle, kittens and mastiffs, roosters and oxen. They brought sundowners, shantymen, sodbusters, and shellbacks, buckaroos and bluenoses, *vaqueros* and *maquereaus*, creoles and Métis, Gaels, Kanakas, Afrikaners, and Suvanese.

They brought wife beaters, lady killers, betrayed husbands, disbarred lawyers, dance-hall beauties, escaped convicts, remittance men, card sharps,

Salvation Army lasses, ex-buffalo hunters, scullions, surgeons, ecclesiastics, gun fighters, sob sisters, soldiers of fortune, and Oxford dons.

They brought men seeking gold and men seeking adventure and men seeking power. But more than anything they brought men seeking escape—escape from a nagging wife, or an overpowering mother-in-law, or a bill collector, or, perhaps, a simple escape from the drabness of the outside world.

And each man brought along a tent. These sprouted everywhere, crowding along the black muck of the waterfront, overflowing across the swamp, spilling into Lousetown, or onto the shoreline opposite Dawson on the west side of the Yukon. They blossomed out on the slopes and hilltops. They straggled by the hundreds along the trails to the gold creeks. From the top of the Midnight Dome above the town, Dawson that spring looked like a field of billowing white—a vast orchard in bloom.

Half a dozen canvas cities had simply been packed up and transferred to the City of Gold. Now sawmills screeched, hammers and saws pounded and rasped, planks and rough timber blocked the roadways, mountains of logs and piles of freshly sawed lumber grew everywhere. Dawson was a city of sawdust and stumps and the skeletons of fast-rising buildings.

Its main street was a river of mud through which horses, whipped on by their owners, floundered and kicked. In between moved a sluggish stream of humanity, men and women trudging up to their calves in the slime.

Land grew costlier. Building lots fetched as much as forty thousand dollars apiece. The cheapest single room on the far edge of town rented for a hundred dollars a month. In those days, a four-room apartment in New York City could have been leased for two years for $120. But an Italian fruit merchant, Signor Gandolfo, paid the same amount for a slender space just five feet (1.5 m) square on the main street. In New York, two baskets of tomatoes could be bought for a nickel. At Gandolfo's fruit stand, they sold for five dollars a pound (0.4 kg).

The town's character and shape changed daily. Tents, cabins, and men were shifted constantly. Because there were no street addresses, it was difficult for new arrivals to find their friends. Those who had spent months in each other's company lost track of one another. Dwelling places with no addresses acquired nicknames such as "the cabin with the screen door" or "the big tent with two stovepipes."

In the crowd of newcomers that summer was hidden at least one murderer, Frank Novak, fleeing from the law. Pressing close behind was a private detective, C. C. Perrin, who had covered twenty-five thousand miles (40,000 km) seeking his man. Now, to his surprise, he found himself in the midst of a gold rush.

The chase had been on since February. Novak had gambled away his firm's funds in Chicago and had killed and then cremated a farmer, in the belief the insurance company would think the body was his and pay off Novak's family. But the corpse was identified, and Perrin was put on the trail, which zigzagged back and forth across the continent.

The detective reached Alaska in June and searched among the climbers for his man. The two actually built boats for the river trip within a few miles of one another. At one point, Perrin's scow actually passed Novak's without either man realizing it.

In Dawson, Perrin doggedly moved from tent to tent, staring into face after face, searching for his man. One tent made him suspicious; one of its occupants only emerged after dark and kept his hat over his eyes. Perrin pounced, and the Mounted Police made the arrest. The detective, who had been six months on the trail, had no interest in seeking gold. Once the prisoner was handcuffed, he made arrangements to leave the City of Gold behind.

By July 1, Dawson had two banks, two newspapers, five churches, and a telephone service. Many made fortunes bringing in papers from the outside world. So great was the hunger for news that bundles of papers were tossed from the upper decks of steamboats before they docked, and the newsboys were able to sell as many as four hundred before the boats tied up. One newsboy was paid fifty-nine dollars in gold for a single paper.

There were now four churches as well as Father Judge's Roman Catholic building. The Church of England, the Methodist Church, the Presbyterian Church, and the Salvation Army all opened that summer.

Banks were rising just as swiftly. The Bank of British North America had raced the Bank of Commerce down the Yukon and won. It opened for business in a tent with a rough plank for a counter and an old open trunk as a safe. Here, in careless piles, lay thousands of dollars in currency to be traded for gold dust at sixteen dollars an ounce (28 g). The Canadian Bank of

Commerce wasn't far behind. It brought an assay plant over the pass, which allowed it to buy gold dust the moment it opened and to make shipments outside ahead of its rival. Within two weeks, it sent three-quarters of a million dollars out of Dawson.

The bank issued one million dollars' worth of paper money brought in over the trail. The words *DAWSON* or *YUKON* were surprinted on each bill in heavy type—a measure taken in case the entire issue should be lost en route. Miners lowered the price of their gold in order to get the less awkward bank notes. And before long paper currency was circulating.

Everything from gold dust to scraps of paper was used for money. The Bank of Commerce on one occasion cleared a three-dollar cheque made from a six-inch (15-cm) square of spruce plank with a nail driven through it for the convenience of the filing clerk. But the medium of exchange continued to be gold dust.

Most men used a so-called commercial dust, heavily laced with black sand. It was valued at only eleven dollars an ounce (28 g), and so customers used it to buy groceries or whisky and could reckon that they were saving five dollars an ounce, since the normal price of clean Klondike gold ran around sixteen dollars. On the other hand, bartenders and businesses weighed the dust carelessly, so that a poke worth a hundred dollars was usually empty after seventy dollars' worth of purchases were made. Thus, as often happened in the Klondike, the supposed gain was non-existent.

CHAPTER FIVE

The Klondike Carnival

BY MIDSUMMER DAWSON WAS CRAWLING WITH PEOPLE. THE LARGEST CITY WEST OF WINNIPEG—AND WINNIPEG ITSELF WAS NOT MUCH LARGER— DAWSON WAS ONLY SLIGHTLY SMALLER THAN THE PACIFIC NORTHWEST CITIES OF SEATTLE, TACOMA, BOTH IN WASHINGTON STATE, AND PORTLAND, IN OREGON. IT DWARFED BOTH VANCOUVER AND VICTORIA. THE MOUNTED POLICE PUT ITS POPULATION AT EIGHTEEN THOUSAND, WITH ANOTHER FIVE THOUSAND PROSPECTING ON THE CREEKS. BUT BECAUSE GOLD SEEKERS WERE CONTINUALLY ARRIVING, CHANGING THEIR ADDRESSES, MOVING TO THE HILLS AND THEN BACK INTO TOWN, AND POURING OFF THE STEAMBOATS, IT WAS HARD TO GUESS AT THE TRUE POPULATION AT ANY GIVEN MOMENT.

The police figured that more than twenty-eight thousand men had passed the Tagish post on the headwaters of the Yukon. Five thousand of these had stopped on the upper river to prospect. But another five thousand had arrived from other points aboard one of the sixty steamboats that made the trip up the river that summer. The *Klondike Nugget* reckoned that sixty thousand persons would reach the goldfields before freeze-up, and that would have made Dawson the largest city north of San Francisco and west of Toronto. That was probably an exaggeration. But it's a good guess that well over half that number did reach the Klondike for a few hours, or a few days, or a few months to form part of the jostling crowd that plodded list-lessly along the main street.

It was as if the vitality had been drained from these crowds. For the best part of a year, they had had their eyes fixed squarely upon the goal. They had put everything into attaining that goal. Now with that goal reached, they seemed to lose their bearings. They eddied about in an aimless fashion like a rushing stream that has suddenly been blocked. Thousands didn't even bother to look for gold. All realized, at last, that none had won the great race. The best ground in the Klondike had been staked out by men who were on the spot before the name became known.

Yet none had lost, for there was a strange satisfaction in the simple fact that they had made it. And so they uncoiled like springs that had been wound too tightly and began to seek out, sheepishly, the former friends with whom they'd quarrelled in the tents during the long months on the trail.

All summer long thousands of aimless men shuffled up and down Front Street still dressed in the faded mackinaws, patched trousers, and high-laced boots of the trail. Their faces, like their clothes, seemed to be the colour of dust. They were like a crowd on a holiday, sightseers at the carnival of the Klondike. Along the board-walk they trudged, and through the sticky ruts of the roadway, bent slightly forward as if the memories of their packs were hanging heavily upon them.

"Gold! Gold! Gold!" the signs read. "Gold dust bought and sold ... Jewellery ... Fine diamond work ... Watches ... Tintypes ... Cigars ... Souvenirs and fine native gold."

Behind them, like a hastily built theatrical backdrop, was the line of false-fronted dance halls and gambling houses, many of them only half finished. A hodge-podge of banners, pennants, signs, and placards, suspended from doors and windows, tacked onto log walls, and slung on poles across the street, advertised the presence of a dozen mining exchanges, transport companies, outfitters, information booths, gold dust buyers, dentists, doctors, lawyers, and merchants.

"Gold! Gold! Gold!" the signs read. "Gold dust bought and sold ... Jewellery ... Fine diamond work ... Watches ... Tintypes ... Cigars ... Souvenirs and fine native gold."

At eight in the evening, the crowd thickened. The dance-hall callers with megaphones stepped outside and barked out the merits of their wares as pianos tinkled and fiddles scraped. Inside, silk-clad women danced, liquor flowed over mahogany counters, chips clicked on green felt tables, vaude-villians cracked stale jokes, stock companies staged badly acted dramas, while Projectoscopes and Animatagraphs, the mechanical wonders of the decade, flashed pictures that actually moved on bed-sheet screens, showing

U.S. soldiers en route to Manila or Gentleman Jim Corbett trying to regain his heavyweight boxing title.

Outside on the crowded street in the light dusk of midnight an enormous magic lantern projected advertising messages on the sides of a frame building. Dogs dashed madly up and down through the mud. Newsboys ran through the crowds hawking the *Klondike Nugget*. And from the wharves could be heard the hoarse whistles of steamboats bringing new arrivals.

If by night Dawson was a great carnival, by day it was an enormous bazaar. Thousands who had thrown themselves body and soul into the task of dragging their ton of goods over the mountains and down the rivers were now trying to sell everything in order to get enough money to go home. The wet sandbar in front of the city was laid out into two streets, known as Wall Street and Broadway Avenue. These were lined with goods selling, for the most part, at half the prices they had fetched in the Pacific coast ports.

After all the shortages, there was a glut of merchandise. You could buy almost anything under the sun during that climactic summer. You could buy clothes and furs, moccasins and plug hats, shoes and jewellery, fresh grapes, opera glasses, safety pins, and ice cream. You could buy peanuts and pink lemonade, patent-leather shoes, yellow-jacketed novels, cribbage boards, ostrich feathers, and oxen on the hoof. You could have your palm read, your picture taken, your back massaged, or your teeth filled with nuggets. You could buy Bibles and sets of Shakespeare and pairs of gold scales by the hundreds, for these had been standard equipment with almost every man. You could buy rifles by the gross at one dollar each; they were worthless in a town where nobody was allowed to pack a gun.

Vegetable and fruit stands, like booths at a county fair, crowded against tents selling dry goods or hardware. Women hawked ice cream made from condensed milk, while others stood perspiring at open bake ovens rich with the odour of steaming bread. Piles of clothing and piles of provisions lay in heaps in the open, unprotected from the summer rains, while inquisitive men picked at them and bargained, Arab-fashion, with their owners.

Just two years before, this flat had been silent and empty, the domain of Carmack and his Indian friends, the province of the moose and the migrating caribou, the croaking ravens and the spawning salmon. Now for two miles along the river it throbbed and quivered like the aspens on the hillsides.

Once again the law of supply and demand was at work. Few had thought to bring in brooms over the trail: these were now so scarce that they sold for seventeen dollars apiece. The building boom was gobbling up twelve million feet (3.7 million m) of lumber as fast as the twelve sawmills could disgorge it, and nails were selling at almost eight dollars a pound. It cost five dollars to cash a cheque in Dawson and seventeen to call a doctor. Gold-dust weighers were paid twenty dollars a day and teamsters one hundred. Lawyers made as much as five thousand a month. (In the rest of North America, working men that year were receiving an average of $1.25 a day, union carpenters about one dollar and a half.)

In July, two wealthy ladies appeared on the scene—the first tourists to reach Dawson City. These were Mrs. Mary E. Hitchcock, the widow of a U.S. admiral, and her companion, Miss Edith Van Buren, the niece of the former U.S. President Martin Van Buren (1782–1862). They were in the habit of visiting various points of interest each summer, and this summer, rather than go to Paris or Shanghai, they chose Dawson City. It seemed the most interesting place to go. Of all the thousands who poured into the City of Gold that season, it's probable that these two were the only ones who came merely as sightseers.

They travelled in style—with an incredible cargo. It included two Great Danes, an ice-cream freezer, a parrot and several canaries, two cages full of live pigeons, a gramophone, a hundred-pound (45-kg) Criterion music box, a coal-oil stove, a zither, a portable bowling alley, a primitive motion picture projector, a mandolin, several air mattresses and hammocks, and box after box of rare foods: paté and truffles, stuffed olives and oysters. This vast cargo was transported some five thousand miles (8,000 km) by water. Mrs. Hitchcock complained endlessly about the freight charges—they were far more than she'd been used to when crossing the Atlantic.

The strangest item of all was an enormous marquee tent that covered twenty-eight hundred square feet (260 sq. m) and was the largest ever brought into the Yukon. There wasn't any space for it in the main town, so the ladies had it raised on the bank on the far side of the Yukon River, where it dominated the landscape. It was so big they found that they had to pitch another smaller tent in one corner in order to stay warm at night.

The two tourists could be seen walking the duckboards of Dawson in their tailored suits, their starched collars, their boater hats, and their silk ties. Sometimes they put on a more picturesque garb—large sombreros, blue serge knickers, and rubber boots, with striped jersey sweaters. They wore heavy cartridge belts to which were strapped impossibly big revolvers—apparently in the belief that Dawson was a wild, gun-shooting town like the American western communities they'd read of.

And here on this frozen strip of riverbank they acted as if they were in Philadelphia or Washington. One English physician, who had known Miss Van Buren's father, wanted to call but had to send a card saying he couldn't do so because he couldn't find a starched shirt. She graciously accepted his excuse and received him anyway in his serge suit.

The Salvation Army had sent a troop to Dawson and asked the ladies if they could use the marquee for the Sunday service. The ladies were happy to oblige. The following Sunday, as the voices were raised in prayer, it was noticed that the pigeons had escaped from their cages and were fluttering above the heads of the congregation. One of them finally perched on the music box, which mechanically responded with "Nearer My God to Thee." At that the entire congregation rose and repeated the grand old hymn.

Mrs. Hitchcock and Miss Van Buren stayed for the summer and then took passage upriver in a tiny little steamer, *Flora*. They were shocked by the primitive cabin. There was only one foot (0.3 m) of space to turn around in between the double bunks in the wall. It was quite impractical to undress, except for the removal of an overcoat. There was nowhere to wash, except for a bucket with a rope attached to it that they had to lower over the side into the muddy river. As the boat departed, the two outraged women were heard complaining shrilly about these arrangements. It certainly wasn't what they had been used to.

CHAPTER SIX

The "San Francisco of the North"

HOLLYWOOD MOVIES HAVE DEPICTED THE KLONDIKE AS LAWLESS AND GUN-HAPPY. NOTHING COULD BE FURTHER FROM THE TRUTH. THANKS TO THE PRESENCE OF THE NORTH-WEST MOUNTED POLICE, NOT A SINGLE MURDER TOOK PLACE IN DAWSON CITY IN 1898. THERE WAS VERY LITTLE MAJOR THEFT. YOU COULD LEAVE YOUR CABIN OR TENT WIDE OPEN AND GO OFF ON A SIX-WEEK TRIP AND RETURN TO FIND EVERYTHING INTACT. A NEW ZEALANDER NAMED JAMES DALZIEL USED TO GO AWAY FOR A MONTH AT A TIME, LEAVING HIS CABIN UNLOCKED AND HIS BEST SUIT HANGING ON THE WALL FOR ALL TO SEE. THERE WAS A SOLID-GOLD WATCH IN A SOLID-GOLD CASE WITH A MASSIVE GOLD CHAIN IN HIS VEST POCKET. IT WAS NEVER TOUCHED.

The nearest thing to mayhem occurred when Coatless Curly Munro had a quarrel with his wife. Both reached for revolvers, which they kept under their pillows, then took one look at each other and fled the premises by different doors. (Coatless Curly was a man who believed in such melodramatic gestures. It was his habit never to wear an outer jacket but to go about in vest and shirt sleeves even in the coldest weather. It was generally agreed, however, that he wore three suits of heavy underwear beneath his outer clothing.)

Nobody could carry a gun in Dawson without a licence, and few licences were issued. One western badman from Dodge City was ejected from a saloon by a Mounted Police constable for talking too loudly. He left like a lamb. The Mountie discovered he was carrying a gun and asked him to hand it over.

"No one as yet has taken a gun away from me," snarled the badman.

"Well," the policeman said mildly, "I'm taking it," and he did without a murmur from his opponent.

So many revolvers were confiscated in Dawson in 1898 they were auctioned off by the police for as little as a dollar and bought as souvenirs to keep on the mantelpiece. The chief crimes were mild ones, such as non-payment of wages, dog stealing, operating unsanitary premises, fraud, unlawfully practising medicine, disturbing the peace, deserting employment, and "using vile language." There were 650 arrests made in the Yukon in 1898, most of them for misdemeanours of that kind. Only 150 were for more serious offences.

To the newcomers, the police often seemed superhuman. There was something miraculous, for instance, about the ability of Inspector W. H. Scarth to work cheerfully in below-zero weather without ever wearing mitts or gloves—and without ever seeming to freeze a finger.

When Superintendent Samuel B. Steele took over command from Inspector Constantine that summer, his reputation had come ahead of him. He had treated the stampede down the Yukon as he would an army manoeuvre, forcing each boat to check in at police posts along the way, in order to keep track of every would-be prospector. He ruled Dawson with the same firm hand.

There were only two punishments. A culprit was either given a "blue ticket" to leave town or was sentenced to hard labour on the government woodpile. The blue ticket was a serious penalty, especially for gamblers and saloon keepers, because it meant they could no longer do business legally. The woodpile kept more than fifty prisoners busy at all times. The police and government offices alone used enough fuel to make a pile two miles (3.2 km) long and four feet (1.2 m) square. All of it had to be sawed into stove lengths.

Steele allowed the gambling halls, saloons, and dance pavilions to run wide open, but he wouldn't allow disorderly conduct, obscenity, or cheating. He told the saloon keepers if he heard of any complaints of unfair gambling he would close them up. He didn't interfere with the liquor traffic—120,000 gallons (545,500 l) came into Dawson during that season. But he did not allow drinks to be sold to people under the age of twenty-one, nor did he allow children to be employed in the saloons. If a man made an obscene or disloyal remark in the theatre, that theatre was fined and could be closed.

To the free-wheeling Americans, Dawson's Sunday was remarkable. On that day, the town went dead. Everything was closed—saloons, dance halls, theatres, and business houses. They were shut one minute before midnight on Saturday and stayed shut until two o'clock Monday morning.

In order to get around the blue laws, some of the theatres began "sacred concerts" at which a collection was taken. A series of "living pictures" of various religious scenes was staged, with scantily dressed performers. The climax was reached on a certain Sunday evening when the curtains parted to reveal a dance-hall queen named Caprice attired only in pink tights and slippers and clinging suggestively to an enormous cross.

Another plan in the summer was the Sunday excursion. The American border was only about fifty miles (80 km) away, and so a boatload of holidayers could easily be transported into Alaska beyond the reach of the Mounted Police. There, on one memorable occasion, some 368 people—gamblers, dance-hall girls, and theatre men—climbed aboard the *Bonanza King* while another hundred embarked on the *Tyrrell.* One boat ran out of fuel, and the other developed engine trouble. Both pleasure ships drifted helplessly downstream into the heart of Alaska until all the liquor was drunk. That Monday Dawson remained a dead town since the liveliest members of its population had gone. Theatres, dance halls, saloons, and gambling houses had to stay closed.

When the two steamers finally limped back upstream and came into sight, the town rushed to the wharf to welcome the returnees. Steamers' whistles blew wide open, and every dog howled in chorus, as several thousand people cheered the girls in their rumpled dresses walking unsteadily down the gangplank.

But the Sunday laws were not relaxed. No work of any kind was allowed on the Lord's Day. One man was arrested for fishing on the Sabbath, another for sawing his own wood. In August 1898, two men were each fined two dollars and three dollars costs just for examining their fishing nets on a Sunday.

On one Sunday, a race was arranged between two famous dog teams. The scene along the Klondike valley road was colourful. In the glittering spring sunlight, scores of dance-hall girls and actresses with their hair piled high on their heads, dressed in their finest be-ribboned silks, lined the course arm in arm with saloon keepers and gamblers in hard hats, stiff collars, and diamond studs. Cheers rang out as the two teams came bolting down the hard-packed road—and then raced neck and neck into the arms of the waiting police, who arrested all and sundry on a charge of offending against the Sabbath.

This was Dawson's climactic year. It was a major metropolis for exactly twelve months: from July 1898 to July 1899. Before that period, it had only been an overgrown frontier community with shacks and tents. Afterward it subsided slowly into a ghost town. But for one glorious winter, it was "the San Francisco of the North."

Even though it lay four thousand miles (6,400 km) from civilization and was the only settlement of any size in a wilderness area of hundreds of thousand square miles, Dawson was livelier, richer, and better equipped than many larger Canadian and American communities. It had a telephone service, running water, steam heat, and electricity. It had dozens of hotels, many of them more luxurious than those on the Pacific coast. It had motion picture theatres operating at a time when the projected motion picture was only three years old. It had restaurants where string orchestras played for men in tail coats who drank expensive wines. It had fashions from Paris. It had dramatic societies, church choirs, glee clubs, and vaudeville companies. It had three hospitals, seventy physicians, and uncounted platoons of lawyers. Above all, it had people.

None of these citizens was ordinary. Almost every one knew how to build his own boat or his own cabin out of green lumber, how to handle a dog team on a narrow trail, how to treat scurvy with spruce-bark tea, how to carry a pack on a tumpline, and how to navigate fast water. Some had more individual accomplishments: there were gamblers ready to bet fifty thousand dollars on the turn of a card and dance-hall girls who could be purchased for their weight in gold.

They came from all over the world and from every background. And there were scores of newspaper correspondents to report on what they did.

A good number of the newcomers came from the American "Wild West." Buckskin Frank Leslie, a famous gunman from Arizona, joined the gold rush. So did Calamity Jane, the camp follower from Deadwood. Irish Nellie Cashman, "the miners' angel," ran a boarding house in Dawson, just as she once had in Tombstone.

For these people, there was nowhere else in the world to go. They'd spent all their lives on the frontier, in towns with names like Deadwood, Tucson, and Cheyenne. The west was no longer wild. The frontier had moved three thousand miles (4,800 km) away. And so they walked the streets of the golden city, many clinging to their fringed gauntlets, and their hide vests, and their broad-brimmed hats.

Captain Jack Crawford, the "poet scout" of the west, turned up with his white goatee, buckskin shirt, long silken hair, and scout's hat. He had fought the Indians in the border wars, hobnobbed with Buffalo Bill Cody and Wild Bill Hickok, and served a stint as a U.S. marshal. Now from a hovel known as The Wigwam, he sold everything from hay to ice cream when he wasn't entertaining by composing a poem about anything or anybody on the spot.

One towering figure on the street seemed to have stepped straight out of a Wild West show. This was Arizona Charlie Meadows, a former rodeo king who conceived the idea of producing a souvenir newspaper that would glorify the wealthy miners. He raised fifty thousand dollars from that scheme and by the winter of 1898–99 was hard at work planning the Palace Grand dance hall and theatre, which, he promised, would be the most lavish place of its kind in the North.

Dawson was a town of nicknames. Half the community, it seemed, went under such pseudonyms as Limejuice Lil, Spanish Dolores, Deep-Hole Johnson, Billy the Horse, Cassiar Jim, and Two-Step Louie. There was Spare-Rib Jimmy Mackinson, so thin that his landlady was said to have refused him sheets for fear that he'd tear them with his bones; and Waterfront Brown, the debt collector who haunted the riverbank in order to capture fleeing defaulters; and Phantom Archibald, who spent twenty-five thousand dollars in gold on a colossal binge and thought himself pursued by a long, black python. Last, as well as least, was that curious little creature known as the Evaporated Kid because he was so small that "he looked like a bottle with hips."

Yet in spite of this apparent diversity, the mix of humanity seemed to belong together. Although they had come to the Klondike from every corner of the globe, and although their backgrounds were entirely dissimilar, they had one thing in common: they were there. Others had given up the struggle and retreated, but each of these desperate citizens had succeeded in what he set out to do.

CHAPTER SEVEN

Dance-Hall Row

ALTHOUGH DAWSON COVERED SEVERAL SQUARE MILES, SPILLED ACROSS TWO RIVERS, AND WAS SQUEEZED UP THE SIDES OF THE SURROUNDING HILLS, ITS PULSE BEAT SWIFTEST IN THOSE THREE OR FOUR SHORT BLOCKS OF FRONT STREET WHERE THE SALOONS, DANCE HALLS, AND GAMING HOUSES WERE CROWDED TOGETHER.

This was the most unstable as well as the liveliest section of town. Here the buildings were continually burning down, being rebuilt, changing ownership, being lost and won in gambling games, sometimes changing both their name and their location, so that the street was seldom the same from month to month.

And yet in another sense it never changed, for anyone who walked inside one building might have been said to have walked inside them all. The outside façade was deceptive. The carved scroll work, the ornate bay windows and balconies, the elaborate cornices and pillars were as false as the square fronts that hid the dingy, gabled log building behind.

Though Hollywood films have presented the dance halls of Dawson with Parisian splendour, the real ones were cheaper and shabbier, and so were the girls who danced within. Like the furniture, they had to be brought in over the mountains and so were plain, sturdy, and serviceable—husky women able to withstand the journey.

The interiors were all the same. Most followed the design of the Monte Carlo, a hastily erected two-storey building with large, plate-glass windows facing the street. On entering, the newcomer found himself in a small, rather dark room dominated by a sheet-iron stove with a long, polished bar to his left. Behind it, the bartenders in starched shirts and aprons with white waistcoats and diamond stickpins stood reflected in the long mirrors at the back.

Beyond this saloon was a smaller room where faro, poker, dice, and roulette were played day and night. Behind that room was the theatre. It consisted of a ground floor with movable benches, a balcony of three rows, with six boxes, and a small curtained stage.

This layout differed only in detail up and down the street. A sign on the balcony of the Opera House reminded customers that "gentlemen in private boxes are expected to order refreshments." It was a mark of wealth for a man to be seen in an opera box surrounded by dance-hall girls, drinking champagne at sixty dollars a quart (1.3 l).

This was one of the great outward signs of success in the Klondike. It showed that these men had won a hand in the hard game of life. The private box in the Dawson dance hall became a sort of symbol. Suspended above the masses on the floor below, a miner, flush with gold, could feel that he had indeed risen in the world. In the Monte Carlo one night, a man who had struck it rich ordered seventeen hundred dollars' worth of champagne to his box.

To many the dance hall was a supreme symbol of achievement. Some men wanted to own one and invested all their gold in a palace of pleasure—not always to their profit.

To many the dance hall was a supreme symbol of achievement. Some men wanted to own one and invested all their gold in a palace of pleasure—not always to their profit. When Charlie Kimball built the Pavilion, it cost him $100,000—everything he had. On opening night, he took in twelve thousand and was so delighted by this new way of mining gold that he began to celebrate. In one three-month bender, he spent $300,000. When he sobered up, he'd lost everything. But for one brief whirl, he had been Somebody.

The bar in the gambling houses ran day and night except on Sunday. The dance hall became alive about eight in the evening and ran till six or seven the following morning. The actual dancing, however, didn't really begin till after midnight. Before that there were lengthy entertainments: a drama first, followed by a series of vaudeville acts.

Many a serious drama found its way to the Dawson stages—everything from *East Lynne* to *Camille*. Sometimes invention was necessary. In *Uncle Tom's Cabin*, the bloodhounds were represented by a single howling malamute puppy hauled across the stage by invisible wires. Newspapers were used to imitate ice floes. But the critics praised the realistic performance of the actress. It was obvious she really had seen people making their way across floating ice.

Arizona Charlie ran a full-blown production of *Camille* at his Palace Grand. He had built the theatre by buying and wrecking two steamboats. To open it, he held a banquet for forty persons and laid a hundred-dollar bank note on each plate. But the stage production was not entirely successful, owing to a serious piece of miscasting. There was obviously no love lost between Armand Duval, the hero of the piece, and his consumptive lady. It appeared that the man playing Duval was the divorced husband of the dance-hall girl playing Camille. She hated him so much she couldn't bear to speak with him off stage. At the end of each performance, she was in a state of nervous prostration from being forced to make love to him on the stage.

When such entertainments failed, Arizona Charlie could rely on his shooting skills. Dressed in his familiar buckskin, with his black locks hanging to his shoulders, the old scout presented a commanding figure. From his position at the far end of the stage, he would shoot glass balls from beneath the thumb and forefinger of his pretty, blonde wife. One night he missed and nicked her thumb. From then on, there were no more shooting exhibitions.

The stage shows in the Dawson theatres brought enthusiastic crowds to Front Street because the town was starved for entertainment. Young Monte Snow and his sister once picked up $142 thrown at them as they danced and sang on stage. Little Margie Newman, a nine-year-old child known as the "Princess of the Klondike," sometimes stood heel-deep in the nuggets after she performed a sentimental song.

In the gaming rooms, the gold never stopped circulating. The entire stampede had been an enormous gamble. When the rush reached its height, men were ready to make any kind of wager for any kind of reason. Two old-timers once bet ten thousand dollars on the accuracy with which they could spit at a crack in the wall.

In the gaming room at the Northern one night in the fall of '98, a neatly dressed man with clean-cut features thoughtfully sauntered over to the roulette wheel and laid a thousand-dollar bill on the red. The black came up. He laid a second on the red. Again the black came up. He laid a third and lost again. Ten times he laid a thousand dollars on the green baize table, and ten times he lost. He showed no emotion but strolled over to the bar and asked for a drink. "I went broke," he told the bartender. He gulped down the whisky, turned about, threw a single fleeting glance at the wheel, walked into the street, and shot himself.

Silent Sam Bonnifield was the best-known gambler in Dawson. His Bank Saloon and Gambling House, at the corner of Front and King across from the Alaska Commercial store, was the most celebrated establishment of its kind in the Klondike. He was a handsome, quiet man in his early thirties, tall and slender, with eyes of a peculiar unfading blue, who never cracked a smile or uttered a word as he pulled in bets of five hundred dollars at the roulette or faro tables.

He once lost seventy-two thousand dollars as well as his gambling establishment in a poker game. At the eleventh hour, a friend arrived and loaned him enough to keep going. Within six hours, Bonnifield had won it all back and cleaned out the customer.

Bonnifield came north with another bold gambler named Louis Golden, better known in the North as Goldie. They ran rival establishments but closed up once a week and played at each other's tables until one of them went broke.

These two took part in the biggest poker game ever recorded in the Klondike. There was fifty thousand dollars in the pot when Goldie raised it by twenty-five thousand. Bonnifield called him and raised again, bringing the pot to a hundred and fifty thousand. Goldie triumphantly laid down four queens. Bonnifield, without a word or change of expression, turned his hand over to show four kings and raked in a fortune.

Harry Woolrich from Montana had the distinction of having won and lost fifty thousand dollars in a game in Butte, Montana. He often played for days on end, taking his meals at the table. In Dawson he ran the gambling concession at the Monte Carlo. One night he cleaned up sixty thousand dollars and determined to give up gambling forever, leave the Klondike, and settle down.

He boarded a parting steamer to the cheers of a crowd of friends who came down to see him off. Alas for him, the boat was delayed. Woolrich went back to the gaming tables and, with a magnificent gesture, pulled a half-dollar from his pocked, flung it on the counter, and cried, "Here's my farewell to gambling, boys; I'm through!" He lost the half-dollar so matched it with another half. He lost again. Twenty-four hours later he was still in the same spot. The boat was long gone. When his money ran out, he pulled out the steamer ticket and flung it on the table and lost that too.

Gambling was the chief amusement in the winter of '98–'99. When a big game was under way, hundreds and sometimes thousands arrived to watch the excitement. If a player had a streak of luck, others would make minor fortunes laying side bets. On one memorable evening, One-Eyed Riley, the night watchman for a navigation company, started a winning streak. Up to this point, he had always lost and was always broke. But now hundreds followed him around as he moved up and down the street from table to table and saloon to saloon.

When Riley started to win, he forgot about his job and stayed at the tables until morning. By then his winnings were in the thousands. He left Bonnifield's to get something to eat, with the crowds following him. Whatever the limit was, he played it and won and moved on. His last stop was the Monte Carlo. Now it was well into morning, but his luck still held. Dealer after dealer was used against him to try to buck his winning streak—without success. A mystic aura seemed to surround him. Scores profited by following his bets with money of their own.

In a last-ditch attempt to stop him, the management recruited a card wizard to deal with him. At that Riley finally called it quits. By then he had piled up twenty-eight thousand dollars and was determined to get out of town as quickly as possible before he lost it all again. He was in such a hurry he didn't even bother to collect his wages. It was midwinter and hard to leave Dawson, but he paid a dog driver a thousand dollars to rush him out over the winter trail.

When he reached Skagway, somebody talked him into a dice game. Riley, flushed with success, lost his fortune in three straight passes.

CHAPTER EIGHT

Death of a Saint

ALL THIS TIME, WHILE THE CARNIVAL RAN DAY AND NIGHT ON FRONT STREET, FATHER WILLIAM JUDGE QUIETLY TOILED AWAY AT HIS HOSPITAL. ALL THE PREVIOUS SUMMER THE STEAMING SWAMP ON WHICH THE TOWN WAS BUILT, RANK WITH UNDISPOSED-OF SEWAGE, HAD SPREAD TYPHOID, MALARIA, AND DYSENTERY AMONG THE STAMPEDERS. THEY JAMMED EVERY AVAILABLE COT IN THE HOSPITAL, FILLING THE VERY HALLWAYS AND CROWDING FATHER JUDGE HIMSELF OUT OF HIS OWN TINY BEDROOM.

The priest had one quality in common with all who descended upon the Klondike: he was a believer in miracles. For him the miracles always seemed to come true. It was his practice never to turn a patient away, and one afternoon he accepted twenty more than he had bedding for, but the miracle came. At nightfall three bales of blankets arrived mysteriously on an unidentified sled and were dumped at the door.

Again, early in the fall, he had so many patients that he was forced to put some of them in the upper rooms, which weren't finished because the roof hadn't been completed. As if in answer to his prayers, the storm ceased, and there was clear weather for three weeks until the last board was in place.

During the winter, he found he couldn't hire workmen to dig a grave in the frozen ground for one of his dead patients. He struggled himself with a pick and shovel until he was about to give up in despair. Out of the gloom two husky miners appeared, told him that they'd heard they were wanted at the hospital, and proceeded at once to complete the grave and cover the coffin.

Father Judge was the conscience of Dawson. Men watched him at his work and felt a little better that they belonged to the human race. It was as if his own example cleansed them of their sins. His little office, which contained nothing more than a narrow bed made of boards, two blue blankets, and a rough wooden drawer in which he kept all his possessions, had long since been turned over to the sick. When he slept at all, he slept curled up in the hallways or in a corner by the stairs. His nurses pleaded with him to take more rest, but he said that only when his work was finished would he have time to sleep.

He rose at five in the morning to hear Mass and to eat a tiny breakfast, frequently sharing his food with others. He did not quit until eleven at night. He always insisted that he be awakened if any patient asked to see him. All through the dark hours, he could be seen moving quietly, like a guardian shade, through the wards.

Judge rarely smiled, yet his face was forever radiant, beaming with what one man called "an indescribable delight." Despite his frailty, he moved with cat-like speed; he did not walk upstairs but always ran.

It would have horrified him to know his hospital was a hotbed of graft. Many of the male nurses waited for a man to die so they could steal his money. It was customary to prescribe a bottle of brandy or whisky for a patient recovering from typhoid, but the attendants drank most of that.

All that fall the feeling grew that something should be done for Father Judge. In spite of heavy donations, the hospital was still in debt, and so the people of Dawson proposed to pay it off as a Christmas present. A benefit was planned, and, although December 25 was the best-paying night of the year, Joe Cooper offered his Tivoli Theatre free of charge for the affair.

As Judge's only garment in all those months in Dawson had been a tattered black cassock, patched and worn, it was decided he must have a new suit of clothes for Christmas. A tailor was sent to measure him, but the priest politely refused. The tailor was told to make the suit anyway, together with a sealskin coat, cap, and gloves. A presentation was made a few days before the show. But Judge, though moved, explained he could not, as a Jesuit, own anything. The presentation committee urged the clothing upon him, pointing out that most of the donors were Protestants. In the end, he relented.

He was reluctant to attend the minstrel show in his honour, but they talked him into it. When George Noble, the master of ceremonies, rose to make a little speech referring to him as the "grand old man of Dawson," the audience went wild. He was taken up on the stage against his wishes, and the cheering continued for five minutes, but this was the only time he appeared in his new clothes. The following day he was seen again in his threadbare robes.

His time was running out, and the whole town knew it. Although he was only forty-five years old, he looked closer to seventy. Overwork had lowered his resistance. Two weeks before Christmas, the word spread across the community that he was ill with pneumonia. A pall settled over Dawson. As if to accentuate the mood, the temperature dropped to fifty degrees below Fahrenheit (−46° C). The snow turned dry as sand, and the smoke from the buildings rose vertically into the still air to hang over the river valley in a pale shroud.

It seemed as if the whole community was slowing to a dead stop. It was so cold the horses couldn't be worked. After a few days, there was scarcely any life in the streets. Moving slowly, like ungainly animals, to protect their lungs, bundled in furs to their very ears, men made brief forays into the cold and then retreated again into the steaming interiors. Windows froze in solid, while cabins even a few yards distant were blurred by the fog that smothered the community.

In the hospital on the hill, the death watch began as Judge clung precariously to life. He sank lower day by day. Hundreds of inquiries poured in asking how he was, while gifts arrived daily, including a case of champagne worth thirty dollars a pint. A wealthy prospector, Skiff Mitchell, made his way to Judge's bedside. He was an old friend of the priest, although a Protestant, and when he saw the wasted figure on the couch the tears rolled down his cheeks.

"Why are you crying?" Judge asked him. "We have been old friends almost since I came into the country."

"We can't afford to lose old friends like you," Mitchell replied.

"You've got what you came for," the priest reminded him. "I too have been working for a reward. Would you keep me from it?"

He seemed anxious to die. When the nuns said they would pray hard for him to stay alive, he answered quite cheerfully, "You may do what you please, but I am going to die."

The end came on January 16. Dawson went into deep mourning. "If the whole town had slipped down the river, it would not have been more of a shock," someone wrote later. Shops and dance halls closed their doors, and even the houses were draped in black.

It took two and a half days to hack the dead priest's grave out of the hard, frozen soil, but there was no shortage of men for the task. When the body was taken to its rest, the grieving population followed. Nothing would do but that the casket cost one thousand dollars and be made of the finest material. It was a gesture in keeping with the general ostentation of the community, though the shrivelled figure within would have shuddered at the thought.

CHAPTER NINE

Money to Burn

MORE THAN ONE VISITOR TO DAWSON REMARKED THAT THE WEALTHIER MINERS SEEMED TO HAVE MONEY TO BURN. THAT WAS TRUE. SOME MEN ACTUALLY LIGHTED CIGARS WITH FIFTY-DOLLAR BILLS. THERE WERE DOZENS OF OTHERS WHO PUT TENS OF THOUSANDS OF THEIR HARD-EARNED MONEY INTO A FRAME HOTEL, A SALOON, OR A DANCE HALL AND THEN WATCHED IT REDUCED TO ASHES.

Dawson's two worst fires occurred in its climactic year. The winter of '98–'99 began and ended with blazes that destroyed, in each case, the most expensive section of town.

The first fire took place almost one year after the Thanksgiving fire of 1897. It was started by the same dance-hall girl. Half a million dollars' worth of real estate went up in smoke because Belle Mitchell set off for Lousetown leaving a candle burning in a block of wood. The fire roared up and down Front Street and back toward the hills, leaping from cabin to cabin, while two thousand men chopped up neighbouring structures to stop it from spreading.

Ironically, in front of the NATT store, the town's newly purchased fire-fighting equipment lay in pieces. It couldn't be used because it hadn't been paid for. Building after building, in which scores of men had flung pound after pound of gold dust, toppled and crumbled because the community wouldn't raise twelve thousand dollars for reels and hoses. Many a man had bet more than that on a single card at the faro table.

The following day a finance company hurriedly signed a note, and a firefighting company of one hundred men went into operation. Dawson breathed more easily. Then, in April, the newly trained firemen asked for better wages, and the town council wouldn't give it to them. The firemen struck. The fire in the boilers died. At this crucial moment, late in the night of April 26, 1899, a tongue of flame shot from the bedroom of a dance-hall girl on the second floor of the Bodega Saloon. Within minutes a holocaust began, far worse than the town had yet known.

Scores dashed to the river in the glare of the flames and tried to break through the ice to get at the water. With the boilers cold, fires had to be set to melt the frozen surface so the water could be pumped to the scene. Half of Front Street was ablaze. The temperature stood at forty-five degrees below Fahrenheit (−43° C), so cold that the heat had little effect on those standing close to the flames. Many discovered their fur coats were scorched and charred, and yet they felt nothing.

> With the boilers cold, fires had to be set to melt the frozen surface so the water could be pumped to the scene. Half of Front Street was ablaze.

There was no breath of wind. The tongues of flame leaped vertically into the air, causing steam to condense in an icy fog that soon covered most of the city. Within this white envelope, the ghostly and frantic figures of the firefighters dashed about. As the dance halls and saloons began to char and totter, large barrels of liquor were overturned, and whisky ran into the streets, where it instantly froze solid in the biting cold.

The men in the river finally burned their way to the water supply. The pumps were started, and the hoses, long in disuse, slowly filled. But, as the water was ice-cold, it froze solid long before reaching the nozzles. There came a ripping, rending sound as the expanding ice tore open the hoses, followed by a moan of despair as the crowd realized the town was doomed.

"What's to be done?" cried Tom Chisholm as the flames darted toward his Aurora Saloon.

Captain Cortlandt Starnes of the Mounties supplied the answer: "Blow up the buildings in front of the fire!"

A dog team raced to the Alaska Commercial Company's warehouse for fifty pounds (22.6 kg) of giant blasting powder. Then the police wrecked the Aurora and another building to leave a blank space in front of the moving wall of flame.

By this time the whole town was involved. Thousands struggled in and out of condemned buildings carrying articles saved from the blaze, until the marsh behind the business section was littered with goods. Many were offering ten dollars an hour for help. Any two-horse team and driver could command a hundred dollars an hour. The manager of the Bank of British North America pledged a thousand dollars to anyone who could save his building. The offer was made in vain.

The town began to shudder with explosions as the dynamite did its work. Firemen, unable to pump water, worked ahead of the explosions, soaking blankets in mud puddles to try to save buildings on the edge of the blaze. At last the groaning multitude saw that further effort was useless. Half freezing, half roasting, they stood like lost souls on the edge of the pit, their faces glowing redly in the reflected light of the flames. Front Street, with all its memories, was being consigned to the inferno.

Bill McPhee's Pioneer Saloon, one of Dawson's oldest log buildings, crumbled to ashes and was gone in a shower of sparks. The piles of gold and stacks of mail piled behind the bar were buried beneath the charred timbers.

"Gather up the money, the town is going to go!" some called as McPhee made a final dash into his building.

But this was not what he was after.

"To hell with the money!" he shouted. "I want to save my moose head." And back he staggered with his prize trophy. It meant far more to him than fleeting gold, for it had hung above the bar since opening day—that day which seemed so long ago, when Dawson was young, and the newcomers had hardly arrived, and his old friends were still alive. Could it have been only two years past?

Harry Ash's Northern Saloon went the way of the Pioneer. Across the street, the Aurora was blown to bits to make a firebreak. Now the Tivoli Theatre was crumbling, and the Opera House, and the Dominion Saloon and Gambling House, where the stakes were so high that eight Mounties sometimes had to be posted to keep order.

Walter Washburn, a faro dealer who had invested ten thousand dollars in the Opera House, watched quietly as it was devoured by the flames. "Well," he said, "that's the way I made it, and that's the way it's gone, so what the hell!"

At this moment, the vault in the tottering Bank of British North

America burst wide open in the fierce heat, and the contents spewed out onto the debris—gold dust and nuggets scooped from the bowels of Bonanza by moiling men, heavy gold watches from the vests of gamblers and saloon keepers, left for safe keeping, jewelled stickpins and bracelets and dance-hall girls' diamonds, bought with favours and with wine and with music and now fused into the molten mass that oozed from the shattered strong box to mingle with the steaming clay.

One hundred and seventeen buildings were destroyed that night. The loss was reckoned at more than one million dollars. The next day the townspeople crept from their homes to view the havoc. The fire had died away, leaving a smoking ruin where the business section had been. On the north edge of this black scar was the Monte Carlo, scorched but still standing. On the south, the Fairview Hotel presented a grotesque sight, completely sheathed in frozen mud. In its lobby, scores of exhausted homeless men and women were sleeping in two-hour shifts.

The river marked the western boundary of the fire, the littered swamp the eastern. In the heart of the city was an enormous gap, from the ashes of which a large number of shapeless, sawdust-covered piles rose at scattered intervals. These were immense blocks of ice that had been cut from the river for summertime use and covered with sawdust as insulation. Of all things, they alone had survived the fearful heat.

At once the town began to rebuild. Within twelve hours after his saloon was lost, Tom Chisholm had erected a big tent labelled "Aurora" and was doing business again. And once again the familiar sound of saw and hammer was quickly heard on Front Street.

The town that rose from the ashes was a newer and sturdier metropolis. Sewers were installed, the roads paved, new sidewalks built. The shops were full of fancy goods displayed behind plate-glass windows. Schools were going up. Scores of handsome women sauntered up and down in fashions imported from Paris.

When the river broke, more and more steamboats lined the river bank—as many as eleven at a time. Already the trip from St. Michael had been cut from twenty-one to sixteen days. Dawson was no longer a camp of tents and log cabins. Dressed lumber and plate glass were replacing bark and canvas.

The dog had had his day. Horses now moved easily through the dry streets drawing huge dray wagons. Houses had parlours, parlours had pianos, pianos stood on carpeted floors. Men began to wear white shirts, polish their boots, shave their beards, and trim their moustaches.

Dawson was no longer the isolated community it had once been. In March one man actually bicycled all the way to Skagway without mishap in a mere eight days. The White Pass Railway from Skagway to the head of the Yukon River was swiftly becoming a reality. Before the year was out, men would be riding in style where two seasons before horses had perished by the thousands.

Now the old-timers began to get an uneasy sensation in their spines. It was as if the whole cycle of their experience was being repeated. That feeling was communicated to the newcomers, who were already thinking of themselves as old-timers. Some had spent the winter in hastily built cabins in distant valleys, sinking shafts on barren claims, far from the golden axis of Bonanza and Eldorado Creeks. Many had gone to work as labourers for fifteen dollars a day or as clerks in stores or as bartenders. And some had done nothing but sit in their cabins, slowly consuming their thousand pounds of food and wondering what to do.

A sense of anticlimax spread among all of them. Thousands walked the wooden sidewalks seeking work, but there was less and less work to be had. A stale taste began to grow in the mouths of these same men who, a year before, had tumbled in confusion from the boats with shouts of triumph and anticipation.

In the outside world, the word *Klondike*, which had once inspired visions of fortune, had become an expression of contempt and derision. The newest expression of disgust was the phrase "Ah—go to the Klondike!" In Seattle gold-pans had been converted to dishpans and were selling at bargain rates.

All through the spring vague rumours of something exciting on Norton Sound near the mouth of the Yukon River had been filtering into Dawson. At first the news was sketchy, as it always was, and people refused to believe it, as they always did. But skeptical or not, they began to trickle out of town and down the river in twos and threes, and then in dozens, and then in scores, searching not so much for new adventure and new wealth, perhaps, but simply for the love of the search.

By midsummer 1899, the news from the beaches of Alaska was confirmed.

On the sands of Nome, just across the Bering Strait from Siberia, a fortune in fine gold dust had been discovered—a fortune that had been lying hidden all the time at the far end of the golden river, on whose cold breast so many men had floated in a search for treasure.

The news roared across Alaska and across the Yukon Territory like a forest fire. A tent city was springing up on the beach at Nome; men were making fortunes and losing them just as quickly; buildings were going up, saloons opening, money changing hands. The beach was staked for thirteen miles (21 km), and the experts were already predicting that the new find would produce two million dollars in the first year alone—more than the Klondike had at the same time in history.

The story was beginning again, like a continuous film show at a movie house. In Dawson, log cabins could be had for the taking as steamboat after steamboat, jammed from steerage to upper deck, puffed out of the town en route to Nome. The saloon trade fell off; real estate dropped; dance halls lost their customers; Arizona Charlie Meadows announced he would float his Palace Grand in one piece down the river to the new strike.

In a single week in August, eight thousand people left Dawson forever. The gaudy gold rush year was over, and the City of Gold began its long decline.

When the author of this book was born, in 1920, Dawson's total population was not much more than one thousand people. Today, with the price of gold going higher, the permanent population has increased to fifteen hundred. Many of the old buildings have been restored for the tourist trade, and these include the oldest dance hall of all. Arizona Charlie didn't make good his plan to float his boat down the river. The Palace Grand Dance Hall can be seen today in Dawson, much as it was in the days of 1898—a symbol of a bygone time, when men believed that a fortune in gold would buy anything. They learned the hard way that it wasn't the gold that counted but rather the adventure of searching for it.

INDEX

The Hub Saloon, one of many establishments of its kind,
was owned by Robert Greaves and Del Bundy, in Dawson
City, Yukon. Klondikers could pay for refreshments
with gold dust and nuggets.

(C018650, LIBRARY AND ARCHIVES CANADA)

KINGS OF THE KLONDIKE

CONTENTS

CHAPTER ONE

Suitcases Full of Gold

THOMAS LIPPY SAT ON THE DECK OF THE STERNWHEELER *PORTUS B. WEARE,* CONTEMPLATING THE YUKON SCENERY AS IT ROLLED SLOWLY PAST. IT WAS LATE JUNE 1897, AND THE BRIEF SUB-ARCTIC SPRING HAD YIELDED TO SUMMER. THE HILLS WERE AFLAME WITH DRIFTS OF CRIMSON FIREWEED, SET OFF BY THE BLUES OF LUPINS AND THE YELLOWS OF DAISIES. THE AIR WAS THICK WITH THE SCENT OF THE BALM OF GILEAD POPLAR. WOODPECKERS DRUMMED AGAINST SPRUCE TRUNKS, WHILE CHICKEN HAWKS AND MOOSEBIRDS WHEELED AND HOVERED IN THE SKY.

Life had been hard for Tom Lippy and his wiry little wife, Salome, who sat beside him on the foredeck. But they both knew that everything was about to change dramatically for the better.

The previous fall they had struck it rich on an unknown creek, now called Eldorado. Eldorado flowed into Bonanza Creek, where the first gold strike had been made a few weeks before on August 16. But Eldorado was richer.

Now they were heading out with news of the new goldfield in the Klondike valley. That name, *Klondike,* was totally unknown. But soon it would be on everybody's lips, and Lippy and his fellow passengers would be known as the Kings of Eldorado or, more often, Kings of the Klondike.

The *Weare* and a second steamboat, *Alice,* were heading for civilization, each loaded with a single cargo: gold. There was gold in suitcases and leather grips, gold in boxes and packing cases, gold in belts and pokes of caribou hide, gold in jam jars, medicine bottles, and tomato cans, and gold in blankets held by straps and cords, so heavy it took two men to hoist each one aboard.

There was a total of more than three tons (2,722 kg) of gold on the two little steamboats. So heavy was the treasure that, on the three-storied *Weare*, the decks had to be shored up with wooden props.

Most of the eighty-odd passengers aboard the two vessels had been paupers a few months before. Now they were rich beyond their wildest dreams. Some had not seen civilization for years. None had heard from their families since the previous summer. One man, imprisoned in the Yukon for two years and reduced to a diet of half-raw salmon, had been planning suicide when he heard of the big strike in the Klondike. Now he was headed for civilization with thirty-five thousand dollars.

In 1897 that was an enormous fortune. You could rent a four-room apartment for $1.25 a week. You could buy an all-wool serge suit for four dollars. A three-course meal in a fancy restaurant cost twenty-five cents. Coffee was thirteen cents a pound. A nickel would buy two big baskets of tomatoes. But labourers made as little as a dollar for a ten-hour day. So the interest on thirty-five thousand would keep a man in relative luxury for the rest of his life.

> *You could rent a four-room apartment for $1.25 a week. You could buy an all-wool serge suit for four dollars. A three-course meal in a fancy restaurant cost twenty-five cents.*

Tom Lippy had a great deal more. He was worth at least one million dollars, and his name would soon be on the lips of every literate American. He had started life as an iron moulder in Pennsylvania, but an almost fanatical belief in physical culture had led him into the YMCA and then on to Seattle as a physical training instructor.

As a volunteer fireman, Tom Lippy had once held the title of world's champion hose coupler, and, like everyone else who had come in over the trail, he was tough, solidly built, dark, and clean-shaven. An injury to his knee had forced him to retire from the YMCA. A strange hunch had sent him north in 1896 on borrowed money. The hunch paid off. Now he had one of the richest claims in the Klondike.

At the old Russian port of St. Michael, near the Yukon's mouth, seventeen hundred miles (2,720 km) downriver from Dawson City at the mouth of the Klondike River, Lippy and his wife left their cramped quarters and switched to the ocean-going steamer *Excelsior*. A second ship, the *Portland*, was also waiting to take the overflow out to civilization.

These two grubby little vessels would bring the first detailed news of the great strike on Bonanza Creek to a waiting world. The Klondike valley was so remote from civilization that it had no telegraph or telephone links with the outside world. That's why it took eleven months for the news of the gold strike to get out.

However, rumours of something big had been trickling down the Alaska Panhandle for some weeks. Had gold been discovered in huge quantities somewhere beyond the mists of the North? No one could be sure until the *Excelsior* arrived.

On July 17, 1897, the word was finally out. It came in the most dramatic fashion. Down the *Excelsior's* gangplank and onto the wharf at San Francisco came the Klondike Kings, literally staggering under their loads of gold.

Here was Tom Lippy and his wife, grappling with a bulging suitcase weighing more than two hundred pounds (90 kg)—all gold. Here were Lippy's neighbours on Eldorado Creek: Frank Keller, a former railway brakeman, and his partner, Jim Clements, who had almost starved to death the previous year. Between them they had eighty-five thousand dollars in gold.

And here was one grizzled miner, fresh off the boat, ordering poached eggs, nine at a time, in a nearby restaurant, tipping the waitresses with nuggets, and hiring a horse-drawn cab to drive him around for twenty dollars a day. He had once pulled a hand sled for fourteen hundred miles (2,240 km), he told the crowd. Now he intended to ride in luxury.

In Seattle the excitement was mounting because Lippy was a local boy. He and his wife took a suite in San Francisco's Palace Hotel, where they found themselves virtual prisoners, the halls outside jammed with people bombarding the doors.

The *Portland* was due in Seattle at any moment. The daily newspaper, the *Post-Intelligencer*, sent a tugboat full of reporters out to intercept her. They tumbled over the ship's rails and into the arms of excited miners who were just as eager for news of the outside world as the newspapermen were of the Klondike strike.

The tug raced back to the city. By the time the *Portland* reached the dock, the paper had rushed three editions off its presses.

"GOLD! GOLD! GOLD!" the headlines read. "68 rich men on the steamer *Portland*. STACKS OF YELLOW METAL."

Five thousand people jammed Schwabacker's Dock at 6:00 AM on July 17 to watch the vessel arrive, and here the scenes at San Francisco were repeated.

John Wilkinson, a coal miner from Nanaimo, who had staked on Eldorado next door to Lippy, had fifty thousand dollars in gold in his leather grip. Although it was tied tightly with three straps, it was so heavy the handle snapped off as he staggered along the dock. Another, who had $100,000 worth of gold dust and nuggets tied up in a blanket, had to hire two helpers on the spot to help him drag it away.

Nils Anderson hoisted one heavy bag down the gangplank and then returned to his stateroom, where he had two more sacks of gold. Two years before, he had borrowed three hundred dollars and left his family to gamble on fortune in the North. His wife, waiting on the docks, didn't know he was rich until he told her he had brought out $120,000 worth of gold.

Staff Sergeant M. E. Hayne of the North-West Mounted Police, who had staked on Bonanza, came down the gangplank and into the arms of newsmen who "clung to us like limpets."

"Let me at least have a thimbleful of Scotch whisky before I suffer the torment of an interview," Hayne cried. Six men seized him and propelled him into a nearby saloon, where each flung a quarter on the bar to treat him.

As the police struggled to hold back the crowds, every prospector found himself corralled by newsmen. Dick McNulty, who had twenty thousand dollars, announced that Klondike placer mining was ten times as rich as California. William Stanley, grey-haired and lame, announced that "the Klondike is no doubt the best place to make money that there is in the world."

Stanley's story was quickly circulated. A bookseller in Seattle, he had made and lost three fortunes in Rocky Mountain stampedes. Fifteen months earlier he had gone north with one son, Sam, on borrowed money and was ready to give up when an Indian drifted past his camp on the Yukon and said that white men had found much gold farther down the river.

Stanley now had $120,000 in gold. During his absence, his wife had been living on wild berries and taking in laundry to keep her six children together. When the news reached her, she told her customers to fish their own things out of the tub, moved with her husband into a downtown hotel, threw out all her clothes, and called in a dressmaker to design garments suitable for the wife of a Klondike King.

From this day on, few of the Klondike Kings knew any real peace. The Stanleys were trailed by such crowds they had to flee to San Francisco. There an avalanche of letters snowed them under. Clarence Berry, a former Circle City bartender, who had dug up a fortune on Eldorado, was tracked down to his hotel room by reporters. "The Klondike is the richest goldfield in the world," Berry declared. The newsmen goggled at four sacks of nuggets on the floor and a variety of jars and bottles on the table, all filled with gold.

Jacob Wiseman tried to get home to Walla Walla, Washington, but the mob that pressed upon him was so insistent he left town secretly to live under an assumed name in Tacoma.

Mrs. Eli Gage, daughter-in-law of the U.S. Secretary of the Treasury, whose husband's company owned the *Weare*, fled to the train station, boarded the train for Chicago, and locked herself in her drawing room for the entire journey.

Frank Phiscator, one of the original stakers on Eldorado, also headed for Chicago, flourishing a big red pocketbook containing a bank draft worth $120,000. When he checked into the Great Northern Hotel, he told the clerk in ringing tones that nothing was too good for him.

After spending thirteen hard years trading along the Yukon, Joseph Ladue found himself eagerly accepted by his sweetheart's parents, who had once rejected him as a ne'er-do-well but were now happy to welcome him into the family.

After all, Ladue had laid out the new town at the mouth of the Klondike, and the papers were calling him the mayor of Dawson City. He was reputed to be worth five million dollars, a figure that established him securely as a man of financial genius. His picture appeared in advertisements endorsing such products as Dr. Green's Nervura blood and nerve remedy. His name appeared as the author of a book about the Klondike, and he was named president of a mining company whose directors included some of the biggest names in New York finance.

Ladue had spent his life searching for treasure from Wyoming to New Mexico to Arizona and on to Alaska. He had begun as a youth operating a steam engine in a mine in the Black Hills. Now, suddenly, he found himself hobnobbing with merchant princes.

It did not last. Thirteen years of trading along the Yukon had taken their toll. Within a year, Joseph Ladue was dead of tuberculosis at the very height of the great stampede that he had helped touch off.

CHAPTER TWO

Poor Man's Gold

BY THE END OF JULY, THE WORD *KLONDIKE* INSTANTLY CONJURED UP VISIONS OF SUDDEN WEALTH. THOUSANDS WERE FIGHTING FOR STEAMSHIP TICKETS TO TAKE THEM UP THE ALASKA COAST TO THE PASSES THAT LED TO THE YUKON. (SEE *THE KLONDIKE STAMPEDE* IN THIS SERIES.) NOBODY WAS QUITE SURE YET WHERE THE KLONDIKE WAS; SOME BELIEVED IT TO BE IN ALASKA AND DID NOT REALIZE THAT THEY WOULD HAVE TO PAY CUSTOMS DUTIES AND OBEY BRITISH LAW WHEN THEY CROSSED INTO THE CANADIAN YUKON.

It was a time for myth and legend—reinforced by interviews with the Klondike Kings, many of whom had made a habit of telling tall stories around the glowing stoves in their primitive log cabins.

In fact the real stories were as remarkable as the false ones. Frank Phiscator, a Michigan farm boy, had worked his way west the previous year, carrying the mail on horseback to earn enough money to go north. He was one of a group of five who had trudged up the little creek that soon became known as Eldorado. Phiscator and his friends were now potential millionaires, for they had staked claims on the richest part of the creek, not far from its junction with the famous Bonanza. But like many others, Phiscator had no faith in his find. He sold half of his claim for eight hundred dollars, only to buy it back a few months later for fifteen thousand when the richness of Eldorado was proven.

Most of those who fought for steamboat tickets in the mad rush to the North had no idea how claims were staked in Canada or how placer gold was mined. Many believed it was lying in piles on the surface of the earth. Some of these gullible people thought they could shovel up the gold as easily as gravel. Indeed, they had brought along gunny sacks to hold their treasure!

After all, hadn't Tom Lippy of the Seattle YMCA, a man who knew nothing about mining, come out with a fortune? If Lippy could do it, anybody could!

Lippy's story was widely circulated. He had given up his job the previous spring on a hunch and headed north with his wife. He staked a claim high up on Eldorado but wasn't satisfied with it. Because his wife was with him, Lippy wanted to live in a cabin and so decided to move farther down the creek where there was more timber.

About a mile and a half (2.4 km) from the mouth of Eldorado, Lippy ran into four coal miners from Nanaimo, British Columbia, who had staked four claims—*Fourteen, Fifteen, Sixteen,* and *Seventeen.* The four Scotsmen—three brothers named Scouse and their partner, John Wilkinson—didn't want to bet everything they had on a single package of ground and so abandoned two of their claims.

Lippy immediately restaked claim number Sixteen. It proved to be the richest in the Klondike. Eventually, it produced for him $1,530,000.

Lippy immediately restaked claim number *Sixteen.* It proved to be the richest in the Klondike. Eventually, it produced for him $1,530,000.

The Scouse brothers had also rejected *Seventeen,* next door to Lippy's ground. A prospector known as French Joe staked it but, having less faith than Lippy, sold it almost immediately for six hundred dollars. The buyer, Arkansas Jim Hall, an experienced prospector who had been ten years in the Yukon searching for gold, knew that at last he had found what he was seeking.

This claim, as it turned out, had the widest pay streak in the country. When Jim Hall discovered what French Joe had given up, he felt sorry for him, and he gave him seventy-five feet of the ground as a consolation prize.

Other stories whetted the appetites of the would-be gold seekers. In the Klondike in the early months, poor men had become rich and then poor again without realizing it, as claims changed hands in the days following the big strike. Jay Whipple had staked at the very point where Eldorado flows into Bonanza—claim number *One.* He sold it for a trifle and later wished he hadn't. Skiff Mitchell, a lumberman from California, bought it. He lived for half a century on the proceeds.

Others hung on. Charles Lamb, who had been fired from his job as a Los Angeles streetcar conductor, refused to give up on his number *Eight*. He and his partner finally sold it for $350,000. George Demars sold half of *Nine* for a mere eight hundred dollars. It was soon valued at a million.

A Chicago newspaperman, William Johns, who had been on the spot when Eldorado was discovered, sold half his claim *Twelve* for five hundred dollars and thought himself lucky to get rid of it. Three months later he sold the other half for twenty-five hundred. It turned out to be one of the richest claims on the creek.

No wonder people talked of "poor man's gold" and beggared themselves in order to join the mad race to the Yukon. (See *Trails of '98* in this series.)

All the gold in the Klondike was placer gold—"free gold," as the prospectors called it. Any man with a strong back, a shovel, and a pick could find it. It was not necessary to drill into the sides of mountains, or blast through ancient rock to reach a vein, for there were no veins of gold in the Klondike. These had long since been ground to dust and nuggets by wind and water through a natural sandpapering process that lasted millions of years.

The gold that bubbled up, molten, from the bowels of the Earth was ground into smaller and smaller pieces, which were deposited in the bedrock of ancient streambeds. This wriggling line of gold was known as the "pay streak." It followed the course of a prehistoric creek, now buried deep beneath a blanket of clay, muck, moss, and shrubbery through which a modern creek flowed.

Few of the would-be prospectors, all agog with tales of sudden riches, realized this. Nor did they realize that to seek and find the elusive pay streak required back-breaking toil and a fair amount of luck. Claim owners had to burn a shaft ten, twenty, even thirty feet (3, 6, 9 m) down, setting fires at night, raking away the thawed earth in the morning, and building another fire to melt the next section of ground.

There were some advantages to mining in the North. No man needed to go to the trouble and expense of sawing wood to build a framework to prevent the shaft from falling in. The sides were permanently frozen, as hard as granite. A poor man's goldfield indeed!

But where was the pay streak? It did not follow the course of the modern creek, which meant that a man might sink two or three shafts before finding it. Sometimes he would have to tunnel from the bottom of the shaft seeking the glittering trail of nuggets and dust—if indeed such a trail existed.

For this was the gamble. Few—certainly none of the amateurs—knew that the bulk of the gold lay in one section of the creek only. The claims near the upper end of Eldorado and Bonanza were empty of gold because the slopes were too steep. The force of rushing water had moved all the gold farther down. When the grade decreased, the larger nuggets began to sink beneath the water, to be caught in the grooves of the bedrock in the streambed.

The heaviest gold—and the richest—was thus deposited first. Farther downstream, where the strength of the old currents weakened, finer gold was deposited. This explains why Tom Lippy's original claim, high up on Bonanza, was worthless, while the one he acquired from the Scottish miners—number *Sixteen*—was fabulously rich.

Few—certainly none of the amateurs—knew that the bulk of the gold lay in one section of the creek only. The claims near the upper end of Eldorado and Bonanza were empty of gold because the slopes were too steep.

At first no one had any idea how rich these claims were. Men had found a few nuggets on the surface, usually on the rim of the creekbeds, but until somebody burned his way down to bedrock to find the pay streak the Klondike was a gamble. A few determined men decided to do just that, and the four Nanaimo coal miners were among them.

The Scouse brothers decided to work *Fifteen*, one of the two claims they had retained. Bill Scouse was on the windlass, and his brother Jack was down in the shaft, hoisting up heavy buckets of gravel, sand, and clay. Suddenly one bucket appeared whose contents were quite different from the others. Nuggets stuck out of the gravel like raisins in a cake, and fine gold glistened everywhere.

"What in hell do you think you sent up, the Bank of England?" Bill Scouse called down the shaft.

"What's up—have we struck it?" came the faint reply.

"Come up and have a look; it will do your blooming eyes good."

The two men sprinkled sand over the two pans of pay dirt to hide what they'd found. Then they went to their cabin and asked the third brother to pan out the gold. When he saw the result, he thought he'd gone crazy. In those two pans was gold worth more than four hundred dollars—at twelve dollars an ounce.

Two industrious men had also sunk shafts to bedrock and found good pay. On *Twenty-One Above* Bonanza (where claims were numbered up- and downstream from the original discovery), Louis Rhodes hit the pay streak on his first try. At the same time, Clarence Berry, a bartender from Fortymile, sank his pan in the crumbling bedrock at the base of his first shaft. From that single pan, he weighed out fifty-seven dollars' worth of gold. Small wonder that his name was on everybody's lips, and his story was being told and retold. (See *Bonanza Gold* in this series.)

These three finds proved the Klondike to be one of the richest mining areas in the world. It was not rich in the total quantity of gold it turned out but certainly rich in the wealth of some of the individual claims. Until this time, ten-cent pans were considered good pay. Before the season was out, some men would be getting as much as eight hundred dollars from a single pan of selected pay dirt.

Most of the greenhorns who heard these tales after the treasure ships docked believed that, even if you couldn't shovel gold into sacks, you could certainly pan it out of the creeks by hand. They didn't realize that once the pay streak was found and the dirt hauled up into a "dump," as it was called, more back-breaking labour followed.

Mining in the Yukon was done in the winter. In the spring, when the snow melted and the hills were a-gurgle with rushing streams, the miners built long sluice boxes and directed the water through them. Day after day, they shovelled the gravel and muck from the dump into the boxes, where it was caught in crossbars and cocoa matting—just as it had once been caught in the coarse bedrock of the old streambeds. Every few days the water was redirected, the matting taken up, and the gold panned out.

No wonder, then, that many claim holders, unsure that they had any gold at all, let their claims lapse or sold them for a song, as Russian John Zarnowsky did. Zarnowsky owned claim number *Thirty* on Eldorado. He thought so little of it that he sold half of it to a big, lumbering Nova Scotian from Antigonish named Alex McDonald for a side of bacon and a sack of flour. There was very little gold above this claim, but number *Thirty* turned out to be fabulously rich—so rich that Big Alex, as he was known, became the wealthiest man in the North, known to everyone as *the* King of the Klondike.

CHAPTER THREE

A Story for Jack London

ALL OVER NORTH AMERICA AND AS FAR AWAY AS EUROPE AND AUSTRALIA, PROSPECTIVE MILLIONAIRES, HOPING TO FOLLOW IN BIG ALEX MCDONALD'S FOOTSTEPS, WERE STUDYING PLACER MINING LAW. ENTIRE BOOKS ROLLED OFF THE PRESSES EXPLAINING THE RULES AND RETELLING STORIES OF SUDDEN RICHES AND MISSED OPPORTUNITIES.

A mining claim, they learned, was five hundred feet (152 m) long, stretching across the creek from rimrock to rimrock. Each claim had to be "located" by planting at each corner a four-foot (1.2-m) stake, known officially as a Mining Location Post, marked with the date, the number of the claim, and the name of the person making the claim.

Each prospector had sixty days to record his discovery at the mining recorder's office in the North-West Mounted Police post at Fortymile, downriver near the Alaska border.

But in those early days few believed there was gold on either Eldorado or Bonanza. Many men staked claims in August and September 1896 and then left the area without bothering to record them. These unrecorded claims fell open in October and late November, and when that deadline arrived a wild scramble followed. By this time, those on the ground realized how rich the Klondike was.

The most memorable incident had taken place on Upper Bonanza. Jack London, then on the verge of a spectacular career as a popular novelist, heard about it even before he reached the Klondike. Later he used it in one of his Yukon stories.

The scene was a bizarre one. An unrecorded claim was about to fall open, and more than a dozen men milled about waiting for the midnight hour, intent on restaking it. So tense was the situation that Mounted Police were stationed there to prevent trouble.

As the deadline approached, the contestants began to give up one by one, until only two were left—a Scotsman and a Swede. Both men had prepared their stakes in advance. Now they moved stubbornly to a starting line where, on the stroke of midnight, a policeman called "time," and the race began. The two men hammered in their stakes and dashed off desperately down Bonanza Creek, neck and neck, heading for the mining recorder's office—some fifty miles downriver.

The two rivals, driving fast dog teams, sped out onto the frozen Yukon, each realizing that the recorder's office closed at four in the afternoon and did not reopen until nine the next morning. Over the humpy ice they slid and tumbled, passing and repassing one another, until hours later the blurred outline of the log town loomed out of the cold fog.

> *The two rivals, driving fast dog teams, sped out onto the frozen Yukon, each realizing that the recorder's office closed at four in the afternoon and did not reopen until nine the next morning.*

At this point, the Scotsman's dogs began to flag. He leaped from his sled, determined to finish on foot. The Swede instantly followed suit. The two men reached the barrack gate in a dead heat.

The Swede, however, was unfamiliar with Fortymile. He raced for the largest building, but that turned out to be quarters for the NWMP officers. The Scot, knowing the layout, let him go, made a sharp turn to the right, and just managed to reach the door of the recording office. He was too exhausted to cross the six-inch threshold. He fell on it, crying with his remaining strength, "*Sixty Above* on Bonanza!" An instant later the Swede toppled across him, gasping out the same phrase.

The police advised the pair to divide the ground, which in the end they did. As it turned out, the disputed claim, being too high up the valley, was entirely worthless.

There were plenty of similar stories going the rounds. But the most unbelievable ones weren't fiction—they were true, like the tale of the Dick Lowe Fraction.

Dick Lowe, a rugged, wiry man, had been a muleskinner in Idaho. He had already made and lost a fortune in the Black Hills of that state and was now in the Yukon, hoping to recoup his losses.

Lowe went to work on Bonanza, not for a wealthy prospector, but for William Ogilvie, a Canadian government surveyor who had been asked by the miners to straighten out the mess on Bonanza Creek. Many claims had been badly measured by the early stakers, and Ogilvie discovered that several were too big. To restore these claims to the regulation five hundred feet, a fraction piece was cut from them. These little pieces of ground were now open for restaking.

Nobody knew it, but the richest fraction of all lay on Bonanza Creek just above George Carmack's discovery. Here, almost at the junction of Bonanza, Eldorado, and Big Skookum Gulch, a prospector had staked *Two Above*. But he had bitten off too much land, and when Ogilvie measured the claim he found a small wedge, only eighty-six feet (26 m) at its broadest point, left over.

Dick Lowe stared at the sliver of land.

"Had you thought of staking it?" he asked Ogilvie.

"I'm a government official and not permitted to hold property," the surveyor replied. "You go down if you like and record."

Lowe didn't know what to do. It was a very small piece of ground. If he staked, he wouldn't be able to stake another claim on Bonanza—a bigger one, he hoped. On the other hand, he had come very late to the Klondike, and there wasn't much left to stake.

Lowe decided to take a chance, but before staking the fraction on Bonanza he decided to look for a larger piece. He could find nothing. The little wedge of property did not excite him. He tried to sell it for nine hundred dollars. Nobody would buy it. He tried to lease it, but again there were no takers. The claim was just too small. In the end, he decided to work it himself.

Dick Lowe sank a shaft and found nothing. He sank another and—*Eureka!*—in eight hours he cleaned up forty-six thousand dollars in gold. The Dick Lowe Fraction, as it came to be called, eventually paid out half a million dollars. It remains, for its size, the richest single piece of ground ever discovered.

It could have been Ogilvie's, but in that incorruptible surveyor's letters and articles, pamphlets and memoirs, there is no hint of regret. Indeed, it's doubtful that the possibility of wealth ever crossed his mind. As far as Ogilvie was concerned, the gold might as well have been on the moon.

This fraction was situated in the most promising spot in the whole district. Two of the richest creeks, Bonanza and Eldorado, met here, pouring down their gold onto the property. A third stream, Big Skookum Gulch, cut directly through another ancient gold-bearing channel, whose presence was still unknown. Just above stood Gold Hill, still unnamed, still unstaked, but heavy with coarse gold, much of it washing down onto the property below.

Lowe's ground was so rich that a wire had to be strung along the border of his claim to prevent trespassers. Whenever a nugget was found along the boundary line, its ownership was determined by a plumb bob, which slid along this wire. In August 1899, a single pan of pay dirt scooped up from an adjoining claim a few feet below the fraction yielded a thousand dollars in gold.

It was said that as much gold was stolen from Lowe's property as he himself recovered from it. In some places, glittering nuggets were visible from a distance of twenty feet (6 m). Alas, like so many others, Lowe was never the same man again. Almost from the moment of discovery he got drunk and stayed that way.

CHAPTER FOUR

The Big Moose from Antigonish

BY THE TIME THE FIRST WAVES OF THE GREAT STAMPEDE REACHED THE YUKON, TWO OF THE MOST DURABLE LEGENDS OF THE KLONDIKE HAD BEGUN TO TAKE FORM.

One was the legend of Big Alex McDonald, the King of the Klondike. The other was the legend of Swiftwater Bill Gates, the Knight of the Golden Omelet. None of the Kings of Eldorado was destined for greater immortality than these two strange figures, so different from each other—the one a towering and sober Canadian, the other a pint-sized colourful Yankee.

Both acquired their fortunes because of the "lay system," which McDonald introduced to the Klondike. He had come to the North after fourteen years in the silver mines of Colorado and a stint in Juneau on the Alaska Panhandle. Although he had no money, he had developed a shrewd sense of values while working as a buyer of land for the Alaska Commercial Company. Now he had an abiding faith in the value of property that amounted almost to a religion.

While other men owned a single claim and worked it themselves, McDonald was determined to own a great many and let others do the work. He had begun by acquiring half of *Thirty* Eldorado from Russian John Zarnowsky for a few groceries. He made no move to mine it. Instead he let a section of it out on lease, or "lay," as it was called. The two men who leased it paid him a percentage of what they found. In the next forty-five days, the pair took out thirty-three thousand dollars in gold. McDonald got half.

With his purchase of claim number *Thirty* on Eldorado, McDonald began his climb from day labourer to Klondike King. Because of his size and his awkward movements, he was known as the Big Moose from Antigonish. He spoke slowly and painfully, rubbing his blue jowls in perplexity, his great brow almost hidden by a shock of black hair, his heavy lips concealed by a huge moustache. But behind those features was one of the shrewdest minds in the North.

While others sold, McDonald bought and continued to buy as long as there was breath in his body. Soon he was famous, renowned on three continents as the "King of the Klondike," and sought out by pope, prince, and promoter.

As fast as the lay men gave him his share, he bought more property. His policy was to make a small down payment and give a promissory note for the balance, payable at the time of the spring cleanup. To raise enough money for these down payments, he borrowed funds at heavy interest. In some cases, he paid as much as ten percent for a ten-day loan, which is a rate of 365 percent per annum.

By late spring, Big Alex McDonald's speculations were the talk of the camp. Cleanup time was approaching. It was no longer possible to work in the drifts and shafts, which were filling with seepage from the melting snow and ice. The miners were building flumes and log sluice boxes and paying a high price for rough lumber.

Everybody waited expectantly. Not until the gold was washed from the gravel of the winter dumps would anyone know exactly how much Big Alex was worth. Until this was done, it was all mere guesswork.

Bets were laid as to whether he would be bankrupt or wealthy by summer. The people to whom he owed money were demanding payment. Often enough he had to pay them off with gold still wet from the sluice boxes.

On one occasion, fate stepped in to save him from ruin. He owed forty thousand dollars to two brothers. When the debt fell due, he still hadn't washed out enough gold to pay his debt. At the eleventh hour, one of the brothers conveniently died. The lawsuit that followed delayed payments until McDonald was able to meet the loan.

Before the summer of '97 was out, McDonald had interests in twenty-eight claims, and his holdings were reckoned in millions of dollars. "I've invested my whole fortune," he remarked. "I've run up debts of $150,000 besides. But I can dig out $150,000 any time I need it."

Nobody knew what he was worth—and that included Big Alex himself. It was said that, if he so much as stopped to look at a piece of property, its value increased at once. He was involved in so many complicated business deals that every time he was introduced to a newcomer he would start out by asking, "Are you a partner of mine?"

Wherever he went, a swarm of hangers-on followed, plucking at his sleeve, waving papers, offering deals, asking for money. Big Alex always answered with an immediate "No!" But that only meant he wanted time to think over the scheme. As often as not, he ended by accepting it, for he had reached the point where he found it hard to turn down any offer.

With his slow speech, his great hands, and his blank features, the King of the Klondike presented a simple face to the world. He rarely showed any emotion, but the deals he made were highly complex.

In June of 1897, he walked into the tent office of Ron Crawford, a former Seattle court clerk who was setting up in a business to draw up legal papers for prospectors. McDonald deposited his huge frame on the three-legged stool in front of Crawford's rough spruce table and announced he wanted to borrow five thousand dollars. Crawford, who had only twenty-five cents to his name, asked him how much interest he was willing to pay.

"I don't want to pay interest," said McDonald in his slow way, rubbing his chin. "Interest is always working against you, and I can't sleep at night when I think of that. But if you let me have the money, I'll give you a lay of one hundred feet (30 m) of *Six Below* Bonanza at fifty percent. I'll also give you thirty-five percent of thirty-five feet (11 m) of *Twenty-Seven* Eldorado and a mortgage on *Thirty* Eldorado as security."

Considering the value of these three claims, it was an enormous sum to pay for the use of five thousand dollars. Crawford stalled for time. He promised to give McDonald an answer by morning. Then he rushed to a neighbouring saloon and raised five thousand dollars from the owner in return for a half interest in the mortgage on *Thirty*. After the loan was made, Crawford sold part of his share of the section of *Twenty-Seven* for five thousand dollars to a Dawson barber. The barber worked it the following winter and took out forty thousand dollars. McDonald's example was widely copied. Claims were carved up like so many apple pies—mortgaged, leased, traded, loaned, lost.

George Carmack, the original discoverer of Bonanza, sold half of his brother-in-law's claim for five thousand dollars. The buyer put five hundred dollars down and went to work. From a fourteen-foot (4.3-m) shaft, he immediately took out eight thousand, from which he paid off the balance. Ogilvie recognized that on this basis the claim could be worth about two and a half million.

"My God," cried the new owner, "what will I do with all that money?"

"I wouldn't worry," Ogilvie told him. "It's hardly possible your claim will average anything like that." And he went on to reason that, if the only wealth on the claim was on the one fourteen-foot strip, there would still be eighty-three thousand dollars in the ground. And that, he added dryly, "is enough to kill you."

CHAPTER FIVE

The Legend of Swiftwater Bill

THE SYSTEM THAT MADE BIG ALEX MCDONALD RICH CATAPULTED SWIFTWATER BILL GATES INTO THE NOTORIETY HE WANTED SO BADLY. GATES WAS ONE OF A GROUP OF SEVEN MEN WHO WERE FINALLY PERSUADED TO TAKE THE LAY ON *THIRTEEN* ELDORADO, WHICH HAD BEEN SHUNNED BY EVERYBODY ELSE BECAUSE OF THE JINX OF THE NUMBER THIRTEEN. THE NEW MEN SANK SEVEN SHAFTS BEFORE THEY HIT PAY DIRT. WHEN THEY DID, THEY SAW AT ONCE IT WAS INCREDIBLY RICH.

They wanted to keep it a secret, so they burned in the sides of the shaft and let it be noised about that they were getting a paltry ten cents to the pan. The owner, J. B. Hollingshead, was delighted that April to sell them the property for forty-five thousand dollars. In just six weeks, they were able to pay him with gold dug out of his own claim.

Until this point, there was little to distinguish William F. Gates from his fellows. He was only five foot five (1.7 m), and his moon face was ornamented by a straggling black moustache that gave his features a comic look. No one ever took him seriously. When he boasted of his former powers as a boatman on a river in Idaho, they laughed and gave him the nickname "Swiftwater Bill."

Like most of his companions, Swiftwater Bill Gates was nearly broke. But all he needed to transform his personality was gold. In 1896 he had been working as a nondescript dishwasher. By 1897 he was a man in a Prince Albert coat, with a top hat, a white shirt, a diamond stickpin in his tie, and the only starched collar in Dawson. It was said that he was so proud of his unique collar that he took to his bed while it was being laundered rather than be seen without it.

All his life Bill Gates had been a small man—a face in the crowd with nothing to set him aside from his fellows. Now he decided to be Somebody.

He didn't wait for his share of the gold to be hauled up the shaft of *Thirteen* Eldorado. He borrowed money at ten percent a month so he could play pool at a hundred dollars a frame, or throw his poke on the faro table and cry, "The sky's the limit! Raise her up as far as you want to go, boys, and if the roof's in the way, why, tear it off."

One night Swiftwater lost five hundred dollars in a few minutes. "Things don't seem to be coming my way tonight," he said, rising from his seat. "Let's let the house have a drink at my expense." That cost him $112. In spite of his losses, he threw the rest of his poke on the bar, lighted a $1.50 cigar, and strolled out.

Like Big Alex, he hired others to do his mining for him. But whereas Big Alex used all his time to acquire more gold, Swiftwater used every waking moment to get rid of his. Like Big Alex, he paid his workers in property rather than in cash, and he paid them well.

One of his helpers, a former milk-wagon driver from Seattle named Harry Winter, worked a hundred days for Swiftwater and received in return a fifty-foot-square (15.2-sq.-m) plot of ground. From that he took five thousand dollars, which he used to buy from Swiftwater a second plot thirty feet square (9 sq. m). That yielded eighty-five thousand. It meant that Swiftwater had, in effect, paid Winter nine hundred dollars a day for his labour.

Swiftwater Bill allowed no wine to touch his lips (though he occasionally bathed in it), but he indulged in other pleasures. It was his habit to escort dance-hall girls to his claim and let them clamber down the shaft to pan out all the gold they wanted. They turned out to be as expert as seasoned miners.

Bill's favourite was Gussie Lamore, a nineteen-year-old who had come to Dawson from Circle City in the spring rush and who shared top billing with him in an incident that has become the liveliest of the Klondike's imperishable legends.

Gussie, it turned out, was very fond of fresh eggs, possibly because they were as scarce as diamonds in the Dawson of 1897. One day, so the tale goes, Swiftwater Bill was seated in a restaurant when, to his surprise and chagrin, he saw Gussie enter on the arm of a well-known gambler. The pair ordered fried eggs, which were the most expensive item on the menu, and it was then that, in a fury of jealousy, Swiftwater achieved a certain immortality by buying up every egg in town in an attempt to frustrate Gussie's cravings.

They called him the "Knight of the Golden Omelet." There are many versions of this tale. Arthur Walden, a dog driver, who claimed in his memoirs to have witnessed the incident, wrote that Swiftwater had the eggs fried one at a time and then flipped them through the window of the café to a rabble of dogs outside, commenting to the gathering crowd on the cleverness of the animals in catching them.

Other versions have it that he presented the entire treasure of eggs to Gussie as a token of his true emotions or that he fed them to other dance-hall girls in order to awaken Gussie's jealousy. Belinda Mulroney, a famous Klondike innkeeper who arrived in Dawson early that spring, recollects that there was about half a case of eggs involved and that these had been brought over the ice from the Pacific coast and were fast growing mellow. Mrs. Iola Beebe, one of Swiftwater's several future mothers-in-law, wrote that there were two crates of eggs and that Swiftwater paid for them with two coffee tins filled with gold.

The details of the story have thus been lost, for there was no writing paper in Dawson at the time to set them down, and no writers either, since every would-be historian was too busy seeking a fortune to attend to such footnotes. Whatever the details, the fact remains that the incident won Gussie over, at least temporarily. She offered to meet Swiftwater Bill in San Francisco that fall and marry him, failing to mention that she was already wed to one Emile Leglice and had been since 1894.

Swiftwater's journey to San Francisco was supposed to be for business. He had gone into partnership with a clever businessman named Jack Smith to establish the most famous of the Klondike's palaces of pleasure, the Monte Carlo Dance Hall and Saloon.

Smith was an old showman who had a variety troupe in Fortymile at the time of the strike. He had reached Bonanza with the first wave, staked a claim, sold it for $155,000, opened up a small saloon on the creeks, and turned a handy profit. That convinced him that it was easier to dig gold out of the miners' pockets than out of the ground.

Smith saw that there were more riches to be mined on Dawson's Front Street than in the creeks of the Klondike valley. He immediately opened the

Monte Carlo in a tent. He made only one error of judgment, but it was a whopper. He persuaded Swiftwater Bill to put up some of the funds for a permanent building. Then he allowed him to go out to San Francisco to rustle up a cargo of furnishings, liquor, and dance-hall girls.

Sending Swiftwater outside to bring back girls was like sending a greedy child to a candy shop and hoping to get a full box back. But the awful realization of what he had done did not begin to dawn on Jack Smith until the following summer.

When Swiftwater arrived in San Francisco, he rented a suite of rooms in the Baldwin Hotel and in the Klondike manner began to distribute gold dust to everybody he met. He tipped the bellboys to walk about the lobby and point him out to hotel guests as the "King of the Klondike." Then he paid a journalist one hundred dollars to publish a lurid account of his own drowning.

In his new Prince Albert coat, and with diamond cuff links and diamond stickpin, he presented to the world a glittering figure, in spite of his small size and his scraggly moustache. Alas for Swiftwater, Gussie Lamore, who had gone ahead of him, refused to go through with her promise of marriage, possibly because in addition to being already married she had a three-year-old child.

Undaunted, Swiftwater then married her sister Grace, bought her a fifteen-thousand-dollar house, and, while it was being fixed up to suit his taste, put her in the bridal chamber of the Baldwin. The honeymoon, however, was short-lived; Grace threw him over after three weeks. Still undaunted, Swiftwater began earnestly to woo the youngest Lamore sister, Nellie.

By this time, he was running out of money and hadn't bought anything for Jack Smith's Monte Carlo. Swiftwater, however, was a born prospector. He was always able to spot a likely piece of ground and, where there was no ground available, to spot a likely looking sucker. His eye fell on a Dr. Wolf, who had twenty thousand dollars to invest. Swiftwater talked so swiftly and smoothly that he was able to get all of it. In return he gave Wolf a ninety-day note promising to pay the astonishing interest rate of one hundred percent.

But Wolf's imagination was so fired by Swiftwater's tale of fortunes in the Klondike that he decided to become a stampeder himself. The two laid plans to organize a trading and transportation company and set off at once for Seattle. There the doctor plunged into the business end of the venture while Swiftwater paraded up and down the street with the girls he'd hired for the Monte Carlo Dance Hall.

He lived extravagantly at the Rainier-Grand Hotel and ordered gallons of champagne, not to drink—for he was a teetotaller—but to bathe in! He splashed about in the tub for the benefit of the press, announcing that a bath was a rare thing in the Yukon. When he left, the bill for damages alone came to fifteen hundred dollars.

> *He lived extravagantly at the Rainier-Grand Hotel and ordered gallons of champagne, not to drink—for he was a teetotaller—but to bathe in!*

Dr. Wolf began to become suspicious. Slowly, it dawned on him that his new partner was not the solid businessman he had thought he was. By the time they reached Lake Bennett, Wolf was thoroughly alarmed. He left Swiftwater behind and sped ahead to Dawson by dogsled to investigate his new partner's background before the main rush arrived. The stories he heard of Swiftwater's escapades in the City of Gold only confirmed his worst fears.

When Swiftwater reached Dawson, both Wolf and Jack Smith were waiting on the riverbank for him. It was, perhaps, the most exotic arrival in the Klondike's brief history. For there was Swiftwater, in the prow of a Peterborough canoe, with two scowloads of girls and whisky towed behind. With a silk top hat cocked on his head, and his Prince Albert coat draped across his shoulders, he extended his arms in a welcome to the crowd who stood on the bank to greet him. Directly behind him a girl was perched on a case of whisky, and on the scow other girls waved and shouted greetings to the onlookers.

Swiftwater stepped ashore in triumph—into the arms of his enraged partner.

"You've got just exactly three hours to pay back the twenty thousand," Wolf told him. "To hell with the interest!"

"I'll have it," Swiftwater gasped.

"Get started!" Wolf rapped back. Swiftwater raised the money. Wolf took the next boat home declaring he'd had all he wanted of the Klondike. Jack

Smith lost no time in taking over twelve thousand dollars of Swiftwater's mining profit in the bank and Swiftwater's share of the dance hall as well.

But nothing fazed Swiftwater Bill Gates. With scarcely an instant's hesitation, he plunged into a new scheme, announcing the formation of a trading and exploration company. He left directly for London to raise the capital. He was not a man whose spirits were easily dampened.

CHAPTER SIX

The Klondike Queen

PAT GALVIN OF BONANZA CREEK SUMMED UP THE SPIRIT OF '98 IN A FEW SHORT
SENTENCES OF ADVICE GIVEN TO HIS NEPHEW WHO'D ARRIVED FROM THE OUT-
SIDE THAT SUMMER. HIS NEPHEW, WATCHING THE WAY GALVIN FLUNG AWAY HIS
MONEY, TRIED TO UTTER A FEW WORDS OF CAUTION ABOUT EXPENSE.

"Expense! Expense!" cried Galvin. "I'm disgusted with you. Don't show
your ignorance by using that cheap outside word. We don't use it here.
Never repeat it in my presence again. You must learn the ways of Alaska.
That word is not understood in the North. If you have money, spend it;
that's what it's for, and that's the way we do business."

That might easily have stood as the Klondike's creed in the year of the
stampede. The gold that had lain hidden for so long in the frozen gravels
now moved as swiftly as the nuggets Galvin gave away like souvenirs to any
passing stranger.

The Kings of Bonanza and Eldorado who'd been common labourers
two years before now saw themselves as captains of industry. They were
determined to invest their newfound wealth. Some built hotels and fitted
them out with Persian carpets and mahogany furniture. Others financed
restaurants that served everything from oysters to sherbet. Dozens were
sucked into mining companies, syndicates, trading firms, and transportation companies.

Galvin, a one-time town marshal in Helena, Montana, was now rich
because of his Bonanza claim. He, too, started a transportation company.
His reputation for free spending was well known. It was said he was good
for two thousand dollars a night in Dawson. On entering a bar, it was his
custom to treat everybody in the house.

"Come on, boys," Galvin would shout. "Open up the best you have, the drinks are on me!" In case he might have overlooked anybody on the street, he would send the bartender outside to drag in any passerby. He was a commanding figure, dressed entirely in black, slender and wiry, with eyes that gleamed from a pale Irish face. A crowd usually followed him, for his generosity was legendary, and he distributed as much as a thousand dollars' worth of nuggets at a time.

Unable to give away all of his money, Galvin bought a steamboat, the *Yukoner*, for forty-five thousand dollars. Others followed his example, becoming, if only briefly, shipping magnates. Big Alex McDonald bought the *W. K. Merwyn* and also acquired the *W. F. Stratton*, named for an eccentric Black Hills mining millionaire.

Nels Peterson, who had grown rich from one of the early claims, formed the "Flyer" line with two spanking new steamboats, the *Eldorado* and the *Bonanza King*. The original name of the *Eldorado* was *Philip B. Low*, but she sank so many times that she was referred to as the "Fill Up Below," and so the name was changed.

Peterson offered a free ticket from Dawson to Seattle to the first person to spot either boat when the two arrived on their maiden voyage from St. Michael at the mouth of the Yukon in the fall of '98. Hundreds who had no other way of leaving the Klondike climbed to the Midnight Dome—the tall hill above the town—straining for the sight of steamboat smoke. One ingenious pair won handily by arranging a system of wig-wag signals from the mountaintop to friends on the main street. Dozens risked breaking their necks in a pell-mell race down the hillside when the *Bonanza King* at last appeared, only to find they'd been outwitted. But Peterson's showmanship was better than his business sense. He sank ninety thousand dollars in the two boats, and that helped to ruin him.

The Kings of the Klondike demanded every luxury. By the end of August, fifty-six steamboats had dumped seventy-four hundred tons (6,600 tonnes) of freight on the new docks—everything from fancy porcelain chamber pots to flagons of Napoleon brandy.

Dawson was no longer a beans and bacon town. The imported San Francisco chef at the Regina Hotel served Rock Point oysters, Lobster Newburg, grilled moose chops with mushrooms, roast beef, and Bengal Club chutney. Its floors were covered with Brussels carpets. Its woodwork had gold-leaf trimming. It rose four storeys, the tallest building in Dawson.

Its chief rival was the equally elegant Fairview, which Belinda Mulroney was constructing on Front Street. Belinda planned to make it the finest hotel in town. It was to have twenty-two steam-heated rooms, a side entrance for ladies, Turkish baths, and electric lights whose power would be supplied by a yacht anchored in the river.

The tables were spread with linen, sterling silver, and bone china. In the lobby, an orchestra played chamber music. The bar was staffed by young American doctors and dentists who couldn't get a licence to practise on British soil but quickly learned to mix drinks instead of medicines.

Belinda was one of the most remarkable figures turned up by the Klondike gold stampede. She was a plain-faced young Irishwoman, rigid in her moral standards but shrewder than most of the men who found sudden riches in the creeks of the Klondike.

She was born in Scranton, Pennsylvania, the daughter of a coal miner. When the great Columbian Exposition opened in Chicago in 1892, she went there to open a restaurant hoping to make her fortune. She was only eighteen at the time.

She earned eight thousand dollars in the restaurant business but lost it all when she went out west to California. That didn't bother her. She shipped aboard the *City of Topeka* as a stewardess. There she quickly gained a reputation for her business sense, her coolness, and the sharpness of her tongue. Once a passenger made the mistake of asking her to black his boots. She said that, if he so much as put them outside his door, she would pour a pitcher of water on them.

On her voyage, a baby had to be delivered. Belinda did the job herself, while the captain stood discreetly outside the cabin door, reading instructions from a medical book.

She was put in charge of purchasing all the ship's supplies, buying everything from machinery to canary birds. For that she charged the captain a stiff ten percent commission. When the ship stopped at the various coastal towns, Belinda was on hand to sell picture hats and satin dresses to the Indian women.

By the spring of 1897, when the first news of the Klondike strike reached the Alaska Panhandle, Belinda had saved five thousand dollars. She decided to invest it all in cotton goods and hot-water bottles. Down the Yukon River she went, on a raft piloted by two Indians. When she reached Dawson, she took her last fifty-cent piece and threw it into the river, swearing she'd never again need such small change. And she was right.

In Dawson she sold her merchandise at a profit of six hundred percent. Then she opened up a lunch counter and hired a group of young men to build cabins for her. She sold those as fast as the roofs went on.

But Belinda wanted to be nearer to the gold, and so she bought a broken-down mule named Gerry and began to haul timber out to the creeks. The town jeered, but Belinda went ahead building a roadhouse. Her friends told her that it was the wrong place—that the only place to open a hotel and a saloon was in Dawson itself. But they were wrong.

Belinda opened her inn in the fall of 1897 at the junction of Bonanza and Eldorado Creeks. A wild little town was already springing up there, servicing those miners who didn't want to make the long trip into Dawson. It was called Grand Forks, and the population reached five thousand. Belinda stood behind the bar, a stern figure in her white shirtwaist and long black skirt, selling eggs at a dollar apiece and wine, cigars, and whisky at the highest prices in the Klondike. She was on her way to making her first fortune.

All this time she kept her ears open to the mining gossip. The Eldorado Kings flocked to her roadhouse. Belinda made a note of everything she heard. Before the winter was over, she had half a dozen valuable mining properties in her name.

She never missed an opportunity to make a profit. That fall a small boat loaded with supplies had been wrecked on a sandbar. Belinda immediately went into partnership with Big Alex McDonald to buy and salvage the cargo. McDonald moved quickly, grabbing all the food and leaving Belinda with nothing but several cases of rubber boots and whisky.

"You'll pay through the nose for this," Belinda vowed. She meant it. The following spring, when the land around the creeks was thick with mud, Big Alex arrived at her roadhouse in a hurry, looking for rubber boots for his workers. She charged him a hundred dollars a pair.

Meanwhile, she was planning her elegant hotel—the Fairview—on Dawson's Front Street. It opened in July of 1898, but more than a year was required to put the finishing touches to it.

All the Fairview's furnishings—from cut glass chandeliers to brass bedsteads—had to be packed in over the White Pass. Belinda, who left very little to others, went personally to Skagway to supervise that operation.

She arrived in the nick of time. Joe Brooks, the packer she had hired, had moved her outfit only two miles (3.2 km) up the trail. Then he dumped it when he received a better offer to transport a cargo of whisky for Bill McPhee's saloon.

Belinda became very angry. She headed for the Skagway wharves and recruited a gang of jobless men. She goaded them into fighting among themselves until she found out which one was the toughest. She elected him foreman, and, that done, she accompanied the gang up the trail to take over from Brooks.

Her men beat up Brooks's foreman, imprisoned him in a tent, set a guard outside of it, and dumped McPhee's whisky on the side of the trail. Then they loaded Belinda's hotel equipment on Brooks's mules and started over the pass. Belinda, mounted on Brooks's own pinto pony, rode at the head of this odd procession. In this manner, she got the entire shipment safely over the mountains and then down the Yukon River on fifteen scows.

Now the Fairview stood complete. It had only one real flaw. The interior walls were made of canvas, over which wallpaper had been pasted so that the slightest whisper anywhere in the building could be heard by every guest.

Thomas Cunningham, purser of the *Yukoner*, once invited Belinda to have breakfast with him at the hotel. She was delighted to accept. When the bill was added up, it came to sixty dollars. That was an enormous sum of money for breakfast at a time when workmen in the outside world were making between a dollar and two dollars a day. Cunningham certainly was staggered.

"Think of a woman ordering champagne for breakfast!" he exclaimed. "It is not done." But it was done in Dawson City in Belinda Mulroney's day.

By 1899 Belinda was one of the wealthiest and most powerful women in the Klondike. In spite of her prim ways and her plain Irish features, she was a good catch for any enterprising bachelor. And such a man duly arrived on the scene. He sported a monocle, kid gloves, spats, a small, jet-black moustache, and a tall, bearded valet.

From an elegant leather case, he produced an engraved calling card:

M. Le Comte Carbonneau
Représentant
Messieurs Pierre Legasse, Frères et Cie
Bordeaux Paris New York

He wasn't a count at all. He was a champagne salesman from Quebec. But he fell for Belinda. Every day he sent her a bunch of red roses at her hotel, and Belinda fell for him.

In October of 1900, the coal miner's daughter from Scranton became a countess. Her husband, of course, was a fraud. Tom Lippy's French-Canadian foreman, Joe Putraw, had positively identified him as a barber from Montreal's Rue Saint-Denis. Belinda didn't care.

Off the couple went to Paris, where they rode up and down the Champs-Élysées behind a pair of handsome snow-white horses decked out with a gold-ornamented harness. An Egyptian footman unrolled a velvet carpet of brilliant crimson whenever they stepped out.

Belinda herself continued to prosper in the Yukon. She became the only woman mining manager in the territory—and of the largest mining company. The Gold Run Mining Company had got into financial difficulties, largely because the owners spent all their profits at a gaming table they were running, while their employees stole gold off the property in order to gamble with it. The local bank manager put Belinda in charge. In just eighteen months, the company was showing a profit.

Belinda's first move was to throw out the roulette wheel and replace it with a bridge table. Her second was to drive all women from the property. As a forewoman, she was a holy terror. One old sourdough retained vivid memories of working for her. He recalled that she wouldn't allow any smoking on the job. He tried to break this rule, but before he had a match lit she gave a low whistle, crooked her finger, and said sharply, "Get off this claim before nightfall." He did.

After the Klondike strike was over, Belinda and her husband went on to Fairbanks during the Tanana mining boom in Central Alaska. In 1910 they left the North at last and bought themselves a ranch near Yakima,

Washington. There, in the style of so many of their fellows, they built themselves a stone castle.

Every winter they went to Europe, where Carbonneau became a bank director and a steamship magnate. They put all their money into the steamship company. But when World War One came, it brought an end to merchant shipping. Carbonneau was killed during the war, and Belinda went back to Washington state, where she lived with her memories until her death in the early 1960s.

But long after the gold fever had died away, hundreds of Yukoners still remembered the plain-faced Irishwoman who dug so much gold, not out of the ground of Bonanza and Eldorado, but out of the pockets of those who had already found it.

CHAPTER SEVEN

The Fate of Kings

By 1899, the Kings of the Klondike had become a distinct social class. In the dance halls, they occupied the royal boxes high above the floor. They drove their fashionable dog teams down the hard-packed snow of the Klondike valley in the same way that British aristocrats drove their Rolls Royces through the streets of London.

The dog team had become a symbol. The Klondike Kings, the saloon keepers, gamblers, and mine owners, all kept expensive teams with expensive harness. One man, "Coatless Curly" Munro, in a single season fed his puppies a total of 4,320 pounds (1,960 kg) of bacon, fish, and flour, at a dollar a pound, hoping they would grow up to be a prize team. Coatless Curly got his nickname because he never wore an overcoat, even in the coldest weather—though, it was said, he did have several layers of underwear.

Jim Daugherty had a prize team of eight dogs worth twenty-five hundred dollars and a sled that had its own built-in bar. That was a specially made tin tank he kept filled with alcohol, which he poured out by the dipperful to mix with hot water and sugar for his friends.

Waste, on a grand scale, went along with wealth on a grand scale. Dick Lowe, the man who had staked the famous fraction on Bonanza, could be seen on Sunday afternoons driving a spanking team of trotting horses along the Klondike valley with a dance-hall girl at his side—or in the evening flinging a fortune on the bars of Dawson's saloons to treat the entire crowd.

On Dominion Creek, two neighbouring miners each installed a butler in his log cabin. On Eldorado, Clarence Berry enjoyed a peculiar luxury: he owned the only cow in the valley, a purebred Jersey, who supplied fresh milk from her sawdust-padded stable and munched hay worth four hundred dollars a ton (907 kg). In front of Berry's cabin, along the Eldorado trail, stood a coal-oil can full of gold and a bottle of whisky beside. A sign between the two of them carried the blunt but inviting message "Help yourself."

Berry's partner, the handsome Antone Stander, who had staked the first of the Eldorado claims, went out to San Francisco with his new wife, a dance-hall girl named Violet Raymond. He planned to take her on a honeymoon to China, and he had a thousand pounds of gold as pocket money in his stateroom. Bit by bit, he gave the gold to Violet; she spent it all.

Charley Anderson, known as the Lucky Swede because he had bought a million-dollar claim while drunk, went off to Europe accompanied by his wife, the same Grace Drummond who had caught the eye of Swiftwater Bill Gates. She married Anderson because he agreed to put fifty thousand dollars in her bank account. They went arm in arm to Paris, London, New York, and then San Francisco, on whose outskirts the Lucky Swede built a monument to his bride in the form of a magnificent castle.

Big Alex McDonald went to Paris, too, and then to Rome, where he was granted an audience with the Pope and made a Knight of St. Gregory, because of his many donations to the Dawson hospital run by the Sisters of St. Anne. Then he went to London, and by the time he returned to Dawson in April 1899 he had a new bride—the twenty-year-old Margaret Chisholm, daughter of the superintendent of the Thames Water Police.

There seemed no end to McDonald's wealth. In Dawson that spring, his fifteen-mule pack train, laden with gold, was a familiar sight on the Klondike River road. One day the pack train went missing. The mules wandered about the hills for two weeks. But no one touched the gold. On one of his claims, a single man was able to shovel in twenty thousand dollars in gold in a twelve-hour stretch. A single payment made by Big Alex to the Alaska Trading and Transportation Company amounted to $150,000.

Big Alex built his own building, which he named after himself, and he lived lavishly on its first floor. On a sideboard, there was a bowl containing forty-five pounds (20 kg) of nuggets. "Help yourself to some nuggets," McDonald said to a young newspaper reporter, Alice Henderson. It was as if he was offering a box of chocolates.

"Take some of the bigger ones," he urged. When she hesitated, he said, "Oh, they mean nothing to me. Take as many as you please. There are lots more."

Back in the outside world, Swiftwater Bill, now hailed in the press as "The Klondike Prince," was publicly offering to bet seven thousand dollars on the turn of a card with anybody who cared to challenge him. He caught the eye of a Seattle widow, Mrs. Iola Beebe, and he also caught the eye of her two young daughters, Bera, aged fifteen, and Blanche, nineteen, both just out of convent school. When Mrs. Beebe's back was turned, he spirited both the daughters aboard his ship, which was about to steam north.

The alarmed mother boarded the boat before it left and discovered Swiftwater cowering under a lifeboat. She rescued the girls and then decided to go north herself to seek her fortune. She and her daughters landed in Skagway, only to come upon Swiftwater lying in wait. Mrs. Beebe awoke one morning to find that he had left Dawson with the fifteen-year-old Bera. Before she could overtake them, the two were married.

Swiftwater gave his bride a gift of a melon, so rare in the Klondike that it cost him forty dollars. Mrs. Beebe soon forgave him. He then managed to borrow thirty-five thousand dollars from her to finance a mining claim in the Klondike. And that was the last she saw of it.

The alarmed mother boarded the boat before it left and discovered Swiftwater cowering under a lifeboat. She rescued the girls and then decided to go north herself to seek her fortune. She and her daughters landed in Skagway, only to come upon Swiftwater lying in wait.

By the end of the year, Swiftwater was magnificently bankrupt, having run up bills totalling $100,000. He fled from Dawson with his child bride, leaving his now destitute mother-in-law to care for a four-week-old granddaughter.

Pat Galvin, the free-spending Irishman who had sunk his profits for his Bonanza claim into a transportation company, was teetering on the edge of ruin by the spring of 1899. So were many others. Galvin's first steamboat, which he designed to be the finest vessel on the river, was a complete failure; she drew so much water she couldn't cross the shallow Yukon flats and had to be abandoned. His second boat lay stranded in the ice fourteen hundred miles (2,240 km) downstream.

Galvin's financial manager, James Beatty, a fast-talking Englishman known as "Lord Jim," also helped to ruin him. Not only did he import the finest china and bed linens for Galvin's proposed chain of Yukon River hotels, but he also imported the best-looking girls to be had in San Francisco for himself. His free-spending habits caught up with him when the company's auditors found forty thousand dollars missing in his books. Beatty was arrested and charged with embezzlement, but Galvin had him released on bail and paid his way across the border into the United States.

Once on Alaskan soil, Lord Jim promptly forged a cheque and headed for South Africa with a troop of detectives on his trail. That was billed as the longest manhunt on record. But Galvin, who had by now lost everything, didn't whimper. When he learned of Lord Jim's troubles, he merely shrugged. "He was a good fellow," he observed.

One by one the Klondike Kings toppled from their thrones. Only a few—Clarence Berry was one—kept their money. Antone Stander, having drunk part of his fortune away and given the rest to his wife, headed north again seeking another Klondike, working his passage aboard ship by peeling potatoes. He got no farther than the Alaska Panhandle and died in the Pioneers' Home in Sitka.

Dick Lowe managed to get rid of more than half a million dollars from his famous fraction. Part of it was stolen from his claim because he was too drunk to take notice of what was happening. Part of it was flung onto the bars of the saloons—as much as ten thousand dollars at a time. He had warned his friends against marrying a dance-hall girl, but in the end he married one himself.

By the turn of the century, Lowe was on his way down, trying to recoup his fortunes in other gold rushes, without success. There is a sad picture of him pawning an eight-hundred-dollar monogrammed gold watch in Victoria, BC. There's another of him peddling water by the bucket in Fairbanks, Alaska, in 1905. He died in San Francisco in 1907.

Others met variations of the same fate. Sam Stanley of Eldorado, the bookseller's son, married a dance-hall girl and died a poor man. Jim Daugherty, who had the fanciest sled in the Klondike—the one with the built-in bar—was broke by 1902. Pat Galvin left the Klondike in 1899 bankrupt and died shortly after of cholera in the South Seas. Frank Phiscator killed himself in a San Francisco hotel.

Even Tom Lippy, the God-fearing YMCA man who did not drink or gamble, ended his days bankrupt, even though he had taken close to two million dollars from his claim on Eldorado. After he sold out in 1903, he and his wife made a trip around the world and built the proudest home in Seattle. Lippy was generous to a fault. When obscure relatives descended upon them, he took them in and gave them jobs. He made large donations to the Methodist Church and the YMCA. He gave twenty-five thousand dollars to the Anti-Saloon League, donated the land on which the Seattle General Hospital was built, and started the drive for Seattle's first swimming pool.

Lippy became a respected citizen, hospital president, port commissioner, senior golf champion of the Pacific Northwest, but he was, alas, a bad businessman. He sank almost half a million dollars in several companies, all of which failed. Lippy was ruined, and when he died in 1931 at the age of seventy-one he had nothing to leave his wife.

Big Alex McDonald was ruined by the very thing that made him rich—his obsession with property. For several years, he kept his wealth, and he became the leading light in Dawson in spite of his awkwardness and lack of social presence. It was Big Alex that the townspeople chose as the key figure in a farewell celebration when the much-loved NWMP superintendent Sam Steele left the Yukon in 1899.

As a special concession, the steamboat on which the policeman was leaving was brought up the river to the front of the barracks. There Big Alex, who had been carefully rehearsed and drilled for several days, was supposed to make a graceful farewell speech and present Steele with a poke of gold. At the last moment, the King of the Klondike lumbered forward sheepishly and thrust the gold into Steele's hand. The farewell speech went as follows: "Here, Sam—here y'are. Poke for you—goodbye."

That wasn't quite what the crowd had expected, but, in spite of it, Big Alex was chosen again to make another presentation to the wife of the Governor General of Canada when his party visited Dawson in 1900. This time the gift to Lady Minto was a golden bucket filled to the brim with curiously shaped nuggets, with a miniature gold windlass above it.

Again Big Alex was carefully rehearsed in a speech written especially for the occasion. Alas, when the awful moment came, the King of the Klondike simply reached out his great ham hands toward her ladyship and said, "Here, tak' it. It's trash."

To McDonald gold was always trash. He continued to use it to buy more land, and as his claims were worked out he bought new ones farther away. He had twenty claims on one creek alone, none worth a plugged nickel. In his last year, he lived by himself in a little cabin on Clearwater Creek still prospecting for gold, his fortune long gone. One day a prospector came upon the cabin and found McDonald's huge form lying in front of his chopping block. He'd died of a heart attack while splitting firewood.

The liveliest Klondike sequel is provided, naturally enough, by Swiftwater Bill Gates. When the Klondike stampede ended in 1899 and gold was discovered at Nome, Alaska, Swiftwater headed for the new strike. There he repeated his success in a mild way by taking a lay on a claim that made him four thousand dollars. He lost it all gambling.

Broke again and back in civilization, he was still the same old Swiftwater. He left his young wife and ran off with a pretty seventeen-year-old named Kitty Brandon. There was the usual wild chase from city to city with an angry mother in hot pursuit. Finally, in Chehalis, Washington, Swiftwater found a preacher to marry the pair. It was complicated, however, by the fact that (1) Swiftwater was still married to Bera Beebe, and (2) Kitty Brandon was actually his stepniece.

He solved that problem by discarding the young woman a few months after the wedding. He was scarcely a free man again when his mother-in-law, Mrs. Beebe, banged on his hotel-room door with vengeance in her eye. Swiftwater was always a fast talker. He persuaded her to pawn her diamonds so he could go back north again to recoup his fortune.

Miraculously, he did just that. He took a lay on number *Six* Cleary Creek, Fairbanks, and made seventy-five thousand dollars, only to find that he now faced two angry mothers-in-law, both of whom had followed him north.

He gave Mrs. Brandon (who was also his sister) the slip, but Mrs. Beebe was not so easy to shake off. She chased Swiftwater down the coast, and when the two reached Seattle she had him jailed for bigamy.

With the help of several bribes, Swiftwater stayed out of jail, his marital problems were untangled, both girls were properly divorced, and Swiftwater moved on. The last we hear of him is in 1935 in Peru. He died that year after he was supposedly wangling a twenty-million-acre (8-million-hectare) silver-mining concession. Swiftwater Bill's story is the stuff of which Hollywood movies are made—but in this case nobody would make it because the truth was simply too far-fetched to be credible. But then the whole story of the mad rush for gold in the Klondike is scarcely believable.

Dawson, a town built to hold some twenty thousand transients, has a permanent population today of some fifteen hundred people. It still straggles along the frozen swamp on which it was built. Much of it has burned or rotted away, but recent work by Parks Canada to restore its most famous buildings has helped preserve the history of the gold rush.

The same cannot be said of most of the communities along the river, such as Fortymile, which have fallen into disrepair. The river itself, empty of steamboats, has given way to the Alaska Highway as the main thoroughfare to the goldfields.

But men still mine placer gold along the famous old creeks. New and more sophisticated mining methods, together with the higher price of gold, have made it practical to seek and find buried treasure in the old workings. Some of these have been picked over two or three times and are still yielding a profit.

The story of the great gold rush is very much a story of human greed and human folly, as it is also a story of high adventure and occasional heroism.

To many men, the gold was like a drug. They could not get enough of it, and they had to give it away in order to get more. One of the lessons of the great stampede is that sudden riches—the pot of gold at the end of the proverbial rainbow—cannot by themselves bring happiness.

Poor men who scrambled all their lives to make a place for themselves in the world found it difficult to bear the weight of the wealth that was thrust upon them. For two or three years, the Kings of the Klondike had a wonderful time spending their money. But most of them ended up as they had begun.

Few of the Klondike Kings ever achieved the immortality of a place name. There are no references to Tom Lippy, Big Alex, or even Swiftwater Bill on the buildings that remain and no plaques to commemorate their passing.

But William Ogilvie is remembered. An Ogilvie Bridge crosses the Klondike River not far from Bonanza Creek. The Ogilvie Mountains can easily be seen from the hills above Dawson. And Ogilvie's original office, the oldest building in Dawson, still stands at the corner of Church and Front. Known for years as the Yukon Hotel, it has been restored by the Heritage Canada Foundation.

The story of Ogilvie and his chainman, Dick Lowe, underlines the lesson of the great stampede. Lowe, as we have seen, died broke and unhappy. Ogilvie, who never made a nickel from Klondike gold, retired to Ottawa, lived out the rest of his life with his family on a government pension, wrote a book about his experiences, and never suffered a moment's regret.

Ogilvie's legacy was greater than that of those he helped to riches. He surveyed the border between Alaska and the Yukon. He laid out much of the city of Dawson. He untangled the mess on the Bonanza claims. He became the second commissioner of the territory—a job equal to that of premier. William Ogilvie died a respected public servant. In a very real sense, he was an uncrowned King of the Klondike.

INDEX

"Sandy's first loaf" is the name given by photographer H. J. Woodside to this picture of prospectors near Teslin Lake, BC. Old prospectors, men who had spent their lives searching for gold in Canada's North and elsewhere, were often called "sourdoughs" after the kind of bread they baked. The men used fermented dough in place of yeast to make bread.

(PA-016141, LIBRARY AND ARCHIVES CANADA)

BEFORE THE GOLD RUSH

CONTENTS

The Trail of Gold

ARTHUR HARPER STUDIED HIS ARROWSMITH'S MAP OF BRITISH NORTH
AMERICA AND ASKED HIMSELF A QUESTION: WHY SHOULD THE TRAIL OF GOLD
THAT HE HAD BEEN FOLLOWING SINCE THE 1850S STOP AT BRITISH COLUMBIA'S
NORTHERN BORDER?

He was a long-time prospector, an Irishman with a square face, shrewd
eyes, and a great beard that would soon turn snow white and give him the
look of a frontier patriarch. He was also a veteran of two British Columbia
gold rushes, first to the Fraser River in the 1850s, and later to the wide-open
Cariboo goldfields in the 1860s.

It seemed to Harper that, if the run of gold stretched from Mexico to
British Columbia, it should continue north beyond the horizon.

Beyond the horizon he went, leaving the Cariboo country and pushing
down the Peace River in canoes hacked out of cottonwood poplar trunks.
With five gallons (22.5 l) of strong rum and five cronies, he followed the line
of mountains on their long northward curve across the Arctic Circle and
into Alaska.

The author of this book was raised in a house on Harper Street in
Dawson. Harper's name and those of other pioneers are still faintly remembered along the Yukon. He was the first of a new breed of adventurer-
explorer, tough, honest, hard-working, far-seeing; men who broke trail for
the stampede that followed; men who were leaders rather than followers.

Harper and his kind were loners. They lived with solitude and thrived
on it. When Arthur Harper started out for the Yukon, he had no idea what
he would find or where the river would take him. In the civilized world, the
very name "Yukon" meant nothing. It lay far beyond the mists of the North,
vast and totally unknown.

Without men like Harper, the stampede to the goldfields of the Klondike could scarcely have been possible. He was the first of the trailblazers, and it is fitting enough that his name should be on a two-block gravel roadway overlooking the river that was his personal highway. Fitting, yes, but scarcely generous. I lived on Harper Street but had no idea who Harper was. The schoolbooks I studied did not mention him.

Harper was right about the run of gold. But it did not begin in the mountains of Mexico; it began much farther south. A glittering trail ran up the mountain spine of two continents from the Peruvian Andes to the Bering Sea.

There was gold everywhere in those mountains, and over a period of three centuries men and women had searched for it—Andean Indians, Spanish *conquistadors*, American frontiersmen, and ordinary prospectors like Arthur Harper. Much of the history of the New World has been shaped by this search for hidden treasure.

The Indians of the Peruvian Andes were among the first to find it. They learned that gold did not tarnish; it could easily be melted down and reshaped for jewellery, masks, and headpieces. By the time the white men arrived in South America, the successors to those first Indians—the people of the Inca—were rich in gold. That was their downfall.

When the Spanish reached the high Andes, they plundered the Inca gold and killed and enslaved the Indians. They searched far and wide for the fabled City of Gold, the lair of the Golden Man—El Dorado. Somewhere, they believed, it lay hidden in the vastness of the snow-capped peaks. They never found it, but they brought the riches of the Andes back to Spain in galleons loaded with bullion.

The golden trail led north to Mexico and the Sierra Madré in the land of the Aztecs and then north again to the former Spanish colony of California. It was the search for California's gold that opened the American West. In 1849 thousands of gold seekers trekked across the empty plains to California. Many moved on north, seeking gold in the streams that ran down the flanks of the Rockies in Colorado and South Dakota. That feverish search spawned Wild West towns with such names as Deadwood and Leadville and Wild West characters like Wild Bill Hickok.

Again the trail led north to the colony of British Columbia. In 1857 men

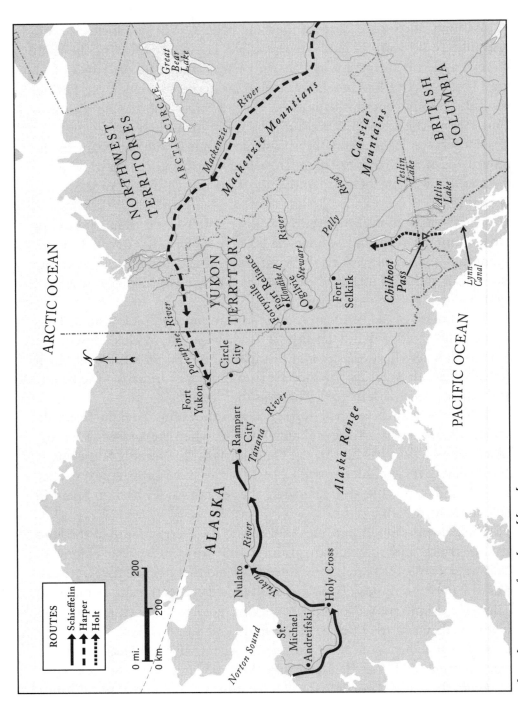

ROUTES
Schieffelin
Harper
Holt

ARCTIC OCEAN

NORTHWEST TERRITORIES

Great Bear Lake

ARCTIC CIRCLE

Mackenzie River

Mackenzie Mountians

Cassiar Mountains

BRITISH COLUMBIA

Teslin Lake

Atlin Lake

Pelly River

Stewart River

Ogilvie River

Klondike R.

Fortymile R.

Fort Reliance

Fort Selkirk

Chilkoot Pass

Lynn Canal

YUKON TERRITORY

Porcupine River

Fort Yukon

Circle City

Rampart City

Tanana River

Alaska Range

ALASKA

Nulato

Yukon River

Holy Cross

St. Michael

Andreifski

Norton Sound

PACIFIC OCEAN

200
200
0 mi.
0 km

The Yukon River Before the Gold Rush

like Arthur Harper rushed to the sandbars of the Fraser River to find more gold, and then north again, following the golden highway to the Cariboo country and the boomtown of Barkerville. A decade later the lure of gold took them even farther north to the Cassiar Mountains on the very rim of the sub-Arctic.

Beyond that lay the valley of the Yukon, unknown and unexplored. But it would be only a matter of time before more prospectors, following the golden spine of the mountains, burst into the great valleys on the ceaseless search for hidden treasure.

Some found what they were seeking. For all along the 2,200-mile (3,500-km) Yukon River there was gold in great quantities. It was hidden in the bottom of ancient creekbeds and in the sands of the smaller river deltas and even high on the benchland above the valleys that marked the pathways of ancient watercourses.

The gold came from the mountains. Eons before, it had bubbled up out of the ground in molten form when the mountains themselves were created. Now the gold was dust and nuggets.

The gold came from the mountains. Eons before, it had bubbled up out of the ground in molten form when the mountains themselves were created. Now the gold was dust and nuggets. Ceaseless erosion—boulder grating on boulder, gravel grinding against gravel, sand scouring sand—had ground down the original deposits.

That process lasted five million years. The metals that had boiled up through the cracks in the Earth's crust were shaved and chiselled away, reduced to muds and clays to be borne off with the current toward the sea. Even the veins of gold that streaked the mountain cores were sandpapered into dust and flour.

The gold did not reach the sea, for it was too heavy. The finest gold was carried lightly on the crest of mountain torrents until it reached the more leisurely Yukon River, where it sank and was caught in the sandbars at the mouths of the tributary streams.

The coarser gold did not move that distance. As soon as the speed of the current dropped, it was trapped in the crevices of bedrock, where nothing could dislodge it.

There it remained over the years, hidden by a blanket of muck growing ever deeper. Thus it lay scattered for the full length of the river—on the hills and in the sandbars, in steep ravines and broad valleys, in underground channels of white gravel, in clefts thirty feet (9 m) beneath the mosses, and in outcroppings poking from the grasses high up on the headland.

There was gold in a dozen tributary rivers that flowed into the Yukon and in a hundred creeks that flowed into these rivers. This veinwork of running water drained 330,000 miles (528,000 km) of streams, creeks, and rivers, stretching from British Columbia to the Bering Sea. There was gold in Atlin Lake at the very head of the river, and there was gold more than two thousand miles (3,200 km) to the northwest in the sand of the beaches on Norton Sound into which the same river empties.

There was gold everywhere. And where there is gold there are always men to seek it. Long before the beginning of the great stampede that we now know as the Klondike Gold Rush, a trickle of men was coming over the mountains, looking for gold along the river. They could not know that hidden in a small salmon stream, not far from the Alaska-Yukon border, gold lay more thickly than in any other creek, river, or sandbar in the whole of the Yukon. But, with the optimism of the true prospector, each knew that somewhere a vast golden treasure lay hidden. And so they travelled north, each hoping that he would be lucky enough to find it.

CHAPTER ONE

The River

MORE THAN HALF A CENTURY BEFORE THE GREAT KLONDIKE STAMPEDE, THERE
WERE WHISPERS OF GOLD SOMEWHERE ALONG A MYSTERIOUS RIVER THAT LED
INTO THE DARK HEART OF THE GREAT ALASKA-YUKON PENINSULA.

The whispers were little more than murmurs, and they fell at first on
Russian ears, for the Russians then owned Alaska. Russian traders had reached
the mouth of the great river, which the Loucheaux Indians called "Yukon,"
or *Yukunn-ah* ("Great River"), in 1834, but they didn't care about gold any
more than did the Native peoples who lived along the river's banks, fishing
for salmon.

But the whispers were heard in Sitka, the Russian capital of Alaska, situated on an island in the Pacific along that strip of coastal land known as
the Panhandle. This was the headquarters of Alexander Baranov, known as
the Lord of Alaska, who had been sent by the Czars to gather a fortune in
furs to enrich the imperial family. In these godforsaken surroundings,
Baranov managed to live like a prince—surrounded by fine books, costly
paintings, and brilliantly costumed officers and women.

Baranov was after seals, not gold. To his Russian-American fur company, they represented a true fortune. The last thing he wanted was a gold
rush—a horde of tough American and British prospectors trampling into
Russian territory and ruining his monopoly. When one of the Russians babbled drunkenly of gold, Baranov, so legend has it, ordered him shot.

When the traders of the Hudson's Bay Company entered the Yukon valley in the 1840s, they too heard whispers of gold along the river. They built
two trading posts on the Yukon. The first—Fort Yukon—was situated at
the mouth of the Porcupine, where the great river makes its majestic curve
over the Arctic Circle. Then they built a second—Fort Selkirk—some six

hundred miles (960 km) upstream, at the point where the Yukon is joined by the muddy Pelly.

This was unmapped, unexplored land. Nobody had yet travelled the full length of the great water highway. The Hudson's Bay traders knew so little about the geography that they didn't realize both forts were on the same river.

Nor did they realize that Fort Yukon was actually deep in Russian territory. They were far from civilization; their crude maps were inaccurate; and nobody could be sure exactly where the boundary was that divided Russian Alaska from British North America.

They had heard whispers of gold, but they took no action. Robert Campbell, the chief trader at Fort Selkirk, actually found traces of it. He wasn't the least interested. Like Baranov, he felt that furs were the real treasure.

We know that another Hudson's Bay clerk wrote home to Toronto reporting that an Anglican missionary, Archdeacon McDonald, had seen so much gold in a small river not far away that he could have gathered it in a spoon. But the minister was not interested in gold either. His task was to translate prayer books for the Loucheaux. As for the clerk, he wrote that he had "often wished to go but can never find the time." Perhaps he was lucky that the gold fever, which destroyed so many men, passed him by.

In 1867, the year of Canadian Confederation, the United States bought Alaska from the Russians. The Americans drove the Hudson's Bay Company out of Fort Yukon, and the Chilkoot Indians, a war-like band, came in from the ocean and drove the company out of Fort Selkirk.

But there were still wanderers who had a burning desire to seek gold. The new territory of Alaska was both a land to conquer and also a wilderness to which a man could flee. The territory was shaped like a kitchen pot—a long strip of coastal land, the Panhandle, was attached to the main body of the Alaska Peninsula, bordering on the Pacific territories of British Columbia. In 1880, at a point midway down this Panhandle, hardrock gold was discovered, and the mining town of Juneau sprang up.

There are two kinds of gold in the northwest. Hardrock gold is discovered in veins hidden in the mountains. It must be blasted free from tunnels driven deep into the rock. To get at this gold, a lucky prospector had to raise large sums of money to form a company to buy the expensive equipment needed to mine the veins.

"Placer gold," or "free gold," was created by the erosion of the centuries. Ground into nuggets and dust by wind and water, it is found deep beneath the soil in the bedrock of ancient watercourses. A single man, if he is industrious enough, can find and mine this gold by sinking a shaft, hauling up the "pay dirt," and sluicing the lighter clays and sands away, leaving the gold behind.

Juneau served as a springboard to the interior Yukon valley. In 1880, when gold was discovered there, the wanderers and adventurers, the Indian-fighters and the frontiersmen of the American West—men who could not sit still—headed north.

These prospectors were men who had spent most of their lives seeking gold. They'd come up through Arizona, Colorado, Nevada, and Idaho, leaving behind names like Virginia City, Cripple Creek, and Tombstone. They had moved up the wrinkled hide of British Columbia, through the sombre canyons of the Fraser and the rolling grasslands of the Cariboo to the snowfields of the Cassiars.

They came at first in twos and threes, and they carried little more than a rucksack, a gold-pan, a short-stemmed shovel, and a vial of mercury to separate the gold from the lesser sands. They lived on beans and tea and bacon. Most were men fleeing ahead of civilization. Whenever they struck it rich, a circus of camp followers crowded in behind them—saloon keepers, dance-hall girls, gamblers, vigilantes, and tenderfeet.

And so, as the horde grew larger and the pioneers moved farther north, valleys became industrial bees' nests, and meadows were transformed into brawling shack towns. The sighing of the wind and the roaring of the river were drowned by the tuneless scraping of dance-hall violins and the crash of butchered timber.

Finally, like the forward patrols of a mighty army, the first prospectors reached the last frontier. In the 1870s and 1880s, they began to move into the Yukon valley.

The Yukon is the fifth largest river in North America. Unlike most great watercourses, it begins just fifteen miles (24 km) from the saltwater of the Pacific Ocean on the eastern side of the great Coastal Mountain wall and then travels on a 2,200-mile (3,500-km) search for that same saltwater. That search takes it on a winding journey across the face of Alaska and the Yukon.

It rises as a trickle in the mountain snowfields that feed the green alpine lakes. From there it pushes incessantly through barriers of rock flowing to the northwest, until it crosses the Arctic Circle. There it falters as if unsure of itself and hesitates on the circle's edge, only to change its mind and turn in its tracks. Now it doubles back, plunging southwestward, defying every obstacle until it spreads itself wide in a mighty delta to pour into the cold waters of Norton Sound across from the easternmost tip of Siberia.

This awkward, roundabout route is the result of the odd tilting of the interior plateau. But without that long and aimless coil of the great river, there would be no water highway into the heart of the northwest.

As with the river, so with the men who sought the gold. They too arrived by roundabout routes. They too often moved hesitantly. And like the river whose quest for saltwater seems futile, their quest for gold brought early disappointment. Yet in the end, like the river, some of them found what they were seeking.

CHAPTER TWO

The Pioneers

THE FIRST PROSPECTORS ENTERED THE GREAT ALASKA-YUKON PENINSULA FROM THREE DIFFERENT DIRECTIONS. THREE ARE FAMOUS BECAUSE THEY WERE THE FIRST.

In 1873, as we have seen, Arthur Harper entered from northern Canada. He had travelled in a roundabout route north and west from the Peace and the Mackenzie River valleys in a wide arc before he reached his goal.

In 1878 George Holt took the shortest route. He came directly in from the seacoast, having climbed the Chilkoot Pass, which at the time was the only known gap in the mountains that screened off the interior plateau from the sea.

In 1882 Ed Schieffelin took the water route by boat, all the way around to the Bering Sea opposite Siberia. He built a second boat—a tiny, stern-wheeled steamboat—and moved up the long water highway of the Yukon River itself.

Harper's name is still remembered in the Yukon. He was, after all, the first white prospector to enter the Yukon valley. For two thousand miles (3,200 km), he and his party had paddled and prospected the creeks on both sides of the great divide that separates the Yukon from the valley of the Mackenzie. It was a back-breaking adventure. They were forced to drag their boats over mountain divides and haul them through the shallow waters of frothing streams—their feet half frozen, their limbs ulcerated from the wet and the cold. But they found nothing.

At last they reached the Yukon River at the point where it coils across the Arctic Circle. For the next quarter of a century, the river was Harper's highway—and he had it all to himself. He roamed it ceaselessly, seeking gold in every stream, testing the gravels, and panning the sandbars, always hoping to find the treasure yet never succeeding.

We know now that the gold was under his nose, but he missed it. He explored four rivers that later yielded fortunes—the Stewart, the Fortymile, the Tanana, and the Klondike. But he didn't make the longed-for discovery.

By the time the gold was discovered and the stampede had begun, it was too late for Arthur Harper. Suffering from tuberculosis, he headed back to the sunlit valleys of Arizona, and there, at the height of the gold rush, he died. A street in Dawson City bears his name.

George Holt didn't find any gold either. Now a vague and shadowy figure, scarcely more than a name in the early history of Alaska, he is remembered for a remarkable feat. He was the first white man to get through the massive wall of angry peaks that seals off the Yukon valley from the north Pacific. These mountains were guarded by three thousand Natives, and no one knows how he got past them.

In this mountain wall, a tiny notch had been ripped out by the shrieking winds. It could be reached only after a thousand-foot (350-m) climb up a thirty-five-degree slope that was strewn with immense boulders. For eight months out of twelve, it was caked with solid ice. Glaciers of bottle green overhung it like huge icicles ready to burst at the end of summer. Avalanches thundered down from the mountains in the spring. In the winter, the snow fell so thickly it could reach a depth of seventy feet (21 m). This forbidding gap was called the Chilkoot Pass. Holt was the first white man to see it. Twenty years later thousands would climb it—over and over again—in a new search for gold.

This was the gateway to the unknown Yukon valley, but the Chilkoot Indians guarded it jealously. These were men of immense strength, squat, sturdy, and heavy-shouldered, able to lug a two-hundred-pound (90-kg) pack across the mountains without a rest. They controlled all the trade with the Han Indians of the interior—a people whom they dominated. It was these Chilkoots who had driven the powerful Hudson's Bay Company from Fort Selkirk back in 1852.

Somehow—we don't know how—Holt got past this human obstacle. He scaled the pass and emerged into that dark land where the Yukon has its beginning. In 1878 he came out with two small nuggets that an Indian from Alaska had given him.

Holt's stories of gold, much of it the result of his own active imagination, excited the interest of newcomers at Sitka. By this time, the old Russian capital was teeming with gold seekers who had originally come north to seek their fortune in the Cassiar Mountains of British Columbia. Now Holt had suggested new fields to conquer. And so twenty prospectors, protected by a U.S. gunboat, headed for the foot of the mountains. There they fired a few blank rounds from a Gatling gun, enough to convince the Indians that the pass should be opened.

In this way, the dam was broken. From 1880 onward, a trickle of men began to cross the divide. The Indians didn't suffer. They charged a fee to pack the white man's outfits over the mountains, and, being clever traders, they always got what the traffic would bear. By the time of the Klondike stampede, they had raised the price to a dollar a pound (0.45 kg). Thus, without ever sinking a pan into the creekbeds of the Yukon, the Chilkoots grew rich.

George Holt, having got past one barrier, now tried to get past another. He moved west to wilder land to invade the copper country of the Chettyna in southern Alaska. The Indians there had no intention of letting him through.

George Holt, having got past one barrier, now tried to get past another. He moved west to wilder land to invade the copper country of the Chettyna in southern Alaska. The Indians there had no intention of letting him through. They had already killed three men. Poor Holt made the fourth.

By this time, some of the prospectors who had followed Holt into the Yukon interior were beginning to find flour gold in the sandbars of the Yukon. Flour gold is just what it sounds like—gold that has been ground into a dust so delicate that it can almost float on the surface of the water.

Placer gold is moved downstream by the force of the rushing water. The coarser gold soon sinks and is caught in the crevices of the bedrock, but the power of the water continues to move the finer gold. By the time a creek enters the Yukon River, only the finest gold—the flour gold—is left to settle into the sandbars at the mouth.

It was not easy to separate this very fine gold from the sands that surrounded it, but some prospectors succeeded. Rumours of their finds began to filter down through the Rocky Mountain mining camps of the western

United States. By 1882 these stories reached the ears of a gaunt scarecrow of a prospector named Ed Schieffelin.

This was no penniless gold seeker. In the Apache country of Arizona, Schieffelin had discovered a mountain of silver and founded the town of Tombstone. This was the same community in which Wyatt Earp and the Clanton Brothers would soon shoot it out at the O.K. Corral.

Schieffelin was worth a million dollars, but he didn't look like a millionaire. His beard and his glossy black hair hung long in ringlets, and his grey, ghost eyes had the faraway look of a long-time prospector.

He had been a prospector all his life, panning gold as a child in Oregon and running off at the age of twelve to join a gold stampede. In the generation that followed, he was in almost every boom camp in the west. He didn't need to look for treasure, but the fever was in him. He wanted to repeat his success in Alaska.

Like Harper, Schieffelin had studied the maps and arrived at an odd theory. He believed that a great mineral belt girdled the world from Cape Horn to Asia and down through the western mountains of North America to the Andes. As we know, he was partially right. Somewhere in Alaska, he thought, the golden highway ought to cross the Yukon valley. He meant to find it.

And so, in the spring of 1883, he and his small party arrived at St. Michael, the old Russian port on the Bering Sea just to the north of the Yukon's mouth. There he built his tiny steamboat, the *New Racket*, and set off up the unexplored river.

See him now, puffing slowly around the coast of Norton Sound and into the maze of the great Yukon delta, where the channels fan out for sixty-five miles (104 km), where the banks are grey with silt, and where long-legged cranes stalk the marshes.

Here were islands that had never been counted. Here a man could lose himself forever in half a hundred twisting channels. At this point, Schieffelin was more than two thousand miles (3,200 km) from the Chilkoot Pass, which Holt had crossed five years before. Before him lay the unknown.

The little boat chugged out into the river proper. This was a land with terraced valleys, sleeping glaciers, and high clay banks pocked by swallows' nests and bright with brier rose and bluebell—an empty land of legend and mystery. So little was known about it that, in London, globes of the world were still being issued showing the Yukon River flowing north into the Arctic Ocean instead of west into the Bering Sea.

Many stories were told and believed of this mysterious country—stories of prehistoric mammoths who roamed the hills with jets of live steam issuing from their nostrils and of the immense bears that prowled the mountain peaks in endless circles, because their limbs were longer on one side than on the other.

To Schieffelin, the broad Yukon seemed endless. It wound on and on, tawny and cold, gnawing through walls of granite and wriggling past mountain ranges, spilling out over miles of flatland at one point, squeezed between black pillars of rock at another.

Once in a while, tiny pinpoints of civilization broke the monotony of the grey-green forest land—deserted Russian missions and Indian graves on the high bank above. For a thousand miles (1,600 km), the little steamer struggled against the current, working its way deeper and deeper into unexplored country—past Burning Mountain, a smoking seam of coal; past the Palisades, cliff-like castles of rock that guarded the mouth of the Tanana River; and finally into the brooding hills known as the Lower Ramparts, where the river channels are gathered into a single rustling gorge.

Here, poking among the mosses on the rock, Ed Schieffelin found some specks of gold, and he was convinced he had stumbled upon the mineral belt he believed encircled the Earth. But there was frost in the air, and Schieffelin was accustomed to the fierce Arizona sun. The bleakness of the Arctic summer had already discouraged him. He decided that mining could never pay along the Yukon.

Back he went, without exploring the rest of the river that drifted for another thousand miles to the gateway of the Chilkoot. And so, as it had eluded Harper and Holt, the gold of the Yukon eluded the gaunt Schieffelin.

For the rest of his life, he would never cease to prospect. In fact he was still seeking a new mine when he died of a heart attack in front of his cabin in the forests of Oregon. The year was 1897, and the world was buzzing with tales of a fortune to be found in the land he had dismissed as frozen waste.

CHAPTER THREE

The Traders

FOR FIVE YEARS AFTER SCHIEFFELIN LEFT THE YUKON, NOTHING HAPPENED.

The land remained silent and empty. Small groups of prospectors continued to dribble over the Chilkoot Pass to test the sandbars along the headwaters. But for eighteen hundred miles (2,880 km), the river was almost untravelled. The only boats on its surface were those of the Natives and of the occasional trader working on a commission for the Alaska Commercial Company, the descendant of the old Russian-American Fur Company.

That's how Arthur Harper scratched out a living. Unable to find a fortune in the shifting sands of the little creeks, Harper had taken to trading tea and flour in return for furs that he trapped along the river. But Harper is remembered in the Yukon to this day because he opened up the Yukon valley to those who followed seeking gold.

Two joined him. They were a strange pair. One was a lean, wiry little thong of a man, the other a six-foot giant with a barrel chest.

The little man's name was Al Mayo. There is a town named after him in the Yukon. He was a one-time circus acrobat driven north by wanderlust, given to practical jokes, and blessed with a dry wit. He used to claim in his later years that he had been in the country so long that, when he first arrived, the Yukon River was a small creek and the Chilkoot Pass a hole in the ground.

The big man's name was LeRoy Napoleon McQuesten, but everybody called him plain "Jack." A ruddy man with a flowing blond moustache, he had all the restlessness of his breed. He had been a farmer in Maine, an Indian-fighter in the West, and a gold hunter on the Fraser River.

Just as Harper was a frustrated prospector, McQuesten was a frustrated voyageur. He had one fierce ambition: he wanted so badly to become a voyageur that he gave himself a course in physical training. He would need that if he was going to perform the incredible feats of strength and endurance for which the early voyageurs were noted.

He signed on with the Hudson's Bay Company in the Athabasca country, only to discover, to his disappointment, that he could not handle the crushing two-hundred-pound (90-kg) loads that his French-Canadian companions hoisted so easily on their backs. So he drifted across the mountains into the Yukon valley, and there he met Harper and Mayo.

The three men became partners. For more than fifteen years, they were alone in the land. The river was their private highway. They could drift down it for a thousand miles (1,600 km) without seeing another white face. In fact McQuesten once recalled he'd gone six years without tasting flour.

They all took Indian wives, but they did not resemble the so-called squaw men who were looked down upon by their fellows. Their wives and families lived in handsome homes with square-cut logs and with neat vegetable gardens at the rear. The wives were partners in a true sense. The children were sent out to be educated in private schools in the United States. Years later, when McQuesten retired, he took his Indian wife to California, where she ran the big family home in Berkeley. When he died, she managed his estate and continued as the head of the family.

The country changed these three. They had been restless and temperamental. But over the long decades, they had developed a serenity that became the envy of those who met them. Frederick Schwatka, a U.S. cavalry officer who was the first man to explore the Yukon River for its full length, came upon McQuesten in 1883. He watched in admiration as the trader bargained for hours with Indians, unruffled by the endless discussions that Schwatka said "would have put Job in a frenzy."

McQuesten, Mayo, and Harper never presented a bill, yet they were seldom short-changed. Once, when a cargo of goods arrived, and a group of miners became impatient for provisions, Harper told them simply to help themselves, keep their own accounts, and hand them in at their leisure. The only missing item was six cans of condensed milk.

They built their first post at Fort Reliance, only a few miles from the mouth of the Thron-diuck, or Klondike, River. It became the focus for future river settlements. Several neighbouring rivers took their names from the distance that separated them from that post. Thus, the Fortymile and the Twelvemile Rivers were named because they joined the Yukon that distance downstream from Fort Reliance. The Sixtymile was so called because it was sixty miles (96 km) upstream from the fort. Later on the towns established at the mouths of these rivers took the same names.

It is ironic that this first river settlement should have been so close to the stream that came to be called Klondike—strange because, though they hunted and prospected along its valley, none of the partners was destined to grow wealthy on Klondike gold. They had come into the country to look for gold, but now they were traders, and gold no longer excited them.

Perhaps this was just as well. Most of those who chased gold in the Klondike in the years that followed died in poverty. But when the madness struck, these three kept their heads. When they died, it was with the respect of everyone who had known them.

In the words of one Alaska Commercial Company employee, they were "typically frontiersmen, absolutely honest, without a semblance of fear of anything, and to a great extent childlike in their implicit faith in human nature, looking on their fellow pioneers as being equally as honest as themselves." This could not have been said of many who came later.

They were "typically frontiersmen, absolutely honest, without a semblance of fear of anything, and to a great extent childlike in their implicit faith in human nature, looking on their fellow pioneers as being equally as honest as themselves."

These men, and a fourth named Joseph Ladue, who arrived a decade later, were the true pioneers and true founders of both the Yukon Territory of Canada and the U.S. State of Alaska. Without their presence, the series of events that led to the great Klondike discovery would not have been possible. Without the string of posts they set up along the Yukon, the early exploration of the river country could not have taken place.

It was they who guided the hands of the prospectors. It was they who outfitted them without demanding instant cash—and sent them off to promising sections of the country. They followed up each discovery by laying out a townsite and erecting and building a general store.

Their little steamboat, the *New Racket*, which they had bought from

Schieffelin, was their lifeline to the outside world. They made a casual arrangement with the great Alaska Commercial Company in San Francisco. In the early years, they were on its payroll, but they remained free to prospect if they wished. Later they operated as independent contractors, buying their goods from the company but trading on their own.

Sometimes they worked together as partners, sometimes separately. There were other traders scattered along the river working with similar arrangements with the company. But it was these men, far more than the others, who were responsible for the mining development in the Yukon and the first of the famous mining camps.

It is not always realized that a series of smaller gold rushes into the Yukon valley took place before the great Klondike stampede. In fact Dawson City was preceded by several mining camps that sprang up along the river in the decade before the great strike. Since all the gold along the Yukon was placer gold—the kind that could be mined by any man with a shovel and a pan and a strong back—it was attractive to the penniless men who made their way north from the civilized world.

By 1886 there were about two hundred miners working their way for three hundred miles (480 km) down the Yukon, from the Chilkoot Pass to the mouth of the Stewart River. In a single year, these men panned out $100,000 worth of fine gold from the sandbars, a sum equal to at least a million today.

McQuesten and his partners built a trading post at the Stewart, suspecting that the human flow would increase. But McQuesten was worried. There wasn't enough food in all of the Yukon to feed the men who would be attracted to the Stewart. He decided to go to San Francisco to order more supplies and equipment from the Alaska Commercial Company.

That winter Arthur Harper persuaded two prospectors to try the waters of the Fortymile River, which joined the Yukon another hundred miles (160 km) farther downstream. Here they found the gold that had eluded Harper— good coarse gold that rattled in the pan, the kind that every miner seeks. At once the men along the Stewart deserted their diggings and flocked to the new strike.

Harper was in a panic. He knew what was coming. As soon as the news leaked back up the river and across the mountain barrier to the outside world, hundreds of men would tumble over the peaks and pour down to the new diggings on the crest of the spring torrents. There certainly wasn't food enough in the land to supply this horde. Harper knew he must get word of the new strike out to McQuesten to increase his order. Otherwise there would be starvation along the Yukon.

He felt like a man in a soundproof prison. To all intents, the interior of the northwest was sealed off from the world by winter. It was virtually impossible to get outside. He might as well be living on the moon.

The nearest point of civilization was John Healy's trading post on Dyea Inlet on the far side of the Chilkoot. But in between lay an untravelled wilderness—a jungle of forest, rock, snow, and mountains. Few men had ever made it in the winter. Who would carry Harper's message?

Of all people, a steamboat man named Tom Williams volunteered. He had no experience in "mushing," as the pioneers called it. But he went anyway with one Indian companion on a terrifying journey.

The two men plunged for five hundred miles (800 km) over the hummocks of river ice and the corpses of fallen trees, through the cold tangle of the Yukon forest, and up the slippery flanks of the mountains. By the time they reached the Chilkoot, their rations were gone and their dogs dead of cold, hunger, and fatigue.

When they reached the top of the pass, a blizzard was raging. Travel became impossible. They clawed a cave out of the snow and crouched in it, their fingers, faces, and feet blackened by frostbite. Their food was gone. They only had a few mouthfuls of dry flour left to keep them alive.

When the flour ran out, the Indian hoisted the exhausted Williams onto his back and stumbled down the slope of the pass until he could carry him no farther. He dropped him into the snow and staggered on until he reached Sheep Camp—a long-time stopping point on the edge of the treeline. We do not know the name of this enterprising Native—nor his history. Nobody bothered to set it down, for in those days the Indians were seen as faceless creatures of the forest—like the caribou or the black bears.

It was now March of 1887. A group of prospectors camped in the shelter of the mountains, hoping for the storm to subside, watched in astonishment as the figure of the Indian loomed out of the swirling snow. They followed him back up the mountain and helped to bring Williams down to Sheep Camp, where they revived him with hot soup.

The Indian borrowed a sled and dragged his companion twenty-six miles (42 km) down the trail to Dyea Inlet. Here the two men finally reached the shelter of the trading post run by the one-time Montana sheriff named John J. Healy. Williams lived for two days, and the men who crowded around his deathbed had only one question: Why on Earth had he made the trip?

It was the Indian's answer that electrified them. He reached into a sack of beans on Healy's counter and flung a handful onto the floor.

"Gold," he said. "All same like this!"

CHAPTER FOUR

A Community of Hermits

ALONG THE HIGH BANK AT THE POINT WHERE THE FORTYMILE RIVER JOINS THE
YUKON—ON THE VERY EDGE OF THE ALASKA-YUKON BORDER—A WEIRD AND
LONELY CANADIAN VILLAGE STRAGGLED INTO BEING AS A RESULT OF TOM
WILLIAMS'S DYING MESSAGE.

This was Fortymile, named for the river that flowed into the Yukon
about forty miles (64 km) downstream from Fort Reliance. It's hard for us
to understand today how far it was from civilization.

For eight months out of twelve, its residents lived as if in a vacuum,
sealed off from the world. The nearest outfitting port was San Francisco—
almost five thousand water miles (8,000 km) away. The only links with the
sea were two tiny sternwheelers: the *New Racket*, owned by Harper and his
partners, and the Alaska Commercial Company's *Arctic*, built in 1889.

There was only time for these boats to attempt one summer trip
upstream from the old Russian seaport of St. Michael, not far from the
river's mouth on the Bering Sea. And sometimes even that wasn't time
enough.

On her first voyage, the *Arctic* was damaged and could not bring supplies to Fortymile. The company sent Indian runners sixteen hundred miles
(2,560 km) upriver to the settlement to warn the miners that they faced
starvation. With no supplies arriving from the outside world, they would
have to escape from the Yukon valley.

As the October snows drifted down from the dark skies, the residents of
Fortymile pressed aboard the little *New Racket*. The tiny vessel made a brave
attempt to reach St. Michael before the river froze, but she was caught in the
ice floes 190 miles (304 km) short of her goal. The starving passengers had

to trudge the rest of the way on foot. Those who stayed behind in Fortymile spent a hungry winter. One man, in fact, lived for nine months on a steady diet of flapjacks.

The only winter route to the outside world was the dreadful trek upstream to the Chilkoot—more than six hundred miles (960 km) away. After Williams's death, very few people had the courage to try it. Four men did attempt it in 1893, but they were forced to leave fifteen thousand dollars' worth of gold dust on the mountain slopes. They were so badly crippled by the shrieking winds and the intense cold that one died and another was disabled for life.

Why would anyone want to wall himself off from the world in a village of logs deep in the sub-Arctic wilderness? Who were they?

In one sense, they were men chasing a fortune—chasing it with such passion that it had brought them to the ends of the Earth. But there was more to it than that. They seemed more like men pursued than men pursuing. The truth is that if they searched for anything it was the right to be left alone.

Father William Judge, a Jesuit missionary in Alaska, described them as "men running away from civilization as it advanced westward—until they'd have no farther to go and so have to stop." Judge met one man who had been born in the United States so long ago that he had never seen a railway. He'd kept moving on ahead of the rails until he reached the banks of the Yukon.

There were veterans of the American Civil War in Fortymile and old Indian-fighters. There were younger sons, black sheep many of them, sent out from England with a bit of money to keep them away—people called them "remittance men." There were prospectors from the far west, many of whom had known each other in the various camps in the Black Hills of Idaho and in Colorado.

They were all nomads, stirred by a wanderlust that seized them at the slightest whisper of a new strike, no matter how flimsy the rumours were. Their natures were such that they each craved the widest possible freedom of action. And yet each was also disciplined by a code of friendship whose unwritten rules were as strict as any law.

Their nicknames, which were far commoner than real names, suggested that none of them was cut from the same cloth. Salt Water Jack, Big Dick, Squaw Cameron, Jimmy the Pirate, Muckskin Miller, Pete the Pig—that was how they were known. In the civilized world, they would have been thought of as very strange.

One man, known as the Old Maiden, carried fifty pounds (23 kg) of old newspapers about with him wherever he went. He said they were "handy to refer to when you get into an argument." Another was dubbed Cannibal Ike because he used to hack off great slabs of moose meat with his knife and stuff them raw into his mouth.

One man, known as the Old Maiden, carried fifty pounds (23 kg) of old newspapers about with him wherever he went. He said they were "handy to refer to when you get into an argument."

One cabin at Fortymile had walls almost as thin as paper because the owner kept chopping away at the logs to feed his fire. He said he did it to let in the light. In another cabin were three partners and a tame moose, which they treated as a house pet. Out on the river, on Liar's Island, a group of exiles whiled away the long winters telling tales that nobody really believed.

This strange little village of log cabins, at the point where the Fortymile River joins the Yukon, was a community of hermits. If the residents had one thing in common, it was the desire to be left alone.

"I feel so long dead and buried that I cannot think a short visit home, as from the grave, would be of much use," wrote William Bompas, a Church of England bishop who was stationed at Fortymile. Bompas was a Cambridge graduate who could read his Bible in Greek, Hebrew, and Syriac. He was the fourth son of a London lawyer.

The clergyman who preceded him had been driven mad by the practical jokes of the miners, but Bompas was too tough for that. He was a giant with a huge dome, hawk nose, piercing eyes, and a flowing beard. He baked his own bread, drank his sugarless coffee from an iron cup, ate from a tin plate with a knife his only utensil, slept in the corner of a boat or in a hole in the snow or on the floor of a log hut.

He took no holidays. His only furniture was a box he used for a seat. He had torn down the shelves and cupboards to make a coffin for a dead

Native, because lumber was so scarce. He thought nothing of making a present of his trousers to an unfortunate Indian who had no pants. The tough bishop mushed all the way home wearing only his red flannel underwear.

He had lived in isolation and was resigned to it. His wife was the daughter of a fashionable London doctor and had been brought up in Italy. When she finally joined him in 1892, they hadn't seen each other for five years. On those dark winter afternoons when she wasn't out on the trail with her husband, she sat quietly in the mission hall with its cotton-drill walls, reading the Italian poet Dante in the original Italian or playing on her little harmonium—that is, if the keys weren't frozen stiff.

Yet this frontier way of life was no more primitive than that of the others. Each miner lived with his partner in a murky, airless cabin whose windowpanes were made from untanned deerhide, white cotton canvas, or a row of empty pickle jars chinked with moss. Knives and forks were made of pieces of tin. Furniture was built from the stumps of trees. Four men often lived year in and year out in a space no more than eighteen feet (5.5 m) square.

Hanging above the red-hot sheet-iron stove, there was always a tin of fermented dough. It was used in place of yeast to make biscuits, bread, and flapjacks rise. That was the origin of the name "sourdough," which was applied to the pioneers in the Yukon to distinguish them from the newcomers—the tenderfeet or *cheechakos*.

Every morning the men left their cabins to crawl into the murky, constricted mine shafts. The mining in the sub-Arctic was unlike mining anywhere else in the world. For here the ground was permanently frozen and had to be thawed before the bedrock, which contained the gold, could be reached. This bedrock lay ten or twenty feet (3 to 6 m) below the surface.

To reach bedrock, the first miners let the sun do the work. That was a tedious, back-breaking process. Each day a few inches of thawed earth were scraped away. Each day the shaft in the permafrost grew a few inches deeper. An entire summer might pass before bedrock was reached.

Later on wood fires replaced the sun. The gold seekers lit them by night, removing the ashes and thawed earth each morning. The fires burned their way slowly down to form a shaft whose sides remained frozen as hard as granite.

The new method allowed miners to work all winter, choking and wheezing in smoky, ice-sheathed dungeons, far below the snowy surface of the ground. When they reached bedrock, they tunnelled this way and that, seeking the "pay streak" that marked an old creek channel. When they hit pay dirt, they hoisted it up the shaft with a windlass and a pail and piled it in a mound they called a "dump."

In the spring, when the ice broke in the creeks and water gushed down the hillsides, the miners built long spillways, or "sluice boxes," to copy the ancient action of nature. Gravel containing the pay dirt was shovelled into these boxes. As the water rushed through the gravel and sand, they were swept away by force of the tide. The gold, being nineteen times as heavy as water, was caught in the crossbars and in matting lying on the bottom. This is exactly what had happened in the creeks eons before, when the gold was caught in the crevices of the bedrock before the ancient streambeds were covered by an overlay of muck.

Every two or three days, the water was diverted from the sluice box, and then each miner panned the residue at the bottom in what became known as a "cleanup."

The entertainments that lightened this monotony were rare and primitive. One of the main amusements was a folk rite known in the slang of the day as a "squaw dance." Josiah Edward Spurr, a U.S. government geologist who visited Fortymile in the old days, has left a description of one of these affairs.

> We were attracted by a row of miners who were lined up in front of the saloon engaged in watching the door of a very large log cabin opposite, rather dilapidated with the windows broken in … They said there was going to be a dance, but when or how they did not seem to know …
>
> The evening wore on until ten o'clock, when in the dusk a stolid Indian woman with a baby in the blanket on her back, came cautiously around the corner, and with the peculiar long slouchy step of her kind, made for the cabin door, looking neither to the right nor to the left …
>
> She was followed by a dozen others, one far behind another,

each silent and unconcerned, and each with a baby upon her back. They sidled into the log cabin and sat down on the benches, where they also deposited their babies in a row: the little red people lay there very still, with wide eyes shut or staring, but never crying …

The mothers sat awhile looking at the ground on some one spot, then slowly lifted their heads to look at the miners who had slouched into the cabin after them—men fresh from the diggings, spoiling for excitement of any kind. Then a man with a dilapidated fiddle struck up a swinging, sawing melody, and in the intoxication of the moment some of the most reckless of the miners grabbed an Indian woman and began furiously swinging her around in a sort of waltz while the others crowded and looked on.

Little by little the dusk grew deeper, but candles were scarce and could not be afforded. The figures of the dancing couples grew more and more indistinct, and their faces became lost to view, while the sawing of the fiddle grew more and more rapid, and the dancing more excited. There was no noise, however; scarcely a sound save the fiddle and the shuffling of the feet over the floor of rough hewn logs; for the Indian women were as stolid as ever, and the miners could not speak the language of their partners. Even the lookers on said nothing, so that these silent dancing figures in the dusk made an almost weird effect.

One by one, however, the women dropped out, tired, picked up their babies and slouched off home, and the men slipped over to the saloon to have a drink before going to their cabins. Surely this squaw dance, as they call it, was one of the most peculiar balls ever seen …

CHAPTER FIVE

The Mounties Bring Order

As the years passed, a thin varnish of civilization began to spread over Fortymile. Some saloons had Chippendale chairs. Some stores even sold *pâté de foie gras*, tinned plum pudding, and other delicacies. Shakespeare clubs were formed to give play readings. A library opened; its shelves contained books on science and philosophy. A dressmaker arrived to fill the latest Paris fashions. An opera house was opened with a troupe of San Francisco dance-hall girls. There was even a cigar factory.

All these institutions were housed in log buildings strewn helter-skelter along the muddy bank above the Yukon and surrounded by a marshland that was littered with stumps, wood shavings, and tin cans.

There were ten saloons in Fortymile, around which the social life of the camp revolved. At steamboat time, the saloons served whisky at fifty cents a drink—heavily watered to make it last. For the rest of the year, they peddled hootchinoo, a vile mixture of molasses, sugar, and dried fruit, fermented with sourdough, flavoured with anything handy, distilled in an empty coal-oil can, and sometimes served hot, at fifty cents a drink. Hootchinoo was sometimes known as forty-rod whisky because it was supposed to kill a man at that distance. (A rod is about 5 m.)

There were strict unwritten rules in the saloons. For instance, a man who bought a drink had to buy for everybody in the house, even though the round might cost a hundred dollars. It was a deadly insult to refuse a drink under these circumstances, but a teetotaller could accept a fifty-cent cigar in its place.

Like everything else, hootch was paid for in gold dust. The prospector who flung his poke of dust on the bar always performed a gesture of turning his back while the amount was weighed out. To watch the weighing was to suggest that the bartender was crooked.

Fortymile thrived on these unwritten rules. It might be said that the community was run informally. There was no mayor or council. There were no judges or lawyers. There was no police, no jail, no written laws.

Yet the people stuck together. Nobody went hungry, though many were broke. Credit at Harper and McQuesten's store was unlimited. If a man had no money, he could still get an outfit without paying.

There were very few "bad men" in Fortymile. In a way, it was more of a Christian community than many towns in the outside world. Men shared their good fortune with their comrades. It was part of the code that he who struck a new creek spread the news to everybody. Each man's cabin was open to any passerby. The traveller could enter, eat what he needed, sleep in the absent owner's bed, and then go on his way. But he must clean up before he left, and he must leave a fresh supply of kindling. That was important. For this was a country in which a freezing man's life might depend on the speed with which he could light a fire.

There was another odd thing about Fortymile. It was inside the Canadian border, but it was really an American town. It got its supplies from the United States without customs payments, and the mail was sent out with U.S. stamps. Some of the mines were on Alaskan soil, and the community itself had all the characteristics of the Rocky Mountain mining camps of the American West.

It was from these parent communities that the tradition of the "miners' meeting" was borrowed. Here was an odd example of grassroots democracy that shows the very real difference between the Canadian and the American character and between the Canadian and the American legal systems.

The Americans were revolutionaries. They had separated from Europe as the result of a bloody war. They wanted to run all their own affairs from the ground up, and that was especially true on the frontier.

The Canadians, of course, had never known the bloodbath of revolution. More often they preferred to have law and order imposed from above—the North-West Mounted Police were a good example—rather than have it spring from the grassroots. That's why the Americans had a "Wild West" and the Canadians didn't.

In the three British Columbia gold rushes, police and courts of justice enforced a single set of laws in the British tradition. The mining law was the same everywhere. The gold commissioner—the man in charge of the camps—had absolute power. The lawlessness that was common in American mining history wasn't known in British Columbia.

In the American mining camps in the Rockies, and later in Alaska, every community had its own customs and its own rules. These were made up on the spot. The miners ran their own community. They held town meetings to dispense justice. Like the placer mining process, these meetings began in California.

Sometimes when a man called a meeting to seek justice, he found himself fined twenty dollars for daring to call one at all. The money was spent at once on drinks.

The American miners' meeting that operated in the Canadian town of Fortymile had the power of life and death over the members of the community. It could hang a man, give him a divorce, send him to prison, banish him, or lash him. In Alaska all these functions were performed. The Fortymilers at one point hanged at least two Indians for murder.

Under the rules, any prospector could call a meeting simply by posting a notice. An elected chairman acted as judge, and the entire meeting acted as jury. Both sides could produce witnesses and state their cases, and anyone who wished could ask a question or make a speech. The verdict was decided by a show of hands. It is doubtful that the democratic process has ever operated at such a grassroots level.

The first saloon served as headquarters for these meetings. That became a problem. Sometimes when a man called a meeting to seek justice, he found himself fined twenty dollars for daring to call one at all. The money was spent at once on drinks.

Finally, one man rebelled. His name was John Jerome Healy, and he was as tough as hardtack. With his cowlick, his Buffalo Bill goatee, and his ramrod figure, he looked the part of the traditional frontiersman. All of his life he had been seeking out the wild places of the northwest.

Healy had been a hunter, trapper, soldier, prospector, whisky trader, editor, guide, Indian scout, and sheriff. He had run away from home at the age of twelve to join a band of bandits who tried to seize part of Mexico and form a new republic. He was a crony of Sitting Bull, the Sioux medicine man. He had built the most famous of the whisky forts in Canadian territory and ruled it like a feudal baron, carrying on illegal trade in alcohol with the Indians. This was Fort Whoop-Up, behind whose log palisades Healy had fought off the wild wolf hunters of the prairie who tried to take it over.

In Montana he was known as the hanging sheriff of Chouteau County. He went after rustlers with a zeal that left some people wondering where crime control left off and lawlessness began. Then, with the frontier tamed, the restless and aging Healy headed north, still hungering for the adventure that had driven him all his life.

He followed gold to Juneau, on the Alaska Panhandle. He pushed on to Dyea Inlet at the foot of the Chilkoot. It was to his trading post that the dying Tom Williams brought the news of the Fortymile strike in the winter of 1886.

Healy saw there was more than one way to get gold out of the Yukon. He went to Chicago, met up with an old Missouri crony, Portus B. Weare, and explained that money could be made in the Alaska trade. These two set up the North American Trading and Transportation Company to break the monopoly of the rival Alaska Commercial Company. They laid plans to establish a series of trading posts along the river and build a fleet of steamboats.

Healy was the boss of Fort Cudahy, the NATT Company's headquarters, just across the Fortymile River from the main town. He was no man to accept quietly the ruling of the miners' meeting, for he had always been a law unto himself. He didn't intend to knuckle under to the miners of this Yukon camp.

He was not popular in Fortymile. He insisted on sending out bills at the end of the month—something Jack McQuesten never did. And so, when his hired female servant hauled him before a miners' court, his enemies were waiting for him.

It was an odd case. The young woman had been brought in from the outside by Healy and his wife. She insisted on staying out late at night, sometimes all night. Healy told her she couldn't go out again to the dances being held in the main town. She disobeyed him and tried to get back into the house, only to find that he had locked her out.

This dictatorial attitude enraged the miners in a town where freedom of action was almost a religion. They decided in favour of the woman and demanded that Healy pay her a year's wages and her full fare back home.

The old frontiersman paid under protest. But he wasn't finished yet. He had an old frontier friend from Whoop-Up days—Superintendent Samuel B. Steele of the North-West Mounted Police. Healy asked Steele for protection under the Canadian law by Canadian police.

At about the same time, Bishop Bompas was sending a similar letter to Ottawa. He said the miners "were teaching the Indians to make whisky with demoralizing effect both to the whites and Indians and with much danger in the use of firearms."

That had come about as a result of a shooting over a poker hand. Jim Washburn, known as the meanest man in town, had slashed a card player across the belly and had received a bullet through the hips in return. Fortymile was in danger of becoming the same kind of lawless community that had formed part of the American Wild West.

The two letters from Healy and Bompas ended Fortymile's free and easy existence. In 1894 Inspector Charles Constantine, a thick-set, gruff, and honest policeman, became the first lawman to enter the Canadian northland. By 1895 he had a detachment of twenty police under his command. When a miners' meeting was held to take away a claim from a man who hadn't paid wages, Constantine immediately reversed the verdict and abolished the miners' meetings forever. He had been eight years on the force and was known for his ability in a rough-and-tumble fight. In Fortymile, he called himself "chief magistrate, commander-in-chief, and home and foreign secretary" of the town.

He was so serious about his work that he had three tables in his cabin, each with a different kind of work on it. He moved from one to the other. Constantine's iron hand was felt in various ways. One of his first acts was to stop the dance-hall girls from wearing bloomers instead of dresses. Another was to collect the tax on all locally made hootchinoo. With these edicts, some of the freer spirits decided the time had come to move again. Once more civilization had caught them up.

CHAPTER SIX

The Rise of Circle City

THE NORTH-WEST MOUNTED POLICE HAD NO SOONER ARRIVED AT FORTYMILE THAN ANOTHER STRANGE COMMUNITY BEGAN TO SPRING UP FARTHER DOWN-STREAM, THIS TIME ON ALASKAN SOIL. IT WAS CALLED CIRCLE CITY BECAUSE IT WAS SET AT THE POINT WHERE THE YUKON RIVER CROSSES THE ARCTIC CIRCLE. AND IT WAS FOUNDED BY JACK MCQUESTEN. (IN AMERICAN MINING LAW, A "CITY" IS THE CENTRE OF A MINING DISTRICT—NOT A METROPOLIS.)

For years McQuesten and his partner, Harper, had been grubstaking men to seek out the legendary "Preacher's Creek"—the one in which a missionary had once seen gold by the spoonful. The gold was finally found, not by white men, but by two mixed-bloods—half Russian, half Indian. It lay on the headwaters of Birch Creek, and within a year the region was producing $400,000 annually—a sum worth ten times as much in today's values. It was here that Circle City took form.

This was the dreariest section of the Yukon valley. It lay 170 miles (270 km) downstream from Fortymile at the point where the river spills over the Yukon Flats. Here the hills seem to sicken and die until they decline to a monotonous waste of sand, while the main river, broad as a lake, moves sluggishly in a huge arc across the Arctic Circle for 180 miles (290 km). There is no real scenery here in this desolate domain—only hundreds of tiny islands and grey sandbars on which ducks and geese and plover nest by the millions.

Circle City was as drab as its surroundings. A hodge-podge of moss-chinked log cabins lay scattered along the curve of the Yukon River, stitched together by a network of short streets, many of which were little more than rivers of mud in the spring.

The gold claims lay eighty miles (130 km) back from the river. Birch

Creek, on which the gold was found, ran parallel to the Yukon before joining it at the southern end of its curve. The trail from the little community to the mines led across a dreadful land of swamp and muskeg and stunted spruce. There was no game here, but in the summer the swamps swarmed with mosquitoes. The insects were so thick they blotted out the sun and sometimes suffocated pack horses by stopping their nostrils. Sometimes they drove men insane.

Here, in this gloomy settlement, Jack McQuesten was king. He owned the most imposing log structure in town—a two-storey trading post from which rose a flagpole. Each year, when the Indian women, by custom, tossed every white man in a moose-skin blanket, McQuesten was honoured by being tossed first. Traditionally, they let him escape. A mock battle followed. McQuesten landed lightly on his feet, no matter how high he was tossed, and only at the last ceremony in 1896, when he was older and bulkier, did he topple onto his back. At that point, the Indian women clustered around him murmuring and patting him as a sign of sympathy.

McQuesten's other partners had scattered. Al Mayo was farther down the river at the mouth of Minook Creek—the same area where Ed Schieffelin had once poked about for gold. Harper and Ladue had poled their way up the river, deep into Canadian territory. But McQuesten staked everything he had on the prosperity of Circle City. He lent so much money that by 1894 the miners owed him $100,000.

For McQuesten continued to give unlimited credit. William Ogilvie, the Canadian government surveyor who established the boundary line between Alaska and Canada, once witnessed his credit system in operation.

Into the store came a miner from the creeks. He asked McQuesten how much he owed.

"Seven hundred," said McQuesten.

"Hell, Jack, I've only got five hundred. How am I going to pay you seven hundred with five?"

"Oh, that's all right. Give us your five hundred, and we'll credit you and let the rest stand till next cleanup."

"But, Jack, I want more stuff, how am I going to get it?"

"Well, we'll let you have it same as you did before."

"But, dammit, Jack, I haven't had a spree yet."

"Well, go and have your little spree; come back with what's left, and we'll credit you with it and go on as before."

The miner had his spree. It took everything he had. But McQuesten, without a word, gave him a five-hundred-dollar outfit and carried a debt of twelve hundred dollars against him on the books. That was the way things worked in those pre-gold rush days.

Indeed, a spree was the high point of social life in Circle City. Every spree was like every other spree. A man on a spree moved from saloon to saloon, swinging a club as a weapon, threatening the bartenders, pouring the liquor himself, treating the house to cigars and hootch, then driving everybody ahead of him to the next saloon, where the performance was repeated.

At the height of such a spree, all the miners would line up on two sides of the saloon and throw cordwood at each other from a pile that stood beside the stove. Then someone would jump on the water barrel to make a speech. He'd upset the barrel and finally roll the stove, red-hot, around the floor.

When the party was over, the man who began the spree would hand his poke of gold dust to the saloon keeper and ask him to take the damages. Such a spree could last for several days. One such bill for damages came to $2,900.

This could have happened nowhere in the world except in Circle City. But here, far from civilization, far from loved ones, far from a man's roots, it was necessary to blow off steam. Everybody understood that.

The only law in the Circle was the law of the miners' meeting. The town, when it opened, had no jail, no courthouse, no lawyers, and no sheriff. But there wasn't a lock or a key in the community.

Circle City had no post office and no mail service either. A letter could take at least two months and sometimes a year to reach its destination and might arrive crumpled and smelly and covered with tar and bacon grease.

Circle had no taxes and no banks, except the saloons, which served as banks. The smallest coin in use was a silver dollar. There was no priest, no doctor, no school, no church. But there were men with Oxford degrees who could recite Greek poetry, especially when they were drunk.

Civilized customs were virtually unknown in Circle. A man might easily rise and eat his breakfast at ten in the evening, because the summers were always light and the winters were always dark. It was light at midnight in Circle in the summer. In the winter, it was pitch dark at noon.

There was no such thing as a thermometer to measure the winter's fierce cold. Jack McQuesten invented one by putting out a series of bottles of mercury, whisky, kerosene, and an all-purpose patent medicine known as "Perry Davis Painkiller." These froze in ascending order, and that's how the miners knew how cold it was. On cold days, even the painkiller froze in the bottles. Then Circle became a ghostly settlement, the smoke rising in pillars to form a shroud that seemed to deaden all sound, except for the howling of the dogs—the wolf-like huskies and the heavy-shouldered malamutes—who dragged sleds out to the mines.

These dogs dominated the town. They were always hungry. They gobbled everything in sight. Leather gloves and harnesses, gun straps and snowshoes, pots of paste, miners' boots and brushes, and even the powdered resin, which they gobbled up as quickly as it was sprinkled on the dance-hall floors.

One man watched a dog eat a dish rag whole for the sake of the grease in it. Another stood helplessly by while a dog rushed into a tent and swallowed a lighted candle, flame and all.

To stop the dogs from eating their precious cakes of soap, the Indians hung the soap from branches of trees. The town's skyline was marked by the silhouettes of log caches built on stilts to keep supplies away from the dogs, whose teeth could tear open a can of salmon as easily as if it were a paper package. Some, indeed, swore the dogs could tell a tin of marmalade from one of bully beef by a glance at the label!

Men crowded into Circle City, claiming they were looking for gold. But actually they came because they were the kind that wished to be left alone. Where else could a man attempt to cut his throat in plain view without anybody trying to stop him?

One did just that. His name was Johnson, and he made a bad job of it because he was drunk. The onlookers, seeing that he was failing, patched him up and told him politely that he might try again if he wished. He didn't. Instead he grew a black beard to hide his scars and ever afterward was known as Cut-Throat Johnson.

If a man's freedom of action got in the way of that of his neighbours, the miners' meetings took hold. The Mounted Police had cleaned up Fortymile, but they had no way of operating on the Alaska side. Once, when a saloon keeper had seduced a young mixed-blood girl, a meeting decided that he must either marry her or spend a year in jail—even though there was no jail. The miners were quite prepared to build one on the spot but were spared this labour when the accused decided to get on with the wedding.

The worst crime in Circle City was not murder; it was theft. When one man stole from a cache, his friends sentenced him to hang. When no one could be found to act as a hangman, they changed the sentence to banishment. The culprit was ordered to live by himself twelve miles (19 km) out of town until the steamboat arrived. The miners took up a collection and bought him a tent, stove, and provisions. Then they said goodbye and never saw him or spoke to him again.

The U.S. government considered these meetings lawful. In fact the verdict of one of them was sent to Washington and confirmed. That was a murder case involving a bartender named Jim Chronister and the same James Washburn whose shooting affair in Fortymile had so disturbed Bishop Bompas. After killing Washburn in self-defence, Chronister went before a miners' meeting trial and was acquitted in just twenty minutes.

Out of these meetings, a Miners' Association was formed, and later the Yukon Order of Pioneers, a fraternal organization whose emblem was the Golden Rule and whose motto was "Do unto others as you would be done by."

That sounds like a Sunday-school pledge, not the kind one usually associates with hard-bitten miners. But it was born of experience by men who had learned, over the years, how important it was to depend on one another. Each member swore to help every other member if the need arose and always to spread far and wide the news of a fresh gold discovery.

In the end, Circle City, though four thousand miles (6,400 km) by water from the nearest city, could not escape the influence of civilized life. By 1896 it had a music hall, two theatres, eight dance halls, and twenty-eight saloons. They called it "the Paris of Alaska." Money was so plentiful that day labourers were paid five times as much as they were outside, as the northerners called the rest of the world.

In the big new double-decker Grand Opera House, George Snow, half prospector, half showman, who had once starred with the great Shakespearean actor Edwin Booth, produced classical plays and vaudeville acts. Snow's children appeared on stage and picked up nuggets thrown to them by miners hungry for entertainment.

One group of vaudeville performers, sealed in for the winter with only a limited program of acts, was forced to go through the same routines nightly for seven months, until the audience howled as loudly as the malamutes that bayed to the cold moon.

As the gold flowed into town, the community grew richer. Miners roared into the bars, flinging down handfuls of nuggets for drink and dancing out the change at a dollar a dance. They kept their hats on and clumped about the floor in their high-top boots. They danced from midnight until dawn, while the violins scraped and the sled dogs howled.

The community grew bigger and bigger. Mixed in with the mud of the rutted streets was a thick porridge of chips and sawdust from the newly erected buildings. By 1896 twelve hundred people were living in Circle. John Healy's NATT Company opened a store in opposition to Jack McQuesten. The Episcopal Church bought land for a hospital. The Chicago *Daily Record* sent a foreign correspondent to the settlement, which now boasted that it was "the largest log town in the world."

Culture arrived. Up from the University of Chicago came Miss Anna Fulcomer to open a government school. The miners established a library. It contained the complete works of such literary giants as Thomas Huxley, Charles Darwin, Thomas Carlyle, and the historian Thomas Babington Macaulay. Here were filed the standard illustrated papers brought in from the outside. There were chess sets for the members and a morocco-bound Bible, as well as an *Encyclopaedia Britannica* and an *International Dictionary*.

In 1896 Circle City had its greatest year. The gold production that season exceeded one million dollars. Lots were selling for two thousand dollars apiece. Who could have believed that before the winter was out this, the Paris of Alaska, would be a ghost town—the saloons closed and barred, the caches empty and left to rot, the doors of the worthless cabins hanging open to the winds, and scarcely a dog left to howl in the silent streets?

CHAPTER SEVEN

On the Eve of the Big Strike

As the winter of '96–'97 wore on, strange rumours began to filter down from the upper-river-country people. Stories seeped in about an almost unbelievable event on a little stream whose name nobody could properly pronounce.

At first nobody believed them. Sam Bartlett floated into town one day before freeze-up on a raft of logs, but all he told his friends was that Joe Ladue, Harper's old partner, was trying to hoax the country so he might make money from the new town he was laying out at the Klondike's mouth.

The town, of course, was Dawson City. It was Ladue who had sent the early prospectors into the Klondike area. Now that they had found what they were seeking, he intended to profit—not from gold but from real estate.

Into Oscar Ashby's smoky saloon, ten days before Christmas 1896, came two traders with a bundle of mail and some gold from a creek named Eldorado in the Klondike valley—a creek that nobody had heard of.

Ashby read one of the letters to a group of seventy-five skeptical miners.

"This is one of the richest strikes in the world," the letter read. "It is a real world-beater. I can't tell how much gold we are getting to the pan. I never saw or heard the like of such a thing in my life. I myself saw one hundred and fifty dollars panned out of one pan of dirt, and I think they are getting as high as a thousand … "

The crowd had heard this kind of talk before. Prospectors are notorious for tall tales. The men laughed, ordered drinks, and forgot about it.

But two old-time sourdoughs, Harry Spencer and Frank Densmore, got a second letter from their partner, a Fortymile saloon keeper named Bill McPhee. Densmore was nobody's fool. He fitted up a dog team and headed upriver to see what was what.

Densmore, who had been fourteen years in the country, had tramped over most of Alaska and was well respected. When he sent back word that the Klondike was really as reported, every man knew that something extraordinary had happened.

By this time, more news had arrived. In January Arthur Treadwell Walden, a well-known dog driver, walked into Harry Ash's saloon, threw a bundle of letters on the bar, and asked for a cup of hot beef tea. (No dog driver would be foolish enough to drink whisky in the cold weather; drowsiness could lead to death on the trail.)

Ash paid no attention but began to riffle feverishly through the mail. He was as much a prospector as a saloon keeper—a veteran of the stampede to the Black Hills country of South Dakota. For some time, he had sensed that something unusual was afoot. At last he found the letter he had been looking for, tore it open, and devoured it, his ruddy face alive with excitement.

All that winter and spring, the residents of Circle straggled up the frozen Yukon in twos and threes, the wealthier men racing behind dog teams, the poorer dragging their sleds by hand.

"Boys," he shouted, "help yourself to the whole shooting match. I'm off to the Klondike."

An orgy followed as men smashed the necks off bottles and drained the contents. Others rushed about Circle trying to buy dogs at any price. Their value leaped from the going rate of twenty-five or fifty dollars to two hundred and fifty and then, as they became scarce, to fifteen hundred.

But cabins valued at five hundred dollars were now worthless as the town was emptied. Only Jack McQuesten stayed behind to look after the handful of miners who continued to work the Birch Creek claims.

All that winter and spring, the residents of Circle straggled up the frozen Yukon in twos and threes, the wealthier men racing behind dog teams, the poorer dragging their sleds by hand. All of Alaska, it seemed, was moving toward the Klondike.

One of these would soon be famous. He was a former Texas marshal, twenty-six years old, who had been one year in the country. His name was George Lewis Rickard, but his friends called him Tex. He and his partner pulled a sledload of provisions up the humpy ice of the Yukon, reached the

Klondike in twenty-six days, and proceeded to get rich. They bought a half interest in a claim on Bonanza Creek in the Klondike valley and sold it almost at once for twenty thousand dollars. They bought a piece of another claim and sold that for thirty thousand.

That was the start of a career that made Tex Rickard the most famous boxing promoter of his day. For it was he who was responsible for the success of the greatest sports palace of that time—Madison Square Garden in New York City.

In the procession up the river that winter were two middle-aged women: a Mrs. Adams, a dressmaker, who would shortly be making thirty dollars a day with her needle, and a Mrs. Willis, an energetic laundress.

Mrs. Willis had gone north in 1895 to support an invalid husband, vowing she would never return until she made her fortune. She did just that.

On reaching the Klondike, she staked a claim and began cooking to finance her mining project. She bought a stove, baked bread, and sold it for a dollar a loaf. She needed starch before she could set up as a laundress. Starch was so scarce a single box cost $250. She cleared that much through the bakery, bought the starch, and set up a laundry. With the proceeds, she paid men to work her claim. She fought off all attempts to jump her claim and, when it began to pay off, refused an offer of a quarter of a million dollars.

Only one member in that ragged procession from Circle City had no interest in gold and no desire for material wealth. This was the Jesuit missionary, Father William Judge, a one-time apprentice in a Boston planing mill, who for the last dozen years had been a servant of the Lord in Alaska.

His fellow travellers eyed him curiously—a skeletal figure with huge, cavernous eyes behind tiny, gold-rimmed spectacles. He was ill fed, for he had loaded his sled with medicine and drugs instead of food, and he trudged along in harness with a single dog to preserve the animal's strength.

Judge knew that the new camp, built on a heaving swamp, would soon be facing plague when summer ended. He was determined to build a hospital in Dawson as quickly as possible. He succeeded but died of tuberculosis before the stampede ended. They called him "The Saint of Dawson."

All that spring, until the ice broke, the ragged procession made its way up the river. In the end, Jack McQuesten joined it, for there was nothing left for him at Circle City. Fortymile, too, was an empty ghost town. Both of these two weird little log villages on the banks of the Yukon had simply provided the prologue to the great drama of the Klondike Gold Rush. Except for a few rotting cabins, there is little now left on these sites to remind the visitor of what they represented.

McQuesten was too late to stake the richest ground in the Klondike, but he managed to secure a small-paying claim that paid him about ten thousand dollars' profit. For him that was enough. After all, it was the largest sum of money he had ever known.

INDEX

About Fifth House

Fifth House Publishers, a Fitzhenry & Whiteside company, is a proudly western-Canadian press. Our publishing specialty is non-fiction as we believe that every community must possess a positive understanding of its worth and place if it is to remain vital and progressive. Fifth House is committed to "bringing the West to the rest" by publishing approximately twenty books a year about the land and people who make this region unique. Our books are selected for their quality and contribution to the understanding of western-Canadian (and Canadian) history, culture, and environment.

Look for the following Fifth House titles at your local bookstore:

The Battles of the War of 1812
   Pierre Berton
Canada Moves West
   Pierre Berton
Exploring the Frozen North
   Pierre Berton
The Golden Trail: The Story of the Klondike Rush
   Pierre Berton
Homemade Fun: Games & Pastimes of the Early Prairies
   Faye Reineberg Holt
Monarchs of the Fields: The Story of the Combine Harvester
   Faye Reineberg Holt
The Nor'Westers: The Fight for the Fur Trade
   Marjorie Wilkins Campbell
Prairie Sentinel: The Story of the Canadian Grain Elevator
   Brock V. Silversides
The Savage River: Seventy-one Days with Simon Fraser
   Marjorie Wilkins Campbell
Settling In: First Homes on the Prairies
   Faye Reineberg Holt
Threshing: The Early Years of Harvesting
   Faye Reineberg Holt

Pierre Berton's History for Young Canadians

"The stories are so real that it's as though Berton is leading us down the surveyor's mountain paths, helping us swing the hammer on the rails, or cut the sod along with the pioneers."
–from the foreword by Arthur Slade, author of *Dust* and the *Canadian Chills* series.

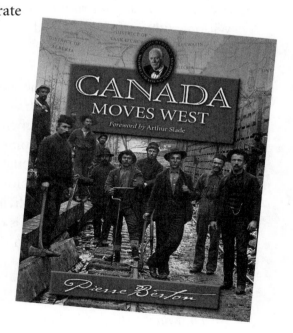

The first book in Fifth House's *Pierre Berton's History for Young Canadians* series is *Canada Moves West*, a rousing collection of five young-adult, non-fiction books by revered author Pierre Berton. These books describe how, back in the days of the pioneers, the Canadian West was won—with blood, sweat, tears, and sheer determination.

Originally printed as separate volumes in the *Adventures in Canadian History* series, the titles in *Canada Moves West* include:

The Railway Pathfinders
The Men in Sheepskin Coats
A Prairie Nightmare
Steel Across the Plains
Steel Across the Shield

Riveting history abounds in the books. Find out about:
* The romantic and gritty adventures of railway pathfinders such as the indomitable Walter Moberly, and railway builders,

Joseph Whitehead and Harry Armstrong, who fought their way from the gnarled rocks of the Canadian Shield to the passes of three mountain ranges in British Columbia;

* The epic tales of the immigrants in sheepskin coats from eastern Europe, who braved hardship and discrimination to create new lives in a new land, successfully settling the wide open spaces of the Canadian prairies;

* The story of those whose lives were forever changed by the coming of the railway: the Cree and Blackfoot peoples, led by Chiefs Piapot, Big Bear, and Crowfoot.

ALSO AVAILABLE—*Exploring the Frozen North*

"Pierre Berton is the perfect writer to take you north. His words pull you into the experience—suddenly you are there ... don't miss the northern adventures recounted in **Exploring the Frozen North***. Pierre Berton makes them come alive."*—from the foreword by Eric Wilson, author of the Tom and Liz Austen Mysteries

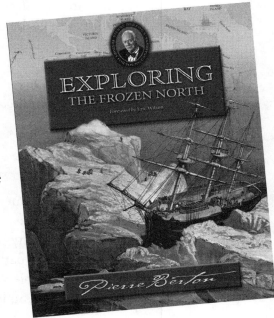

Exploring the Frozen North is the second omnibus in the *Pierre Berton's History for Young Canadians* series. It documents the amazing lives of the men and women who mapped the Arctic at great personal cost. Berton tells the stories of the explorers, but he does not ignore those people living in the Arctic—the Inuit. The titles in this omnibus include:

Parry of the Arctic
Jane Franklin's Obsession
Dr. Kane of the Arctic Seas
Trapped in the Arctic

In *Exploring the Frozen North* incredible Arctic adventures come alive. Join Berton as he writes about:

❧ William Edward Parry, the first white man to attempt exploration of the Arctic islands;
❧ Jane Franklin and her relentless search for her lost explorer husband, John Franklin;
❧ Elisha Kent Kane, the sickly American doctor, who sought the legendary ice-free passage to the North Pole; and
❧ Robert John McClure, whose ambitious and aggressive race for the North West Passage almost ended when he and his crew were trapped in the ice for two long years.

The Battles of the War of 1812

"When Pierre Berton describes a battle, you are right there. You get to know the commanders; you meet some of the eager young soldiers; you *care* about what happens to them … The War of 1812 helped create the Canada we see today—a Canada that the late, great Pierre Berton loved."—from the Foreword by Charlotte Gray

The third book in the series is a seven-book collection that captures the history and the characters of the War of 1812.

Titles in *The Battles of the War of 1812* include:

The Capture of Detroit
The Death of Isaac Brock
Revenge of the Tribes
Canada Under Siege
The Battle of Lake Erie
The Death of Tecumseh
Attack on Montreal

In *The Battles of the War of 1812*, facts and figures, historical characters, and battle strategies blend seamlessly into an exciting history lesson. Join Berton as he tells about:

* John Richardson, the fifteen-year-old "gentleman" volunteer, who rushed to serve his country in June 1812;
* General Isaac Brock, a man now made into a legend, who died defending Upper Canada at the Battle of Queenston Heights;
* The commander of the British fleet at the Battle of Lake Erie, Robert Heriot Barclay, whose nine ships were built from the forests around the lake;
* The great Shawnee leader Tecumseh who dreamt of forming a strong alliance of tribes that would protect Native lands from American troops and settlers; and
* A few hundred men who managed to fight off the tired Americans at the Battle of Châteauguay.

Berton's accounts of heroism, deception, loyalty, and espionage make for exciting reading and are highly recommended for every Canadian.

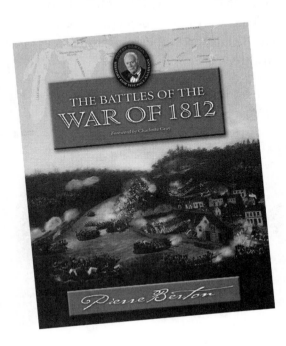